PRAISE FOR THE FIRST EDITION OF *THE SECRETS OF COLLEGE SUCCESS*

"If I had my way, I'd give this book to every single college student, of any age, and *make* them read it. A book that moves from 'How to Turn a B into an A' to '10 Surefire Ways to Piss Off Your Professor' is beyond just 'helpful.' It is 'the Missing Manual' for turning a merely 'okay' college experience into a delicious adventure. I laughed, I took notes, I loved every page. And I'm not even in college. If you are, don't even think about not buying this book. It will be the best thing you ever did for yourself."

> —*Richard Bolles, author of* What Color Is Your Parachute?

"Along with shower flip-flops and a very loud alarm clock, this book should be on every freshman's college packing list. The professors have outlined solutions for all the major fears that students face when they start college."

> —*Marjorie Savage, parent program director, University of Minnesota and author of* You're on Your Own (But I'm Here If You Need Me): Mentoring Your Child During the College Years

"Psychologically sound tips for thriving, not just surviving, in college. Lynn's and Jeremy's tips will make your college experience a spectacular success."

> —*Chuck Snowden, director of honors program, University of Wisconsin*

"Clear, practical, comprehensive—and caring. These authors want you to succeed. Listen."

> —*Judy Genshaft, president, University of South Florida, and past president, American Council on Education*

"Riddled with humor and witty in presentation, this lighthearted 'easy read' could be the most helpful, honest resource for today's college student."

> —*Scott H. Reikofski, director, fraternity/sorority affairs, University of Pennsylvania*

"*The Secrets of College Success* needs to be required reading for anyone starting college, regardless of age. A great source of practical advice that could mean the difference between success and failure."

—*Eduardo J. Padrón, president, Miami Dade College*

"The students who are most successful in college are those who are most prepared. *The Secrets of College Success* reveals what students need to know from the perspective of the professors who teach them. It pays to know the rules of the game before you play."

—*George R. Boggs, president and CEO, American Association of Community Colleges*

"This volume provides a banquet of tips. Easy to read, easy to locate what you need, this book will be helpful throughout your undergraduate years. I highly recommend it."

—*Sharon J. Hamilton, professor and former director, Indiana University Faculty Colloquium on Excellence in Teaching*

"Accessibly written and logically organized; there's something here for everyone. This handy volume will help students focus on what it takes to be successful."

—*Peter H. Quimby, deputy dean, Princeton University*

"This book provides sound advice in a great format on how to get the most from your college education, starting on Day 1 of your freshman year."

—*Martha O'Connell, executive director, Colleges That Change Lives*

"High schools focus on getting their seniors TO college but they rarely teach them how to get THROUGH college. Professors Jacobs and Hyman fill this gap with a series of high-energy, digestible, and practical tips that any student can master in one sitting. This book should be required reading for every college-bound student so that they will be equipped with the 'under-the-hood' expertise they need to succeed in higher education."

"*The Secrets of College Success* is an easy-to-read, highly informative book. In my experience, many students come in to Stanford unprepared for the realities of college life. With bite-sized and digestible tips, this book provides substantial advice applicable to any college student."

Professors'
Guide™

THE SECRETS OF
COLLEGE SUCCESS

Second Edition

THE SECRETS OF
COLLEGE SUCCESS

Second Edition

Lynn F. Jacobs and Jeremy S. Hyman

Cover design by JPuda and Tom Hapgood
Cover image: © skodonnell/istockphoto

Copyright © 2013 by Professors' Guide, LLC. All rights reserved. Professors' Guide name, the male and female professors icons, and the trade dress are trademarks of Professors' Guide, LLC.

Published by Jossey-Bass

A Wiley Brand

One Montgomery Street, Suite 1200, San Francisco, CA 94104-4594—www.josseybass .com

Jossey-Bass books and products are available through most bookstores. To contact Jossey-Bass directly call our Customer Care Department within the U.S. at 800-956-7739, outside the U.S. at 317-572-3986, or fax 317-572-4002.

Wiley publishes in a variety of print and electronic formats and by print-on-demand. Some material included with standard print versions of this book may not be included in e-books or in print-on-demand. If this book refers to media such as a CD or DVD that is not included in the version you purchased, you may download this material at http:// booksupport.wiley.com. For more information about Wiley products, visit www.wiley .com.

Library of Congress Cataloging-in-Publication Data has been applied for and is on file with the Library of Congress
9781118575123 (paper), 9781118575130 (ebk.), 9781118575154 (ebk.), 9781118618035 (ebk.)

Printed in the United States of America

SECOND EDITION

PB Printing   10 9 8 7

MEET THE PROFESSORS

Dr. Lynn F. Jacobs is professor of art history at the University of Arkansas. A specialist in Northern Renaissance art, Lynn previously taught at Vanderbilt University, California State University, Northridge, the University of Redlands, and NYU. She has received the National Endowment for the Humanities Fellowship twice and the University of Arkansas Prize for distinguished academic advising.

Jeremy S. Hyman is founder and chief architect of *Professors' Guide*™ content projects. An expert in early modern philosophy, Jeremy teaches at the University of Arkansas, and has previously taught at UCLA, MIT, and Princeton University. He received the University of California Regents' award for distinguished teaching.

Lynn and Jeremy are coauthors of the book *Professors' Guide to Getting Good Grades in College* (HarperCollins, 2006). They write a column at *U.S. News & World Report*, WWW.USNEWS.COM/PROFESSORSGUIDE, and contribute to *Reader's Digest*, the *New York Times'* "Choice" blog, *Huffington Post*, and *Fox Business.*

Lynn and Jeremy live in Fayetteville, Arkansas, with their son, Jonah. Their website is WWW.THESECRETSOFCOLLEGESUCCESS.COM and they tweet at @professorsguide.com.

CONTENTS

PREFACE TO THE SECOND EDITION

To the student—that is, *you.*

Much has changed at college since the first edition of this book, just three years ago. Online courses and e-readers, picking majors at the beginning of college, increased emphasis on first-year experience and capstone courses, booming enrollment in community colleges, and mounting worry about how to pay for college and whether, in the end, it's worth it—all of these are new to the college scene. And we have tips for all of them.

But much hasn't changed at college. Taking tests and writing papers, managing your time and making deadlines without undue stress, knowing when—and how—to go see the professor, applying to grad school or finding a job—all of these are things that will always be a part of college. And we have tips for them, too.

We offer you a simple promise: *if you follow the tips, techniques, and strategies in this book, you will succeed at college.* Tens of thousands of students have read the first edition of this book and benefitted from it (we know; we get e-mail from students all over the United States—indeed, from all over the world—every day). And we've presented the ideas in this book to thousands of additional students at orientation programs at dozens of colleges (to see clips from our *The Secrets of College Success* campus presentation, visit WWW.GIMMEANA.COM).

We're out to change college in America; to change it from a place in which students sit like sponges in large lecture courses, passively absorbing content dished up by professors, to a place where students know what the professors are really thinking and, using this information, take charge of their own learning—and succeed. Hence, *The **Secrets** of College Success.*

But more than any of that, we'd like *you* to succeed. That is why, if you come to a tip you don't understand—or a technique or strategy you're not sure how to use—we want you to ask us about it. E-mail either of us at lynn@professorsguide.com or jeremy@professorsguide.com. We're here to help.

And if you have a tip that's worked especially well for you, share it with the other twenty million college students in the United States. Tweet it to @professorsguide. Hey, we haven't cornered the market on tips for college success.

College is a journey—one you're perhaps thinking of starting on (if you're a college-bound high school student), just starting on (if you're entering in the fall), or are already well into (if you're already at college). Whatever the case, the over eight hundred tips, techniques, and strategies in this book—from things to do the summer before college all the way through to how to get a job and pay off your student loans—will ensure your success on the college journey. We guarantee it—which is why we sign our names below.

Lynn and Jeremy

INTRODUCTION

You might not know this, but you're going to college at the very best time in the last five hundred years. New media, twenty-first-century technologies, better professors, government funding for college—all of these go together to make this a wonderful time to be at college.

That is—if you know what to do.

You might have thought professors and advisers would tell you all you need to know. You wouldn't be right. Some professors think part of college is figuring out on your own what's expected. Others think it's a waste of class time to go over how to manage your time, study, prepare for tests, or write papers. Still others think that if they tell you what to do, you'll think it's a recipe for an A, which, if you don't get, will result in a colossal grade dispute—something no professor wants.

And, at some colleges, the booming enrollments have simply made it impossible for professors, advisers, and staff to give you the advice and attention you need and deserve—no matter how much they'd like to.

And so we've written *The Secrets of College Success*—the first book to offer quick tips, all written by professors, that'll help you achieve your full potential at college. Whether you're a beginning or advanced student; whether you're at a four-year college, community college, or taking courses on the Web; whether you're already doing pretty well at college or maybe not as well as you'd like; even if you're a high school student just beginning to think about college—this book is for you.

The secrets we reveal and the tips that we offer are the product of over thirty years of teaching experience at eight different colleges—big and small, private colleges and state universities, good schools and not-all-that-good schools. Over ten thousand students have tried the tips—and we can tell you they really work.

Most of all, this book is fun to read. You'll find yourself not only strategizing about college—figuring out how you can apply our tips to your own college experience—but also making up tips of your own and even wanting to share them with others. And you'll enjoy your success when you find that the tips—both yours and ours—have changed the way you approach college.

Congratulations. This is a wonderful time to be at college. Make the most of it.

Top 10 Reasons to Read This Book

#10. The tips are really good. Written wholly by professors, the tips in this book give you high-value information about what to do at college—and what not to do.

#9. The information is not available elsewhere. No professor, adviser, or college guide will tell you the insider secrets we reveal in this book.

#8. The information is quick. Top 10 Lists, Do's and Don'ts, To-Do Lists, How-to (and How-*not* to) Guides—all the advice is bite-sized and easy to digest. And our *Professors' Guide*™ icons will help you navigate your way through the book.

#7. The tips are practical. No abstract theories here, just concrete, easy-to-follow tips that you can use to guarantee your success at college.

#6. We tell you everything you need to know—and only the things you need to know. From the summer before college to the crucial first year of college, from picking a major to finding a job—all the key moments of college are covered.

#5. The tips are up-to-date. All the new realities of college are included. And we give you links to useful websites, so you can find out the latest information about special topics.

#4. Each tip stands on its own. You can use as many—or as few—of the tips as you want and still get excellent results. And you can follow the tips in any order. Pick a tip that interests you and then move on to others, or just randomly flip to a page and start reading.

#3. We tell you what to do. Like a good undergraduate adviser (something sorely lacking at many colleges), we tell you not just what you might do, but what you should do. In a friendly and supportive voice, of course.

#2. The tips are time-tested. The advice in this book has worked for thousands and thousands of students. And it will work for you.

And the number-one reason you should read this book:

#1. The tips are fun to read. You'll enjoy thinking about different strategies for college success as you read through our tips. And, in the best case, you'll LOL as you read some of our attempts at humor. (At least you won't be bored.)

The Professors' Guide™ Icons

Here are the icons used in this book—and what each of them means:

 EXTRA POINTER. An additional tip that fills out another tip or applies to a special situation.

 5-STAR TIP. A really high-value suggestion that you should be sure to use. One of the best tips in the book.

 BEST-KEPT SECRET. One of the things that no one wants you to know, but that will help you do really well at college.

REALITY CHECK. An invitation to take a step back and assess what's really going on.

IOHO (IN OUR HUMBLE OPINION). We get on our soapbox to bloviate—that is, give our expert opinion—about controversial issues at college. Not all professors will agree.

 RULE OF THUMB. A general principle that will work in most, but perhaps not all, situations.

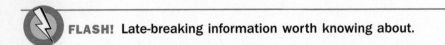

ON THE WEB. A useful link for getting more information or buying a product or service online.

BONUS TIP. For those who can't get enough, one more tip.

FLASH! Late-breaking information worth knowing about.

Except for websites that are very familiar (such as Google, Amazon, Barnes & Noble, or eBay), we've given the entire web address; for example, WWW.OCW.MIT.EDU. Some URLs, for who knows what reason, omit the "www"; these appear as, for example, HTTP://OCW.ND.EDU.

THE SECRETS OF
COLLEGE SUCCESS

Second Edition

1 *THIS* IS COLLEGE

Going to college is a very special sort of experience. A time of tremendous personal growth. A time when some students get their first serious taste of independence, while others find their BFFLs, increase their Facebook friends exponentially, or even meet up with their future spouses. But even more important, college is also a time of great intellectual growth. A chance to study things you didn't even know existed or to delve into topics you do know about at a level of detail and sophistication that you've never before imagined.

Because college is so special, it's important to make the most of it. To squeeze all the juice out of it and drink it all up. Especially when it comes to the academic side of things, where students often don't reap all the benefits college has to offer. This chapter will help you understand what college is all about—to get a real picture of what you are about to go through or are already going through. And it will offer basic tips about the things that matter most at college—no matter what kind of college you're going to.

In this chapter you'll learn:

▶ 10 Things You Need to Know About College (but Probably Don't)

▶ What's New at College? Fun Facts

▶ The 15 Habits of Top College Students

▶ The 10 Worst Self-Defeating Myths

► The 11 Secrets of Getting Good Grades in College

► 20 No-Brainers to Save Money at College

► 14 Ways to Ensure You Graduate in Four Years

► Top 10 Tips for Community College Students

► 10 Best Tips for Engineering School

► Top 10 Tips for Applied Arts and Design Colleges

► The College Student's Bill of Rights

10 Things You Need to Know About College (But Probably Don't)

1. **You're in charge of this thing.** For many students, the most striking thing about college is that there's no one there to hold your hand. Picking courses, getting to class, doing the reading, and figuring out what's going to be on the test and what's expected on the papers—all of these are things you're going to have to do pretty much on your own. Sure, there are profs (and, in some schools, TAs) who'll give instructions and offer suggestions from time to time. But you're the one who'll have to take responsibility for hauling your butt out of bed when it's ten degrees below zero—or one hundred and five above, depending on what school you're at—and doing what you need to do.

2. **Your parents may not be much help.** Some students are on their iPhone five times a day looking for advice from Mom or Dad. But even the best-intentioned parents can lead you astray. Colleges are different—and, in many cases, much improved—from what they were twenty-five years ago, and professors' expectations have changed accordingly. Suggestion: tune down (or, in some cases, tune out) the parents until you have a firm handle on what's expected at your college—today.

3. **Attendance isn't required—but is expected.** One of the first things many students discover is that college classes can be huge: 100, 200, and, at some state schools, even 700 students in a lecture. In such an anonymous environment, it's the easiest thing in the world to tell yourself there's no good reason to bother going to class. (Even if your school has small classes, attendance typically counts for only a tiny percentage of the grade, if at all.) But professors assume you've made all

the classes, and they have no hesitation about asking a midterm or final question that focuses on the contents of a single lecture. Kinda makes you want to go, doesn't it?

4. **Content is doled out in large units.** You may be used to getting your content in short, entertaining blasts: the one- to three-minute YouTube video, the abbreviation-filled IM, the 140-character tweet. But the professor is thinking in terms of the fifty-minute lecture, divided into only two or three main segments; and the author of the journal article is thinking in terms of twenty-five pages of densely written argument, divided into perhaps three or four main sections. Bottom line? You've got to adjust your focus from quick bursts of content to sustained argument. And retrain your attention span to process long—very long, it'll seem—units of content.

5. **Up to two-thirds of the work is done outside of class.** Contrary to what you might have heard, the lecture portion of the course is the least time-consuming activity. That's because (with the exception of a few very basic, introductory courses) the professor is expecting the bulk of the work to be done by you, on your own. Doing the reading and homework; preparing for the quizzes, tests, and presentations; doing research and writing papers—all of these are activities that can easily eat up more than half the time you put into any given course.

6. **A C is a really bad grade.** Many first-year college students— and even some students who've been at college for a while— think that if they get C's in all their classes they're doing just fine—or at least adequately. But what these folks need to know is that in some college courses the grade distribution is 20 to 30 percent A's, 30 to 60 percent B's, and only 15 to 30 percent C's. Set your sights accordingly.

7. **Not everyone who teaches is a prof.** At many state universities—especially those where the student-faculty ratio is 15 to 1 or greater—much of the teaching is done by graduate students. At some of the better state schools (the University of

California and the University of Texas, for instance), only very advanced graduate students are allowed to teach their own courses. But at other schools (we won't mention names because we want to keep our jobs), the lecturer can be a first-year graduate student who might not even have majored in the field in college. Moral? Whenever possible, take courses with regular faculty, who'll be more experienced and, in the best cases, will actually have done research in the subject they're teaching.

BEST-KEPT SECRET. Colleges don't always list the name of the instructor in the course description or at the online registration site. Sometimes it's because they've made last-minute appointments, hiring some adjunct or TA a few weeks before the semester starts. But sometimes it's because they don't want to highlight how few of the courses are taught by the regular faculty. Go to the department office the week before classes start and ask who's scheduled to teach the courses you're interested in—and what his or her status is.

IOHO. Graduate students at universities are often compared to residents at teaching hospitals. But the analogy is misleading. Residents are full-fledged doctors who have completed their medical degrees; graduate students are not professors and have not completed their terminal degrees (in most fields, the PhD).

8. **It's the product that counts.** Many students think that *effort* counts. That's why, when papers are returned, there's always a line of students waiting to argue how many hours they worked, how many articles they read, and how hard they've been trying in the course. The thing is, in college what counts most is the *product:* the paper (not how it was produced), the test (not how

much you studied for it), and the oral presentation (not how much you knew about the subject, but couldn't quite get out).

9. **Understanding is more than just memorizing.** While some intro courses require some memorizing (vocabulary in world or foreign languages, theorems in math, names and dates in history), other beginning courses will include essays on the exams. And in virtually every advanced or upper-division course, you'll be asked not just to regurgitate what you've memorized from the lecture or textbook, but to do some analysis, apply the concepts to some new cases, or organize the material or data in some new or interesting way. Pretty different from what you may be used to.

10. **The prof's on your side—and *wants* to help.** Many students see the professor as an enemy to be defeated—the person who'll trick you with all sorts of gotcha questions on the test and who's very stingy come grade time. But really, the professor is eager to teach you and (believe it or not) would like to see you do well. That's because, in many cases, he or she has forgone a much more lucrative career in business or industry for the sole purpose of educating college students—like yourself. So when the prof invites you to come to an office hour, go to a review session, or just communicate by e-mail, Skype, or Facebook, consider the possibility that the professor really means it. Because he or she probably does.

What's New at College? Fun Facts

- There are almost 21 million students enrolled in U.S. colleges—a number growing at 4.5 percent a year.

- Almost 60 percent of college students are women, and 40 percent of college students are over the age of twenty-five.

- Community colleges are booming: over 40 percent of college students go to one.

- The *average* list price for tuition at a private college is $29,000; at a state university, $8,600 (for in-state residents; $21,700 for out-of-state students); and at a community college, $3,100—*a year.* (At some schools, the prices are considerably higher.)

- College tuition at state universities went up by an average of 4.8 percent in 2012-13—and about 6 percent a year in the decade before (community college and private college tuition grew at an average rate of only 3 percent a year in the 2000–2010 decade).

- About 75 percent of full-time college students receive financial aid. Averaged across all colleges (public and private), students in 2011–12 received about $13,000 in financial aid, of which $7,000 was in grant aid, $5,000 in loans, and $1,200 in tax credits and deductions.

- The average college student graduates with about $27,000 of student loan debt. This year, for the first time, total student loan debt is higher than total credit card debt.

- A recent study pegged the lifetime increased earnings potential of someone with a college degree at $279,893 (not a million dollars, as previously claimed).

✔ Over 90 percent of college students are on Facebook; 20 percent are on Twitter. (You'll get a laugh if you ask college students whether they're on MySpace.) The average college student spends about half an hour a day on social networking; 82 percent of college students log into Facebook several times a day.

✔ Ninety-one percent of colleges have their own Facebook pages, 88 percent use Twitter, and 79 percent make their own YouTube videos.

✔ Only about 10 percent of college students belong to a fraternity or sorority.

✔ Many colleges have new first-year experience courses or freshman seminars to help students find their place in the college community. Sometimes they have a "common-read" (a book that all first-year students have to read), sometimes they're taught in sections with different subjects or topics in each, and sometimes they're just introductions to the campus and to student life in general.

✔ Many students fulfill their language requirement with Mandarin Chinese, Arabic, or Japanese—not Spanish, French, or German.

✔ The most popular majors are business, psychology, nursing, history and social sciences, biology, education, and communications. (Classics, astronomy, film studies, aviation, and chemical engineering have the fewest takers.)

✔ The most lucrative majors are petroleum engineering and civil engineering. (The job prospects aren't so good in English, classics, philosophy, and art history.)

✔ E-textbooks and e-resources are rapidly replacing print books and brick-and-mortar libraries. Many students read their textbooks on e-readers, and some students even rent their books.

✔ "Smart" classrooms allow professors to incorporate PowerPoint presentations, videos, and other content into their lectures. Some professors use "clickers" that allow students to offer instant input on how well they've understood the lecture.

✔ A third of all students took an online course for credit in 2011. (Some students wonder why they should go to class at all.)

✔ Massive open online courses (affectionately called "MOOCs") enroll tens of thousands of students (70 percent from abroad) in not-yet-for-credit courses. Some college students take them in order to study with marquee professors or to take courses not offered at their home institutions.

✔ Many colleges offer service learning programs: you get college credit for volunteering to do community service.

✔ Some schools require a year of study abroad: globalization comes to college. The most popular destination is England (they speak English there).

✔ The graduation rate at U.S. colleges is only slightly more than 50 percent—something we hope to change with this book.

The 15 Habits of Top College Students

What makes some college students successful, while others—well, less so? Sometimes it's a question of intelligence or insight. And sometimes it's sheer good luck. But a lot of the time it's good habits: things you do on a regular basis that set you apart from the hordes of other, more scattered students. In the hopes of separating the sheep from the goats, we offer our top 15 habits of the most successful students. You'll find that these folks . . .

1. **Have a goal.** They have a definite reason for being in college—and know what it is. Could be a future career, graduate or professional school, or just wanting to further their education. But it's almost never because their parents told them to go to college, or because it's the next thing to do after high school, or because they're too unimaginative to think up anything else to do with their time.

2. **Set priorities.** For every student, college is a balancing act between going to classes, doing the homework, having a social life, and, for many students, holding down a job. But the successful student knows how much time to allot to each of these activities—and how to set limits. Maybe partying is held down on weeknights, or an employer is told that hours have to be cut back during the jam-packed midterm week, or the family Thanksgiving dinner is jettisoned in favor of extra work on the term paper. Look, there are only 168 hours in the week—and not one of them can be spent twice.

3. **Divide up the work.** Readings get broken up into manageable chunks (not 200 pages in one sitting). Quizzes and tests are studied for over the course of a week (not at 3 a.m. the night before). And paper ideas start gestating when the assignment is handed out (not two days before the paper is due, when you

can barely formulate an idea, much less think through an issue).

4. **Are organized.** Successful students have gotten used to the fact that, in college courses, there's not a lot of redundancy or "going over." So they make it their business to make it to most of the lectures (and they don't cut the sections, either). They take really good class notes (and keep them in super-neat condition). And they always get their work turned in on time (no one-week extensions that only make it harder to complete the work in their other courses).

5. **Work efficiently.** Each task is done well—and once. There's no listening to the lecture a second time on their MP3 player (they paid careful attention the first time). No copying over all their notes (why would they do that if they have a good set from the lecture?). No doing the reading three times (once for a general overview, once to understand the argument or direction, and once to focus in on the finer points). In a fifteen-week semester, with four or five courses on tap, who has time to do things twice (or, in the case of some students, thrice)?

6. **Are consistent.** They do the work every week—even when nothing is happening on the grading front.

7. **Are persistent.** They know that sometimes the going gets tough. Maybe there's a problem set that requires serious hard thinking, or a paper that has to go through a number of painful drafts, or a presentation that has to be rehearsed 'til one really has it down. But whatever the case, the successful student doesn't flinch at the extra effort needed or the uncertainty of the result while he or she's still working on it. This student's mantra: *I'll get this thing right if it kills me.* (Which it usually doesn't.)

8. **Challenge themselves.** Successful students are intellectually energetic. So, when they read, they think actively and critically about what they're reading (not just slog their way through to get the plot). When they go to class, they actively think about, and question, what the professor is saying (not just taking it all

in like a giant sponge). And when they write papers, they probe more deeply into nuances of the issue (not just looking for the most basic, "yes/no" answer). Above all, they get the wheels and springs of their mind moving—and keep them moving throughout any intellectual task.

9. **Hang out with smart friends.** Successful students know that peer support is as important as getting good grades from professors. Finding friends who are intellectually engaged and eager—in some cases, taking the same classes as you—can stimulate and reinforce your own intellectual drive. On the other hand, spending lots of time with dorm mates who don't know what courses they're taking—or even why they're in college at all—can create an atmosphere so toxic that any attempts to do well immediately wither and die.

10. **Are open to feedback.** The best students realize that the returned papers and exams are a golden opportunity: these are the times in the semester when the professor is giving one-to-one, customized feedback on their level of achievement. So instead of tossing away the graded papers and exams, or conveniently forgetting to pick them up, these students pore over the comments and redo the missed problems in the hopes of really learning where they went wrong and how they can do better next time. All with a nondefensive and genuinely open frame of mind. (Hard for everyone, but somehow these students manage to do it.)

11. **Engage the professor.** Successful students realize that the prof isn't just some content-dispensing machine, pouring out what he or she knows during lectures, but is a working scholar who's happy to work with you on the content and materials of the course. So these students go to office hours, talk to the professor (or TA) after class, and email questions about things they didn't understand. In the best case, they forge a two-way relationship with the professor and, in so doing, learn more than the average college student and defeat the anonymity of the (for some students) alienating mega-university.

12. **Don't kid themselves.** When they study, they're really studying—not flitting between the e-article, their Facebook page, and the football scores. When they've messed up a test, they figure out where they went wrong—not just hope it'll go better next time. And when things aren't going quite according to plan, they diagnose the problem and, if need be, adjust their plan.

13. **Manage their emotions.** It's difficult to excel at college if you're feeling inadequate, bummed out, or doomed to fail. So successful students know how to focus on their own positive achievements—rather than on their failure to get a check-plus on the quiz that counts for only 2 percent of the grade. And they're not hypercompetitive or concerned to find out how everyone else did on that just-returned piece of work. They know that, for every assignment, there'll probably be someone doing better than they did—and many doing a whole hell of a lot worse. (And even if not, there's nothing they can do about it, so why add negative emotions to a less-than-stellar situation?)

14. **Visualize success.** For any multistep activity—especially one that's spread out over five years and forty-odd courses—it's helpful to imagine the end product: that is, to really picture what it'll be like, and to experience the good feelings that will come with it. That's why the most successful college students repeatedly picture what will come at the end of the road for them: their dream job, their acceptance to a prestigious graduate or professional school, or simply the next stage in their life. This provides motivation and energy, especially when you're in a rut, and makes it all seem worthwhile.

15. **Strive for excellence.** No matter what the task, successful students aim to do it well. Could be the term paper, the midterm, or even the (seemingly dumb to others) weekly quizzes, problem sets, or daily homework. No matter. *If I'm going to put my name on it*, top students think, *I might as well do it well*. Which they usually do.

The 10 Worst Self-Defeating Myths

The semester's just about to start and you've got a clean slate. And yet, some students beat themselves down before the first class has even met. Burdened with negative self-impressions and defeatist attitudes, they think up all sorts of ways in which the semester is going to go badly—and in the process ensure that it *does* go badly. Sound familiar, perhaps? Here are the 10 most common—and most destructive—things students tell themselves:

Myth #1. **"I'm just not good at math [or science or foreign language or some other required course]."** Many students have dubbed themselves bad at certain subjects, based on past experiences, future expectations, or what you've been hearing since you were six years old. But the past doesn't have to dictate the future. Maybe your difficulties were generated more by bad teaching than by any fault in your brain. Or maybe, bored to tears, you didn't pay attention in class or do the work at home. But now you have a new chance, so get psyched, do the work, and, most important, view the course as something you can do. Because you probably can.

Myth #2. **"Everyone in this place is smarter than me."** It's easy to look at the 500 students in the lecture hall and think that everyone is a better student than you—and that *they'll* be carting off all the A's. Especially if someone steps up to bat at the first lecture and asks a smart-sounding question. But don't panic too soon. Usually, the first-day showoff is more of a blowhard than a good student, and anyway, you have no way of assessing how much ability—or lack of ability—the other students have.

Myth #3. **"I don't learn well in big classes."** If you're going to a large state university (as most students are), it's easy to be buffaloed by the sheer size of the lecture: except for the lack of cheerleaders, there's not too much difference between sitting in this class and sitting in row 246 of the football stadium. But although big classes aren't the best learning environment on the planet, there are concrete things you can do to lessen your sense of alienation: take really good notes throughout the lectures (doing something defeats bad feelings); get to all the discussion sections (smaller environment and a chance to talk with other real people); and hoof it on over to your professor's office hours (one-on-one communication, always a winner).

Myth #4. **"This required course is a killer—half the people always fail."** Before you totally psych yourself out, keep in mind that the college rumor mill isn't always totally accurate. So don't necessarily trust the grade "curve" provided by your buddy (even if he or she really did fail the course last year). Also, most professors are way too scared to run courses in which half the students actually get F's (and besides, in most college courses there are significantly more A's and B's than C's and D's). But in the extremely rare case where you encounter that sort of class, why can't *you* be in the half that passes?

Myth #5. **"I just don't test well."** Tests are stressful—for everybody (except perhaps for the most laid-back surfer dude). And virtually all college courses come with tests, at least a midterm and final. But some stress and pressure can lead to good performance and improvement of skills (ask any competitive gymnast). Do what you can do to tone down the volume: use the study questions to construct and take a practice test the night before; budget your time carefully during the exam itself, paying careful attention to the weightings of the various questions; and realize that some questions are designed to be more challenging, so don't blow a gasket when confronted with a harder question (that's how professors distinguish the A and B answers).

Myth #6. **"I'll be able to ace this course by just cramming the night before the tests."** This is one of the most dangerous—and most common—myths, especially among students who're just starting college or have been in college only a year. Sure, perhaps in Earth Sciences 102 or Sociology 107 you got away with memorizing facts from the textbook the night before the test. But as you move up in college you're likely to get courses that are cumulative—that is, where the ideas depend on one another and require time to be assimilated into your mind. Besides, there can be essay questions that, to properly prepare, take more like a week than a night. So get rid of your bravado and face up to how things really are: it's not a 15-week semester for nothing.

Myth #7. **"I can't write papers."** Many students suffer from paper phobia: they try to avoid at all costs any course that even smells of writing. And when they do have to put their fingers to the keyboard, they spend more time feeling like they're about to be sick than they do getting any words on the screen. But relax: there are many things you can do to ease the pain. Get started working right when the paper is assigned—that way you'll plenty of time for your ideas to jell and to write drafts. Go see the professor (or TA) if you're not sure what to do or you get stuck—they're happy to help, and you may get a better grade, to boot. And, most important, realize that for many students (perhaps you) writing papers is an acquired skill—one that you can get on top of with repeated practice in different courses.

Myth #8. **"I'm too shy to talk in class."** It's perfectly fine to be shy. But that's no excuse for not participating in class. Shy or not, there will be times in life when you have to speak up, not just in classes that require discussion or presentations, but in life itself—whether it's to say "I do" at your wedding or to make a good impression at the interview for your dream job. And one of the purposes of college—as with any interpersonal or group activity—is to learn to present your ideas to other living, breathing human beings (for which talking is usually required). Most classes and professors are very supportive of students who make an effort to participate, even if they don't spout a steady stream of pearls of wisdom—so take advantage of the opportunity.

Myth #9. **"I don't need to go to class—I'll just watch the lectures on YouTube."** It's no secret that there are professors who post their lectures on the Web. But thinking you can rely on the Web instead of going to class is risky business. Shocking as it may seem, it's actually much easier to get to class M, W, F at 10 than to get it up at home to watch the lectures— because, at home, no time ever seems to be the right time. Also, working from the Web affords the constant temptation to listen to five lectures in a single evening—never a good way to learn.

Myth #10. **"I'm overwhelmed—it's all too much."** You're in distinguished company here: fully one-third of all college students report being overwhelmed after just one semester. But relax; this too will pass, especially if you adopt an upbeat attitude, get whatever help you may need (consider any of a myriad of campus resources), and plan for a successful semester— without your defeatist attitudes, which probably aren't true, anyway.

The 11 Secrets of Getting Good Grades in College

Grades are the measure of college success. Like the salary at a job, a batting average in baseball, or the price of a stock, your GPA is an objective indicator of how you're doing. And yet, there's surprisingly little good information—least of all from professors—about just what you should do to get good grades. We go where others fear to tread. And so, here are the eleven secrets of getting really good grades in college (A's, we mean):

1. **Take control of your destiny.** Your grade destiny, that is. There's no teacher or parent to remind you every day what you need to do or to make sure you've studied for exams. It's all in your hands. So step up to the plate and take responsibility. The grades you get will depend on what you yourself do.

2. **Don't overload.** Some students think it's a mark of pride to take as many course hours as the college allows. It isn't. Take four or, at the most, five courses each semester. That way you'll be able to devote all your energies to a manageable number of subjects, and you won't have to sacrifice quality for quantity. (For our best tips on which courses to take, see "Do's and Don'ts for Picking Your Courses" on p. 68.)

3. **Get your a** to class.** Most students have a cutting budget: the number of lectures they think they can miss in each course and still do well. But if there are thirty-five class meetings, each class contains 3 percent of the content: miss seven classes, and you've missed 20 percent of the material.

BEST-KEPT SECRET. Some not-so-nice professors want to penalize students who blow off the class right before Thanksgiving or spring break. So they pick an essay question for the final exam from that very lecture. End result? You can do really major damage to your GPA for the price of missing just one class.

4. **Take really good notes.** In many intro courses, the professor's lectures form the major part of the material tested on the midterm and final. So as you're taking notes, you're really writing the textbook for the course—which in many cases is more important than the official textbook. Be sure to get down everything the professor says and to maintain your notes in an organized and readable form. After all, these are the notes you'll have to study a number of times later in the course. (For primo note-taking tips, see "10 Secrets of Taking Excellent Lecture Notes," p. 109.)

5. **Study like you mean it.** There's a difference between studying and "studying"—and you know what it is. When you're really studying, you're 100-percent focused on and engaged with the material—a total immersion in what you're doing and a strong desire to get it right. When you're only half-heartedly studying, you're really only 35 percent involved, with the other 65 percent of your attention divided among tweeting your friend about how much you're studying, scoping out the surrounding tables to see who else might be around (and how attractive they are), and daydreaming about all the fun things you'll do when you finish this awful studying. Look, we know studying can be painful, but all students who get A's do it—no matter what they tell you. (For our best study tips, see "The How *Not* to Study Guide" on p. 104.)

6. **Do all the homework.** You may think the homework and problem sets—each of which is worth maybe 0.1 percent of

the grade—are just busywork: something the professor assigns to make sure you're doing something in the course each week. But really, the homework provides applications of the concepts, principles, and methods of the field to actual examples—the same sort of examples that will come up on the bigger tests. If you do well on the homework—that is, get ten out of ten on the problem sets or a check-plus on the little writing exercises—you're putting yourself in a good position to get a 100 when it really counts: on the midterm or final.

7. **Take each test three times.** When done right, taking a test is really three activities: preparing for the test, taking the actual exam, then going over the comments to see what mistakes you made. Each activity furnishes important—and grade-improving—information: the studying gives you practice in questions very similar to the those that will be on the test; the actual test is where the A is earned (at least in the best case); and the review of the comments (often accompanied by a visit to the professor's office hour to clear up anything unclear) is an investment in an A on the next test. (For our best advice about tests, see "12 Tips for A+ Test Preparation" on p. 166, "'So What's Going to Be on the Test Anyway?'" on p. 171, and "Top 13 Test-Taking Tips" on p. 174.)

8. **Always answer the question asked.** More points are lost on tests and papers by not answering the question asked than by giving the wrong answer. That's because students often have strong—and wrong—preconceptions about what the professor should be asking. "How can the question be so specific?" they wonder. "How can the professor *not* be asking a question about last week's classes, especially since he (or she) seemed so interested in that topic?" "Can the professor *really* be asking about that journal article we were supposed to read, or about the discussion in section___?" Don't try to psych out the professor or distrust what you see before your very eyes. Answer the question, as asked, head-on. (If you're not sure what's meant, always ask—and rescue your grade.)

9. **Play all four quarters.** Many college courses are "back-loaded." More than half the grade is left to assignments due the last month of the semester: a third test, 15 percent; the term (or research) paper, 25 percent; the cumulative final, 30 percent. You get the idea. Pace yourself and don't run out of gas just as you're coming into the home stretch.

10. **Do all the "extras."** In some courses, there are special end-of-the-semester activities that can improve your grade. Review sessions, extra office hours, rewrites of papers, extra-credit work—all of these can be grade-boosters. Especially in schools where there are no pluses and minuses, even a few extra points can push your borderline grade over the hump (from, say, a B+ to an A–; that is, an A).

11. **Join a community.** Many students improve their grades by working with study buddies or study groups. Try to meet at least once a week—especially in courses in which there are weekly problem sets or quizzes. And if your school offers "freshman clusters" in which a group of students all take the same section of some required courses, sign up for them, too. Students can improve their grades one level or more when they commit to working in an organized way with other students.

5-STAR TIP. Resolve to get at least one A each semester. Getting even a single A will change the way you think about yourself: you'll be more confident about your abilities and more energized for future semesters. If you're at all close in even one course, work really hard to get that A. It will change things forever.

20 No-Brainers to Save Money at College

For some, it costs about as much as a Lexus ES. *Every year.* For others, about as much as a Honda Fit. And some will get change from a $5,000 bill. It's college, and, whichever way you slice it, it's very expensive. But cheer up. We've got twenty tips to help you save money at college. Even if you're laying out big bucks, at least you'll get more bang for your buck. Here's how:

1. **Cut the costs of textbooks.** The average student spends $1200 a year on textbooks. You needn't. You can save a bundle if you order ahead and don't depend on the campus bookstore. Compare all the alternatives: print books (plus buyback), e-books, book rentals, and marketplaces. For print and e-books, check out WWW.AMAZON.COM, WWW.BN.COM, WWW.ABOUTFOLLETTEBOOKS.COM, and WWW.HALF.COM, as well as your brick-and-mortar campus bookstore. Rentals are available at WWW.CHEGG.COM, WWW.BOOKRENTER.COM, and WWW.CAMPUSBOOKRENTALS.COM. And for marketplaces (purchases from and sales to real people), go to WWW.TEXTBOOKSRUS.COM or WWW.TEXTBOOKX.COM.

5-STAR TIP. For all book modalities (print, e-, and rentals), check out the aggregators (sometimes called meta-sites): these are websites that compare the prices of many other bookselling websites. Two we especially like are WWW.CHEAPESTTEXTBOOKS.COM and WWW.BIGWORDS.COM (others include WWW.BESTPRICEBOOKS.COM, WWW.CAMPUSBOOKS.COM, WWW.TEXTBOOKS.COM, and, for rentals, WWW.TEXTBOOKRENTALS.COM).

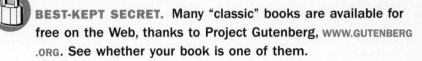

BEST-KEPT SECRET. Many "classic" books are available for free on the Web, thanks to Project Gutenberg, WWW.GUTENBERG .ORG. See whether your book is one of them.

2. **Get a cheaper device.** Many students starting college lunge at the most expensive devices: a fancy, full-sized tablet or one of the new, and expensive, Touch or Ultrabook laptops. In many cases, though, you can make do with much less: a mini tablet, a less powerful (and less expensive) laptop, or sometimes a mere e-reader. Check out "10 Things to Consider Before Buying a Tablet, E-Reader, or Laptop for College" on p. 62 for our best suggestions.

5-STAR TIP. Be sure to check out all sources—and look for "academic" or "educational" pricing—for all your hardware purchases. Always start with your campus computer store; often they have special back-to-college pricing. But if you're thinking Apple, consider the Apple Store for Education (HTTP:// STORE.APPLE.COM/US/BROWSE/HOME/FINDYOURSCHOOL); Dell, Dell University (WWW.DELL.COM/COLLEGE); and Hewlett Packard, the HP Academy (HP.FORCE.COM/EXTERNAL/HPACADEMY). Also, of course, Amazon and WWW.MACMALL.COM.

3. **Get academically priced (or in some cases, free) software.** If you're wedded to Microsoft Office (which includes Word, Excel, PowerPoint, and a number of other programs), you'll be pleased to learn that most years Microsoft offers a special discount for college students (search "Microsoft Office Academic" for a link). For those watching their pennies, Apache's OpenOffice and the open source LibreOffice are downloadable, absolutely free (can't beat that). If you're expecting to do heavy graphics,

search for Adobe Creative Suite at a student price (search the Web or check your campus computer store—they're likely to know).

BEST-KEPT SECRET. Discounted software for students is available at WWW.ACADEMICSUPERSTORE.COM and WWW.JOURNEYED .COM. Good values, always.

---

4. **Get some apps.** If you're one of the hundred-million or so people worldwide who own an iPhone, you'll want to get some apps especially tailored to college (most of them will set you back a buck or two or three). Some we like include:

   ▶ *iStudiezPro* (organizing your schedule)

   ▶ *PocketList* (to-do lists)

   ▶ *EverNote* (notetaking)

   ▶ *Wikipanion* (Wikipedia)

   ▶ *MentalCase* and *FlashCard++* (flashcards)

   ▶ *Chegg* (study help)

   ▶ *Graphing Calculator* (just like the handheld model, and includes screenshots)

   ▶ *The Chemical Touch* (periodic table)

   ▶ *Instapaper* (stores web pages)

   ▶ *iTranslator* (translations for your language courses)

   ▶ *Dictionary.com* (lots of words you don't know)

   ▶ *BlackboardLearn* (hooks up with your school's course management and grade reporting system)

   ▶ *My GPACalculator* (includes "what if" scenarios so you can fantasize about getting an A in that killer statistics course)

5. **Use e-services.** Try Amazon, eBay, and Overstock for just about any merchandise (Amazon often offers special shipping discounts for students); Priceline, Hotwire, and FLY.COM for airline tickets; CARRENTALS.COM and, at some colleges, Zipcar for car rentals; Netflix and Amazon for streaming movies; and Pandora and iHeartRadio for music.

6. **Tame your phone.** If you're like most students, you'll be spending every waking moment (and then some) on your phone. Be sure to get a plan that offers unlimited web, data, messaging, and e-mail. Not all plans do. And while you're at it, be sure your phone has reception in all the places you're likely to drive to (even if they include Wyoming, South Dakota, or Western Texas).

 5-STAR TIP. The major carriers (AT&T, Sprint, T-Mobile, and Verizon) almost always offer student discounts of around 10 percent (at least if your college is on the "approved" list).

7. **Eat in—and pack a lunch.** If you're living in a dorm, by all means eat there—or at some other dorm, nearer to your classes, that will accept your meal plan for lunch. Or have your dorm's food service pack you a lunch. An often-not-very-good lunch that you buy at, for example, the Student Union can easily set you back $15. Why pay twice?

8. **Take your own coffee.** If you're addicted to coffee, get a stainless steel thermos, a burr coffee grinder, and the roast of beans you like best, and make your own coffee to take to class (tea aficionados will want to get a good strainer or infuser; white, green, oolong, or black teas; and a stainless steel insulated mug). Saves four dollars a day or more (really adds up) and will give you a modicum of pleasure as you sit through the otherwise soporific lectures you're stuck in.

9. **Get there in a different way.** Instead of taking your own car, and paying $600 a semester for the preferred, on-campus parking, consider public transportation or, better, bicycling. If you can't give up driving, at least carpool with a friend or two, which saves lots of money and helps you cement your relationship with that friend or two.

---

⑤ **5-STAR TIP.** To save on gas, check out WWW.GASBUDDY.COM or buy your gas at Walmart, Costco, or your own local discount station.

---

10. **Check your car insurance.** Especially if you live in a big, freeway-laced city, car insurance can be super-expensive. Try to stay under your parent's policy, if you're of appropriate age. If not, ask your insurance agent for a "Student" or "Good Grades" discount (that is, assuming you have good grades). Also, if you're driving only a few miles per day, make sure your policy is rating as "pleasure" driving; your rate will be cheaper.

ⓌⓌⓌ **ON THE WEB.** Be sure to check out web-based insurance companies; for example, 21st Century, GEICO, and USAA (if you have a military background). They're likely to be cheaper than in-person agents.

---

11. **Use the facilities.** No, not *those* facilities. We're thinking about the recreational and academic services you paid for as part of your student fees—Olympic-sized swimming pools, Apple-endowed computer labs—not to mention the free tutoring service, writing center, and math lab. And if you're not feeling up to par, or college isn't turning out to be quite the happy experience you expected, be sure to check out the university

health service or counseling center. You've already paid for them, too.

12. **Think about flying the coop.** At many schools first-year students are required to live in the dorms. But after that, you're on your own. Consider living off-campus in an apartment or a cooperative living arrangement. You can often save bundles on food (at many colleges the food service is overpriced and is used as a means to subsidize the expense of the dorms). And hey, you might enjoy playing Rachael Ray, not to mention doing dishes once a month.

EXTRA POINTER. If you're really serious about saving money, consider adding a roommate—three people instead of two, four people instead of three.

REALITY CHECK. It's much harder to get along with three people than it is with two.

13. **Consider house-sitting.** In many college communities it's possible to house-sit for a professor who has a sabbatical or is on leave for the year—often for free or at a greatly reduced rate. Hey, these profs probably live better than you, so not only can you save a bundle of dough, but you can also increase your socioeconomic standing—at least for a year.

14. **Entertain yourself cheaply.** At many colleges, there are concerts, plays, speakers, cookouts, and all sorts of other events at student prices—and sometimes for free. Check out your college's Web site, student newspaper, or posters around campus for dates and prices. If you're in a big city, you might also find "rush tickets" (last-minute tickets at greatly reduced prices) for wonderful events. And if you're in a college town,

you might be able to work as an usher at concerts in exchange for free attendance.

EXTRA POINTER. If you're at a big football school and have bought season's tickets (but are not all that eager to go to all the games), you may be able to sell the ticket to the "big" game at a price sufficient to offset your costs for all the other games.

---

15. **Skip a trip.** Travel, especially airline travel, can be very expensive, especially if you want to travel at peak times. If you're a little short on cash—and don't have terribly magnanimous parents—consider forgoing the trip home for Thanksgiving. You'll see your parents in just three weeks for Christmas, so save your $500 and tell your parents to freeze the pumpkin pie.

5-STAR TIP If you're still dead set on making a trip, see whether you can get a student discount. Some good sites to start with are WWW.STATRAVEL.COM, WWW.TRAVELOSOPHY.COM, and WWW.STUDENTUNIVERSE.COM. If you like surface transportation, it's good to know that Amtrak and Greyhound offer student discounts. And if you're driving, see whether your school has a real or virtual "ride board" where you can hook up with other people driving to the same place.

---

16. **Join the workforce.** At many colleges, there are special work-study jobs to be had. Some of these—like being a museum guard or the checkout person at the college library—have long periods of down time, when you are on duty but can do your homework at the college's expense. And you'll make friends with other student workers.

17. **Travel on their dime.** Wanna see the world? Consider the study abroad program. Many colleges have special scholarships or stipends to enable students to do research abroad or to take courses at "sister" universities. This can be a wonderful opportunity to improve your language skills, to do research in countries where the materials actually exist, and to take courses at colleges where they actually specialize in what you're interested in. (For more information on study abroad, see "Top 10 Myths About Study Abroad" on p. 268.)

18. **Drop early.** Many students procrastinate about everything, including dropping a course they know they're doing badly in and will never finish. At schools at which you're paying by the course (or credit hour), you'll get a much bigger refund if you drop in an early week of the semester. So bail early, and save.

19. **Buy a prepaid debit card.** One of the easiest ways to save money is to set yourself a monthly budget. And one of the easiest ways to set a monthly budget—and stick to it—is to buy a prepaid debit card such as the Vanilla Visa or MasterCard. We prefer the off-the-rack *non*reloadable cards (sometimes called gift cards) available in various denominations at office supply stores (Office Depot, Office Max, Staples), pharmacies (Walgreens and Walmart Neighborhood Markets), and many supermarkets. (Why avoid reloadable cards? They are subject to a very complicated application process, thanks to the Patriot Act, and what's the point of reloading if you're trying to stick with the money you have?)

20. **Hit up your uncle.** Uncle Sam, that is. To some degree, the pain of out-of-control tuition increases has been lessened by a slew of recently introduced tax advantages, including the American Opportunity Credit, and the Lifetime Learning Credit—as well as the Tuition and Fees Deduction and the Student Loan Interest Deduction. Be sure to educate yourself about all of these; then, come April 15, calculate your deduction or credit for each to see which one gives you the maximum benefit (many tax-preparation software packages will do this for you automatically).

ON THE WEB. Very good information about all of these government tax breaks (including family-income caps and other requirements) is available at the Sallie Mae web page WWW.COLLEGEANSWER.COM/PAYING/CONTENT/PAY_TAX_BENEFITS.JSP and at the IRS' own Tax Breaks for Education: Information Center, WWW.IRS.GOV/UAC/TAX-BENEFITS-FOR-EDUCATION:-INFORMATION -CENTER. Gluttons for punishment can read the entire 87-page IRS publication at WWW.IRS.GOV/PUB/IRS-PDF/P970.PDF.

Ways to Ensure You Graduate in Four Years

College seems to be taking longer and longer to get through. The average time-to-degree at the (so-called) four-year college hovers at about five years, with only one-third of students graduating in four years and another third taking six or more years to finish. The situation at community colleges is no better: only 50 percent of students graduate within two to four years, while a full quarter take more than four years to complete their associate degree. All those extra years cost money and delay your entry into the workforce. It's not all that hard, though, to complete your program in the traditional four- or two-years if you follow our 14 tips for getting college done on time:

1. **Make a financial plan.** With the sticker price of some private colleges running upward of $40,000 a year and some state schools coming in at about $10,000, it's important to have a firm conception of how you're going to pay for your four years. What combination of gift aid, loans, parental help, and off- or on-campus employment is going to net the amount you need to pay for tuition and room and board? You wouldn't want to have to take time off from college just because you were short on funds. (Besides, realizing how much each year of college is really costing you can be a great motivator in getting you to complete your work in a timely fashion.)

2. **Assess the value of outside employment.** Needless to say, given the cost of college and current economic conditions, many students have to work part- or full-time just to make ends meet. But if you can at all swing it, it's much more time-efficient—and often more financially advantageous—to put all your efforts into finishing your coursework so that you can

more quickly land that real job with a real salary. Weigh the amount you're going to make from that part-time job against the cost of another year of college.

3. **Consider loans.** Even if you didn't take out any loans when you started college, it could be a good idea to borrow money at later stages of your college career. Do the math and see whether it's a good idea to take out small loans now if it means you could get a good job next year—as opposed to two or three years later. Knowing about the job prospects in your major—and how much they pay—will be instrumental in your assessment. (For more information about taking out loans during college, see "Top 9 Tips for Taking Out Student Loans" on p. 272.)

EXTRA POINTER. In some cases you may be able to land a "completion loan" from your parents or some other relative: you promise you'll finish college this year, they lend you the money.

4. **Apply for scholarships and prizes.** In many universities there's a surprising number of scholarships, awards, and prizes reserved for continuing and upperclass students. Check out your major department, the study abroad office, nontraditional students or veterans' office, honors college, or general university financial aid office for details. Often the fellowships are very fine-grained (for instance, for students studying ancient Greek, or food security and economic growth), so if you fit the bill, it can be easy to win.

ON THE WEB. You might also consider fellowships from sources outside your school; WWW.SCHOLARSHIPMONKEY.COM is an excellent source for upperclass fellowships.

5. **Get what's coming to you.** If you've taken AP courses or an international baccalaureate (IB) program, cash in your chips: apply to have these credited to the degree you're working on. Also, consider taking one of the 33 College Level Examination Program (CLEP) exams, if you're especially strong in some field and your college accepts these exams for credit. And if your college allows credit for life experience (for instance, work experience, summer internships, or, believe it or not, political campaigning), claim these, too.

6. **Fight for your transfer credits.** If your current college isn't your first one, make sure you get at least distribution (or core or general-education) credit for the work you've done (in some cases, you won't be able to get credit in your major, since the faculty want you to take those courses at their school). Usually, this will go through pretty smoothly, especially when there are "articulation agreements" in place (see "Transfer Tips—from Community College to Four-Year College" on p. 261 for an explanation of what these are and how they work). But even if your courses don't automatically transfer, don't give up hope. Most schools have appeal procedures that you should use. What have you got to lose?

7. **Consider the eight-semester plan.** Many colleges now offer you the option of contracting for a prepackaged program of courses in exchange for guaranteed places in each of them. If you're 100 percent sure what major you want, the eight-semester plan can facilitate your finishing in four years. The downside? You have to commit to a major before having taken any college-level courses in that field, you must take the courses in the order prescribed, and you have to stick to the letter of the program (there's no leeway to drop a course or to change your major).

8. **Don't set yourself back.** In sequences of courses aimed at developing skills—world (or foreign) languages and math, for example—many students have the strong inclination to start again at the very beginning, even if their placement test shows that they should enroll in a more advanced course. "After all," they figure, "what's the harm? And I'll learn it better this time." But there's a hidden cost. If you start the sequence again, you're signing on to extra, unnecessary courses and buying yourself more time in college. Not a good idea, if you're planning to finish in four years.

9. **Don't be a serial dropper/adder.** If you drop a class in the twelfth week, you've wasted a ton of time and have no credits to show for it. Avoid this situation either by bailing out when there's still time to add a replacement course or by more carefully researching your choices when you first sign up (see "10 Questions to Ask Yourself the First Week of Classes" on p. 82 for more on sizing up your classes).

10. **Don't double (or triple) major.** If you're serious about getting out in four years, you should stick with one major. Each additional major increases your requirements to the tune of between 10 and 12 courses. Given that the standard course load is between 8 and 10 courses a year, you don't have to be a statistics whiz to see how many years an additional major can add to your time-to-degree.

11. **Don't fail a requirement.** If you're ever in danger of getting the dreaded "F" in a required course, take emergency action to be sure you that you pass. Have a serious talk with the professor to find out what you need to do to pass the class, and then follow the instructions exactly. If you can eke out a D (or in some schools a C), you won't have to retake the requirement and retard your progress.

12. **Use the summers.** Summer is a great time to get in some extra courses and build up some added speed toward completion of your degree. Not going to be hanging around your college over the summer? No problem. Consider gaining credits through online courses or credited internships or job experiences. (For more on the advisability of summer school, see "Summer School Pros and Cons" on p. 264. For more on

online courses, have a look at "10 Tips for Online Courses (and MOOCs)" on p. 154.)

13. **Keep on top of your degree progress.** Many students have their degree delayed after discovering there were requirements they didn't know about. Check in with an adviser regularly to make sure you're on track and haven't overlooked any of the more obscure requirements. Many schools have online checklists or degree planners. Use these and make sure you read the fine print (including any footnotes at the bottom of the page, which can be more important than they might look at first glance—especially when yours is the exception treated in the note).

14. **Consider a five-year dual degree program.** One really time-efficient plan is to do a five-year combined BA/MA degree, which will save you at least a year or two of MA training. You can get these combined degrees in many fields, including economics, public policy, public health, engineering, and world languages. Also, some schools offer combined professional degrees, such as BA/DDS (dentistry) and BA/JD (law) plans. OK, it's not four years, but it's a really fast track into fields that require advanced degrees.

Top 10 Tips for Community College Students

Community colleges are hot: almost half of all college students are enrolled in one. And the 2009 American Graduation Initiative substantially boosted government funding for community colleges, and set the goal of increasing the number of community college students by five million by 2020. So if you're enrolled at a community college—with the idea of either getting a degree or ultimately transferring to a four-year college—well, you're in the vanguard. Here are our 10 best tips for getting started on the right foot:

1. **Figure out why you're there.** Especially at community colleges, where there is a broad variety of students with many motivations for being there, it's important that you figure out what *your* goals and aspirations are and how best to achieve them. If you're looking for vocational training—either to start in a profession or to refine or upgrade your skills at some existing job—it's important that you focus on that. If you're looking in the end to transfer to a four-year college, be sure to take the courses appropriate to that goal. And if you're just taking a few courses out of interest or to broaden your horizons, construct your program with that in mind. There's no "one size fits all" at community college, so be sure to tailor your program to your individual goals.

2. **Know your A.A.S. from your A.A. (and your A.S.).** One distinctive feature of community colleges is that they offer both the Associate in Applied Science degree (A.A.S.) and the Associate in Arts (A.A.) or Associate in Science (A.S.) degree. The A.A.S. degree is a two-year vocational degree, preparing you for a career such as nursing or other health care,

business, criminal justice, fashion, culinary, design and graphic arts, information technology, or paralegal work. The A.A. and A.S. degrees, on the other hand, provide you with basic, lower-division liberal arts coursework that parallels the program a four-year college and prepares you for transfer to that sort of institution. Be sure you pick your track appropriately. Once you start on an A.S. or an A.A. it's very, *very* difficult to shift to an A.A.S. (and vice versa).

3. **Get on top of the "developmentals."** Though almost all community colleges offer open admissions (that is, any high school graduate or GED holder can get in), they also require you to take "developmental courses" (or, as they used to be called, "remedial courses") if you're not up to college snuff in math, reading, or writing. For a nursing degree, for example, you might (in the worst case) have to take pre-algebra, beginning algebra, intermediate algebra, and only then, college algebra. Tip? Start taking your developmental courses right away the first semester, especially if you have a lot to make up. (For more on remediation, see "Facing Up to Remediation: Top 10 Strategies" on p. 149.)

EXTRA POINTER. In most community colleges they'll offer you testing in reading, writing, and math when you enter, in order to place you in the right level course. Don't disregard these results. You won't be happy if you find yourself drowning in a course that's way over your skills level.

---

4. **Know what transfers.** If you're planning on continuing your education at a four-year college, make sure that all the courses you're taking can transfer. If the course is too easy or is in a subject not taught at the four-year college, you may find that the college won't accept your community college course(s) for transfer credit. Luckily, there are usually agreements in place for which courses will transfer, usually called "articulation

agreements." Look for a list on the websites of both your community college and your prospective four-year college. And when in doubt, ask before you leap. (For more information about transferring, flip to our "Transfer Tips—from Community College to Four-Year College," on p. 261.)

BEST-KEPT SECRET. In most states, the department of education maintains a tool that allows you to see what will transfer. To see one of the best, visit WWW.VAWIZARD.ORG. Then check out the American Association of Collegiate Registrars and Admissions Officers website, WWW.AACRAO.COM (search for "Transfer and Articulation"), for a link to your state's site (worth a careful look).

---

5. **Expect to attend every class.** One possibly surprising feature of community colleges is that classroom attendance counts a lot in the grade. Sometimes up to 40 percent. That's because professors want to motivate commuter students to make all the classes and, in addition, tend to emphasize in-class learning over homework (because in some cases, working students don't have all that much time to prepare at home). You can really put yourself behind the eight ball if you've missed 16 of the 30 classes—even if you cram before the final and somehow manage to get an A on it.

6. **Prepare to be active.** Community college professors often see the class as an occasion to get the students actively involved in the learning, rather than treating their students as sponges to sop up what the professor is dishing out. Be prepared to participate in discussions, make a presentation, play simulation or role-playing games, design experiments, and in some cases even do community outreach or service programs.

7. **Don't work yourself to death.** Most students at community colleges are both working and going to school. Which is great. Keep in mind, though, that you can't both work full-time and go

to school full-time. And if you're also a parent, that's one more pressure. Make a plan that integrates your work, school, and home needs.

8. **Use the college resources.** One of the best aspects of most community colleges is the broad variety of services they offer. Especially good is the career counseling service—a trained professional (often a counselor, psychologist, or business person with years of experience) can help you find the career that's right for you and will make specific suggestions about courses to take. Be sure also to check out the advising center, writing center, tutoring center, and, if need be, the health and psychological services center. Part of your tuition and fees prepays for the services, so why not make use of them?

5-STAR TIP One of the facilities you might not have thought of is the learning resource or computer center. Here people will offer you advice about how to recover lost data, how to convert data from one program to another, how to use a spreadsheet, and how to interface with the various college web destinations (registration, grade reporting, course web pages, electronic library resources, and so on). And if you don't have a computer, you'll usually find free computers at which you can burn the midnight oil while preparing your papers.

9. **Go see the prof.** One of the great things about the community college is the tremendous number of hours the professors are required to sit in their offices to help students: at many schools professors are available, without appointment, for ten hours and up each week. Take advantage of this one-on-one help before the test, before a paper or assignment, and especially when you feel lost in a course (as many students do). The profs want to see you do well and are ready to help you do so.

REALITY CHECK. At many community colleges, professor-student relations take on an air of informality. But don't think that just because your prof is friendly and nice, he or she wants to be your BFF. It's sometimes good to keep your professor posted on what you're doing in your life. It's another thing to make him or her your confidant for all your problems.

10. **Join the community.** Community colleges realize that most students are commuters and don't have the social benefits that they might have at a four-year college. That's why the colleges try to compensate by providing "cohort" programs and "study buddy" programs that will put you in touch with other students taking the same courses. Make full use of these wonderful opportunities to meet students with goals and lives similar to your own, as well as those from different socioeconomic backgrounds, from different countries, and with different life experiences. The melting pot that is the community college is one of the great features of American college life. Make sure that, even if you don't melt in, you join the stew.

10 Best Tips for Engineering School

As engineering enrollment has steadily increased over the past 20 years, more and more students are realizing that engineers are creative problem-solvers who help to shape the future. Indeed, more than one-third of college students today are enrolled in either an engineering or a science program. Before you embark on your journey of discovery, design, and innovation, it'd be good to know how to prepare yourself for the trip. So we asked Bruce Mendelsohn, director of communications and outreach at the Bernard M. Gordon Engineering Leadership Program at MIT, to hit up some of his colleagues and friends—not to mention himself—for key advice on how to succeed at engineering school. Here are their ten best ideas:

1. **Find an engineering discipline that motivates you intrinsically.** Whether you opt for chemical, civil, mechanical, industrial, biological, or biochemical engineering, choose an engineering discipline in which you are genuinely interested. Your major most likely represents your career path, so by all means, be pragmatic—but also remember to follow your heart.

EXTRA POINTER. As you make your way through the intro courses in the various fields of engineering, pay attention not just to the grades you get but also to how much you enjoy (or don't enjoy) working in each field.

2. **Understand the first principles and never simply memorize.** Concentrate on internalizing the first principles of engineering: the basic concepts that lie beyond the problems you're trying to solve. Challenge yourself to describe engineering concepts effectively in layman's terms to your nontechnical friends—after all, you'll have to do so when you

get into industry. A neat party (or bar) trick for engineers is distilling complex concepts into cocktail napkin–sized diagrams and explaining them to nonengineers. (Really. It works.)

3. **Intern with different engineering companies and in different industries.** A three-month summer internship helps you convert classroom knowledge into engineering know-how and gain real-world engineering experience. Try different industries and corporate cultures to see which one works best for you.

5-STAR TIP. Ask around to see what programs are available and the companies where your department has successfully placed students in previous years. Also, if your department has bulletin boards—either physical or on the departmental web page—check them out too. And if you (or your parents) have a friend in the community who's working in some engineering discipline, reach out to him or her. Leverage any contact or relationship that you can.

4. **Network, network, network.** Start making contacts while you're in school as an undergrad and continue to do so after you graduate. The professional network you build during your time as an undergraduate (through your internships, externships, co-ops, professors, advisers, and so on) will complement your paper diploma. Whether online or at career fairs offered by your school, aggressively seek networking opportunities.

ON THE WEB. LinkedIn—not Facebook. Facebook is for fun; LinkedIn is for professional purposes. Also, check out your school's career services website and ingratiate yourself with the people who work in that office—good relationships are key, both on- and offline.

5. **Diminish your digital distractions.** Most engineering students think they're prolific digital multitaskers, capable of answering

the phone, reading, sending texts or email, and listening to music all while doing problem sets. But most aren't as good at it as they think. According to Stanford University research, these activities can negatively impact your ability to retain and accurately recall information. When it's crunch time, study in a quiet environment without digital distractions. And never cram. According to a recent UCLA study, sacrificing sleep for extra study time—whether it's cramming for a test or plowing through a pile of problem sets—is actually counterproductive. Ample sleep is critical for academic success—especially for aspiring engineers.

6. **Be single-minded.** Every engineering school has a required curriculum of introductions to the various areas of engineering: concentrate on doing well in all of them, not just the one(s) you most like. Also, rather than double major—as many go-getting engineering students seek to do—choose one major and pack in as many relevant courses as you can.

7. **Take leadership classes.** It's not enough for tomorrow's engineers to be technically proficient: you must also learn how to lead teams of people with diverse skills, from different cultures and socioeconomic backgrounds. As engineering teams transcend national boundaries and time zones, devote yourself to developing the engineering leadership skills that will help you lead a multinational project or an international team.

BEST-KEPT SECRET If you know what you're planning to go into after you graduate, and if it essentially involves work in other areas of the world, it's not a bad idea to build up a competence in the relevant language. If you plan, for example to do transportation engineering in Saudi Arabia, you could benefit from knowing some basic Arabic. And don't forget to brush up on the technical terms needed for your field of interest. Lots of people worldwide know some English, but in certain cases you could get a leg up if you can communicate with your coworkers.

8. **Take courses in majors that complement your primary study.** Knowing more about adjacent systems will help you see the big picture of the design and understand the constraints (or areas of flexibility) that characterize the overall product. For example, if you're an electrical engineer, think about the mechanical packaging requirements of your components, the heat transfer challenges of a design, the interference on sensitive communications or audio circuits.

9. **Take writing classes.** You may have thought that engineering was all numbers and calculations, but when I ask recruiters what attribute they most look for in a new hire, their resounding answer is "writing skills—we have to write about everything we do—we take the engineering knowledge for granted." Rather than avoiding English and communications classes when fulfilling your arts and humanities requirements, challenge yourself to become the effective communicator that employers seek. If you can't communicate in writing, your education can come up short.

10. **Ask, ask, ask.** Although engineers are naturally curious about the topics they're working on, sometimes they're not as curious about other areas. Be actively curious about people not like yourself and about topics unrelated to engineering. Take classes in topics you know nothing about. Challenge assumptions. As an engineering student, you may find it easy to fall in love with technology; however, engineering is about relationships—specifically, between technology and society. Get an engineering *education*, not just a degree.

Top 10 Tips for Applied Arts and Design Colleges

The creativity of designers can be seen almost anywhere you look, from innovative product packaging and apparel design to 3-D characters in movies and artfully displayed cuisines.

For creative people interested in the areas of industrial and advertising design, fashion, media arts, game design and animation, interior design, and the culinary arts, the right mix of education, imagination, and motivation can lead to a fulfilling career—starting with an applied arts or design college (or else a design or arts program at a four-year liberal arts college). We invited Jonathan DeAscentis, dean of academic affairs at the Art Institute of California–Los Angeles, to share some tips about how to succeed at an applied arts college. Here's what he recommends:

1. **Treat class like a job.** For many applied arts courses, the demands of class are intended to mimic industry expectations and collaborative work environments. Prepare to treat your classes and coursework like a job.

   REALITY CHECK. Consider how your boss and work colleagues would react if you showed up unprepared and late, or not at all, for a consultation session with a client. Now think of your professor as one such client.

2. **Start your portfolio.** An effective portfolio must demonstrate the skills and knowledge of a student just as well as it represents a student's personal brand and identity. Whether you are a graphic designer, fashion designer, web, or other designer, the key questions to ask (and answer) as you start your collection of work include: "Who am I?" "How am I

unique?" "What artistic strengths do I bring to the project?" "What am I passionate about?" and, most generally, "What is my goal as an artist and creator?" Reflecting on these questions as you assemble your portfolio of creative work will not only keep your work centered on your own identity as an artist but also help you amass the work that is going to go into the portfolio of your work.

 5-STAR TIP. Train yourself to talk about your work. A career in any creative art will require you to express—in words and to other people—what you have in mind as a creator. Practice communicating, orally and in writing, what your goals are as an artist and how you think your work manifests them.

3. **Participate and volunteer.** Attend class, join campus activities, and show up to professional clubs and organizations to share your work and ideas with fellow artists and designers. Also, try to volunteer for community service and industry-related events to start showing your work more broadly and to make the connections you will need when you are ready for a job. For instance, budding web designers need to befriend great coders; beginning chefs will do well to connect with savvy restaurant managers; filmmakers will benefit from linking up with visual effects and 3-D artists. Particularly in emerging industries and fields, connections are what help someone put together a team for a freelance project or young company, and they can be instrumental in helping you find work.

4. **Identify a faculty mentor.** Remember that your instructors are experts in their fields, with lots of insight to share. Pick one you admire and seek out a mentoring relationship.

5. **Intern.** To gain real-world experience, develop connections, and grow as an artist, become an intern or look for a job in your field of study—at the best place you can. Search for these openings early, and when you secure the position, give it all you have.

5 **5-STAR TIP** Seek out your campus career center as soon as possible. The advisers there are dedicated to providing local resources and helping you gain valuable work experience. Also, if you know someone in the community working in your field of choice, seek out that person. Often acquaintances outside college feel very warmly when people they know, in a college they know, want to join their team.

6. **Become financially literate.** Do this right away. It is important to educate yourself on your financial choices and outcomes. Moreover, individuals with creative talents such as graphic design, photography, or video production, for example, also have opportunities to freelance. Consult with your career services department to see what guidance they can offer regarding ad hoc assignments (such as going rates and tax considerations).

7. **Apply yourself.** There are many, many design and art competitions out there looking for emerging talent and student participation at no cost. Keep an eye open for the next "call for entries" and apply. A win or recognition will make for a great work sample for your portfolio and an accolade for your resume. And it'll make you feel better about your work: after all, the contest probably had lots of entries that were judged to be less good than yours.

8. **Be your own publicist.** Don't be shy about sharing your accomplishments with faculty, mentors, and club colleagues. They may pass along your good news and lead you to a great opportunity.

EXTRA POINTER. If your school or program has a newsletter or does an e-mail blast from time to time, be sure to get your achievement noted. You never know who reads these things.

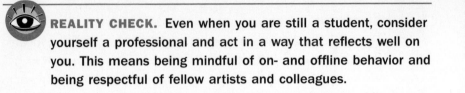

REALITY CHECK. Even when you are still a student, consider yourself a professional and act in a way that reflects well on you. This means being mindful of on- and offline behavior and being respectful of fellow artists and colleagues.

9. **Stay inspired.** The road to graduation is challenging for many reasons. Even the best designers and artists feel overwhelmed and discouraged at one point or another (indeed, often the most gifted students set themselves the highest standards and are most unhappy when they don't quite live up to them). Remind yourself of your goals and why you are at school in the first place: to earn your degree and continue on the path to reaching your goal, be that becoming an executive chef, establishing your own fashion label, or achieving some other creative success. Then tap the network of students and faculty that you have created for support.

10. **Stay connected.** Don't let all the time and effort you've spent developing relationships go to waste once you graduate. Plan to stay connected with your fellow alumni, mentors, and faculty. Build up your own personal website and/or Facebook page. Sign up for newsletters, collect contact information, connect via social media. And if you have occasion to show your work, be sure to invite all your friends and acquaintances to have a look. Invite them to look at the ads you've designed, the meal you've cooked, the clothing you've designed, or whatever the product of your creative talents is.

ON THE WEB. To see some lists of applied arts or design colleges, check out HTTP://ARTSCHOOLS.COM/, WWW .ALLARTSCHOOLS.COM/, and WWW.ARTINSTITUTES.EDU/LOS-ANGELES/ DEGREE-PROGRAMS/DEFAULT.ASPX.

The College Student's Bill of Rights

As a college student you don't just have responsibilities; you have rights. But figuring out what these rights are—and what they do and don't include—is often no simple matter. Here's our (semi-) humorous take on what you are—and aren't—entitled to at college:

Article 1. You have the right to annual tuition that is less than the price of a Lexus IS C convertible—at least the one that doesn't come with the HDD navigation system.

Article 2. You have the right to comprehensible, easy-to-fill-out FAFSA and Profile® forms—or at least ones that don't require a PhD from Wharton or Sloan School to get past page two.

Article 3. You have the right to affordable textbooks—that is, if you think $600 a semester is "affordable."

Article 4. You have the right to professors who are basically knowledgeable about the material—just not ones who can hold their own against Adderall in keeping you awake.

Article 5. You have the right to professors who sometimes offer up something funny—just not ones making regular appearances at WWW.COLLEGEHUMOR.COM.

Article 6. You have the right to a professor who dresses neatly and professionally—just not one who never wears "mom jeans."

Article 7. You have the right to professors who don't hit on students—just not ones who rate a chili pepper at WWW.RATEMYPROFESSORS.COM.

Article 8. You have the right to adjunct instructors or TAs who are courteous, friendly, and nice—or at least would be if they were making enough to live indoors.

Article 9. You have the right to a "smart" classroom that is equipped with twenty-first-century technology—just not a prof who has any idea how to use the stuff.

Article 10. You have the right to nod off, zone out, or IM once in a while during lecture—but not the right to play Pocket Rockets on your iPhone right under your prof's nose.

Article 11. You have the right to express your views in discussion section—just not to hold court in your astronomy course on why the moon landing was a hoax.

Article 12. You have the right to an exam with questions reasonably related to what was talked about in class—just not one that covers only the classes you bothered to show up for.

Article 13. You have the right to dispute your paper grade and get a clear explanation of why you got the grade you did—just not to have your grade raised simply because "you paid good money for this stinkin' course." (We've heard this argument more times than we care to remember.)

Article 14. You have the right to get an extension on your paper if you have a serious medical emergency or a death in the family, or you wind up in jail (no kidding, it really happens)—but not if your Internet connection failed just as you were downloading page six from WWW.COLLEGEPAPERMILL.COM (not a real site, so don't bother).

Article 15. You have the right to talk to a professor about the term paper during his or her office hours—just not at 5:45 p.m. on the third Thursday of the month (the one time you can make, given your jam-packed schedule of work, intramural sports, and hooking up).

Article 16. You have the right to a comfortable working environment in which to take your final exam—or at least enough space so that your classmate sitting next to you (who hasn't showered in three days) isn't pouring sweat onto your paper.

Article 17. You have the right to spaces in courses you need for your major—at least *some* time in the next seven years.

Article 18. You have the right to a seamless transfer of credits from a community college to a four-year college—in your dreams! (Get ready for hours of pitched battle when you try to transfer that graphic design 101 course you took back in 1994.)

Article 19. You have the right to a living, breathing professor—if your college hasn't yet discovered the money-saving potential of online courses and MOOCs.

Article 20. You have the right to professors who don't attempt to tell lame jokes—a right you can promptly exercise by turning the page.

2 IN THE BEGINNING . . .

There's always a huge amount to do when you're getting ready for the college year. Luckily, your to-do list needn't include re-creating the heavens and the earth (though it can be quite long). Getting supplies for college, meeting your roommate, planning your commute, picking your courses and major, and getting settled into college—all of these are part of the back-to-college grind. There's no need, however, to run around like a chicken without a head. Or to get so freaked out by what's to come that you end up paralyzed, unable to even start on what there is to do. Our tips will help you focus on what's most important at this time and guide you through the key decisions you'll need to make.

In this chapter you'll learn:

- ► 7 Things to Do the Summer Before College

- ► 15 Things to Do the Week Before College

- ► 10 Things to Consider Before Buying a Tablet, E-Reader, or Laptop for College

- ► Do's and Don'ts for Picking Your Courses

- ► Top 12 Tips for Picking a Major

- ► Top 10 Secrets of the Syllabus

- ► 10 Questions to Ask Yourself the First Week of Classes

- ► The 13 Warning Signs of a Bad Professor

- ► Tips and Tricks for Improving Your Course Schedule

7 Things to Do the Summer Before College

Some students—and their parents—can't start on college soon enough. And it's a good thing. The more you do the summer before college, the less you have to do come crunch time: the week-before-college rush. To help all you early birds (and just about everyone else college-bound), here are our seven best things to do the summer before college:

1. **Get to orientation—early.** Almost all colleges offer summer orientation programs—typically day-long affairs, some as early as June—in which students and their parents can tour the campus, visit with a few faculty members and academic advisers, and, most important, pick their courses (ideally it's the students doing the picking, not the parents). Many colleges follow the airline model, offering only a limited number of spaces, especially in large, required first-year courses that, when filled, are closed. Tip: go to the very first orientation session you can make, for your best shot at the courses you want.

> **BEST-KEPT SECRET.** If you get into an honors program or declare your major or (at some colleges) sign up for a four-year time-to-degree, you might qualify for special places reserved for these "privileged" classes of students. Find out whether you're eligible.

2. **Get some hardware.** If you don't already have a computer—preferably a laptop, tablet, or e-reader—now's the time to get one. If you opt for a laptop, whether you choose a PC or Mac, we think your computer should weigh no more than three or four pounds, have at least a six-hour battery life (a must for taking notes in lectures throughout the day), have a webcam

and good speakers, and have a full-size (or at least 92 percent of full-size) keyboard. (For our best ideas on what to think about when buying a device, see "10 Things to Consider Before Buying a Tablet, E-Reader, or Laptop for College" on p. 62.)

3. **Get some software.** You'll want to get some good word processing software. Microsoft Word is the college standard (try the new 2013 version), though many students like the free OpenOffice or LibreOffice alternatives. If you're buying more task-specific software—say, for your business, graphic design, or urban planning course—we strongly recommend that you hold off until your course has started and your instructor tells you what to buy. It'd be a shame to spend $329 on the wrong program, only to find that it's nonreturnable.

4. **Surf the college website.** Sure, you've had a peek and watched the glossy propaganda videos when you were choosing a college. But now have a look at the academic side of things. Go to the college portal of the university you'll be attending; look for the *academics* or *for current students* tabs; then search for the *college requirements,* the list of *majors and minors,* the individual *departmental home pages* (where you might even find syllabuses for the courses offered), and the *course schedule* (the actual list of courses to be offered in the fall—not to be confused with the course *catalogue,* which is the list of every course ever offered at the school). The more you know about the structure of the school, the easier it'll be to navigate, once you get there.

---

⑤ **5-STAR TIP. Master the academic calendar.** It's worth checking out when classes start and end, when finals are held, the dates of those all-important fall and spring breaks, and whether your school celebrates Martin Luther King Day, Robert E. Lee Day, or Tu B'Shevat. Now's the time to try to make sure that your sister's wedding or the family ski trip to Steamboat Springs doesn't get scheduled smack in the middle of final exams week.

---

5. **Dust off your language skills.** Most every college has a foreign or world language requirement, usually a four-semester sequence in a language of your choice. Now would be a good time to brush up on a language you learned in high school or speak around the house. If your summer plans include travel abroad, resolve to speak only the language of the country from touchdown to return home. Better language proficiency will not only save you some of the distribution requirements, it'll actually be a boon if you major in one of those fields that use other-than-English language resources—European or Asian history, international marketing, Slavic literature, or premed or other health care professions.

EXTRA POINTER. If your school assigns summer reading for the first-year experience course or the freshman seminar, plan to get it done. You don't want to be behind before the race has even started.

---

6. **Reach out to your roommate.** It's always a good idea to find out whom you're going to be sharing your digs with for the next nine months. If you're planning to live on campus, your college may be sending you all sorts of information about your assigned roommate; even if they don't, you can check him or her out on your own. You don't have to scour WWW .BACKGROUNDCHECKS.COM or WWW.BEENVERIFIED.COM; a simple Google search or glance at his or her Facebook page should give you more dirt—er, information—than you need (provided your roommate hasn't set the privacy settings too high—which is a fact about the roommate, too). Once you get to know your new roommate a little—or if you're rooming with a good friend from high school or from previous years at college—it wouldn't be a half-bad time to make some room rules: When do lights go on and off? What will the "do not enter (you wouldn't want to see what's going on in here)" signal be? And how much noise and partying is too much (or not enough)?

WWW **ON THE WEB.** If you don't yet have a roommate, try one of the online roommate-finding services: WWW.ROOMSURF.COM, WWW.EASYROOMMATE.COM, or WWW.ROOMSYNC.COM.

---

7. **Pursue your passion.** The summer before college is one of the last times you'll be able to do what you most enjoy doing, for 100 percent of the time. For Lynn, age seventeen, it was reading Russian novels. For Jeremy, age eighteen, it was working in a camera store. And for our son Jonah, age fifteen, it's designing bridges and reengineering the New York City subway system for greater efficiency. Getting in touch with your true passion—and cultivating it without the demands of school—will put you in a really good, and motivated, mood for college in the fall. And, with any luck, it'll net an elective course in Tolstoy, marketing, or civil engineering that you'll actually look forward to going to.

5-STAR TIP. The secret of college success is integration—lining up what you want to do with what you have to do. If you succeed at this, you will succeed at college.

---

15 Things to Do the Week Before College

The semester's just about to start. And you're all geared up for fifteen weeks of great courses. Or maybe you're still in vacation mode and haven't even had a thought about the semester that, now that you think of it, begins next week. Either way, you're guaranteed the best semester ever if you follow our 15 must-do's for the week before college:

1. **Figure out where you're going and how you're going to get there.** Your college experience will be off to a bad start if you discover on the first day that there are no spaces left in Lot 32 or that the bus doesn't stop at Lincoln and Nebraska. Always have a Plan B. And while you're at it, figure out where your classes are going to meet. You wouldn't want to show up at 411 Old Main, only to find the class is at 411 New Main.

2. **Figure out where you're going to eat.** Are you going to be taking lunch to classes or going back to your dorm or apartment to eat? And what about Sunday nights, when (for who knows what reason) the food service in the dorms is closed? Hey, you can't do this college thing without proper nourishment.

3. **Plan an exercise routine.** Colleges invest gazillions of dollars in world-class exercise facilities. Go over to one of them, pick up a barbell, and imagine yourself doing this three times a week. (At least you'll have a sound body in which to preserve your, we hope, sound mind.)

4. **Get some proper beverage equipment.** Every lecture or discussion section will go better with a piping hot caffeinated drink. So hoof on over to the local superstore or coffee bistro and buy the biggest spill-proof stainless steel thermos you can find. Even if the lectures are not so hot, at least you'll be

awake and not spilling coffee on the legs of your pants (or worse). (Non-coffee-drinkers should consider tea, vitamin water, and five-hour energy drinks.)

5. **Buy the tomes.** Get the list of required textbooks from either your college bookstore or online course page. Then check out prices at both brick-and-mortar bookstores and online sites. (For our best ideas on where to search, see "20 No-Brainers to Save Money at College" on p. 22.)

6. **Start calendaring.** Get a good electronic or print calendar and start entering your time commitments right away: when your classes meet, when you plan to study, what the assignments are, and when they're due (often these can be found in advance on the course web page). Some e-calendars we like are Google Calendar, iStudiez, AirSet, 30 Boxes, and iCal (for Mac). Of course, if you have an iPad or iPhone, do your calendaring there.

7. **Learn to Skype.** If you've never tried real-time video conferencing, try out the free program at WWW.SKYPE.COM. You'll be able to talk to—and see—high school friends at other campuses, professors holding virtual office hours and individual conferences, and even your parents and siblings back home, if you're so inclined. (If your computer doesn't have a built-in web cam and mic, you'll need to buy one for about $30 at your campus computer store.)

8. **Get the word.** You'll need a password to access the university portal (which is where you'll find course web pages, library e-resources, your enrollment status and grades, and online registration in semesters to come). Get it now. Also take advantage of your free university e-mail account: professors will be happier getting papers from jeremy.hyman@ucla.edu than from jeremythestud@mondohotbodies.com.

9. **Visit the books—including the electronic ones.** Make your way over to the library and see where the books and journals are shelved. And while you're at it, look at the electronic

resources at your library's home page: see how the databases and e-resources are organized, and imagine yourself actually using them. With any luck, you will. (You'll find more details about this in "14 Techniques for Doing Research Like a Professor" on p. 190 and "Top 10 Tips for Doing E-Research" on p. 196.)

10. **Scout out the services.** When you have some extra time, make a campus tour and check out the various "offices": advising center; writing center; math and computer labs; tutoring center; and centers for nontraditional students, first-generation students, international students, single parents, and veterans. Hey, who knows, you might actually want to use one someday.

11. **Find yourself a cave.** You won't want to spend much time during the semester trying, then retrying, all kinds of study places. Figure out where you think you'll study best, then christen this place as your study spot.

12. **Rein in the folks.** Set some limits on your parents, especially if your dad—or mom—is the type who'll be texting you the two hours a day that he or she isn't calling you. And up the privacy settings on your Facebook page if your parents are the intrusive type—or if you think you'll have stuff going on that you don't want to become a family affair. You might prohibit them from posting messages on your wall or tagging you in family photos—or refuse to "friend" them altogether. (Of course, if they're paying for your college and they know the ins and outs of Facebook, your folks might not be all that happy about your banning them from your page.)

13. **Meet the prof.** For the really bold, there's the visit to the professor's office to find out a little more about the course and distinguish yourself from the nameless masses. Don't be put off, though, if the professor is too busy to visit with you (he or she might be rushing to polish up the syllabus or figure out what to say in the first week of lectures).

14. **Go clubbing.** While you still have some free time, it's nice to see what kinds of student clubs and teams your college has to offer. You might just be dying to join the Jews for Jesus or the Wiccans, the Young Green Republicans or the Democrats for Sarah Palin, the Rock-Paper-Scissors Club or the Death Cab for Cutie fan club. And even if you don't want to join in on the fun, the look-see will give you a better feel for what's going on at the school and what the students are like.

15. **Take a breath.** Fifteen weeks is a long haul. Don't get wound up too quickly. There'll be plenty of time for panic once the semester sets in.

10 Things to Consider Before Buying a Tablet, E-Reader, or Laptop for College

Devices are quite the rage at college (and just about everywhere else). iPads and iPad minis; Kindles, Nooks, and Kobos; Nexus, Galaxies, and Surfaces—there are more choices than you can shake a stick at. But which is best for college? And which is best for *you* at college? You'll avoid a tech wreck if you carefully follow our ten best tech recs:

1. **Decide your budget.** Before deciding on any models, you need to figure out how much you're willing to spend. Least costly are e-readers, which can run anywhere from just under $100 to about $300; next are tablets (including mini-tablets), which run in the $200–$600 range; finally, there are laptops and netbooks, which start at about $350 and can run up to well over $1,000.

REALITY CHECK. Consider who's paying. If it's your parents or grandparents who are shelling out the bucks, tell them it's "an investment in your future" and you really need something good. So too, if your scholarship is paying, you might want to spring for a premium product. But if you're going to have to pay it off yourself from your $10-an-hour job at the library or pizza store—well, you may want to buy a more basic and less costly device.

2. **Decide how you're going to use it.** Hype aside, *tablets* are basically ancillary or secondary devices: they're really portable

media players good for watching movies, listening to music, playing games, checking Facebook, sending and receiving email, Skyping friends, and browsing the Web—in short, all the *entertainment* you'll want at college. But when it comes to the *work* of college, with a tablet you're going to come up short. You won't be able to use programs as basic as Microsoft Word, Excel, or PowerPoint (although you can *view* .ppt documents, you'll need to move to apps to get greater functionality—and even then, you might not get all the functions); Adobe Photoshop (full version) won't run on a tablet, and Flash won't work, either; not to mention computation programs such as Mathematica, MATLAB, and Maple. Tablets are not made for power users. Laptops are.

3. **Decide whether you're going to use it only for reading.** Many students buy dedicated e-readers in the hopes of saving money on (e-) textbooks and also (for the really motivated) taking books to class. For those purposes, these devices fit the bill. They offer access to millions of e-books, often at a price cheaper than their print counterparts; they typically come with a 6- or 7-inch screen, more than large enough to read from; the ability to enlarge the font, making reading even easier; and a long battery life, typically 10 hours or so—more than enough to read the day's portion of even *Crime and Punishment.*

IOHO. On some e-reader models, you can save $20 if you agree to a constant barrage of advertisements. Don't.

4. **Decide *where* you're going to read.** If you're thinking of reading in bright light, say in the library or outside on the grass, you'll want to get an E-Ink display: not only does it look most like paper, but it also doesn't have annoying reflections, and the display doesn't "wash out." (Keep in mind, though, that you're giving up color for readability.) If, on the other hand, you're planning to read in your dark and dingy dorm room—or in your man- or woman-cave—opt for a backlit display. Not only will it be easier to read in low light, but it will also bring the added benefit of color—useful for studying the 3-D human anatomy models required in your biology course, not to mention the magazines, comic books, and web content that are not.

5-STAR TIP. If you decide to bypass the e-reader in favor of a tablet, make sure you try reading an e-textbook on the tablet before plunking down your money. Some students find many tablets' displays to be annoyingly bright, and you wouldn't want to get a migraine while doing your last-minute reading before the midterm.

FLASH! Some E-Ink e-readers now come with edge-lighting. Good for reading in bed or in other dark places.

5. **Decide what functionality you need for reading.** You may not have thought of this, but reading at college involves a multitude of tasks: turning from page to page; perusing the footnotes and flipping back to the body of the text; taking e-notes and, in certain classes, sharing them with your friends; highlighting key passages; and annotating and referring to page numbers (which are variable, depending on the device). Check to see how many of these functions are smoothly—and easily— performable on your device of choice.

6. **Find out what e-books are available for your device.** There are almost as many book formats as there are devices: EPUB (Open Standard), KF-8 (Amazon), iBook (Apple), and, in some

cases, PDF. Check whether the books for your courses will work on the device you're planning to buy. Get a sampling of ISBNs from your college bookstore or assorted course web pages. Then search on the Web (just enter the ISBNs in your search engine) to find out what formats each book comes in. You wouldn't want to spend $300 for a device, only to find that the publisher hasn't deigned to produce the book in the format you need.

7. **Consider the pros and cons of a mini-tablet.** For some students, the 7-inch mini-tablet represents an excellent compromise: true portability, availability of apps, and reasonably good processing power, all at one-third to one-half less than its full-size, 10-inch counterpart. Keep in mind, though, that convenience comes at a (small) price. The mini may have a lower-resolution screen than its bigger brother (not so much a problem for reading, as you can increase the font size, but a bigger problem for HD videos); and in some cases, it might have a slower processor (could be an issue depending on what you're running).

FLASH! A number of tablet makers are beginning to give serious thought to how textbooks display on their devices—in particular, the aspect ratio (the ratio of length to width). Be sure to try out an e-book before buying any devices made specifically for college use.

EXTRA POINTER. If you decide to buy an Android-based tablet, make sure it has the latest version of the OS: currently 4.0 and, in time, higher. It's hard enough to be sure your app of choice will work with Android without having to worry whether it'll run on 2.0.

IOHO. If you're planning heavy road use (and have the money), consider getting a model with 4G capability. Although you may think WiFi is enough, once you've searched for a Starbucks for an hour, only to find that there's nowhere to sit when you get there, you'll wish you had coughed up the extra hundred bucks or so for 4G. And consider getting more memory than the minimum amount; the few extra bucks are more than made up for by the diminished future headaches.

8. **Decide whether you're planning to do any writing.** Writing requires keyboards, and there are all kinds: virtual and physical, full-sized and tiny, detachable and built-on. Whatever device you're planning to buy, try out the keyboard—not just for as long as it takes you to tweet, but as long as it would take you to write, say, a paper. Keyboard fatigue can be a problem, and if your super-thick fingers don't work well with tiny, close-set keys, you'll average over one error per line—a tremendous time-waster and pain in the butt.

EXTRA POINTER If you're not happy with the keyboard that comes with your device, or if you're only an occasional writer, consider an accessory keyboard. Check out your college store or local computer store for Bluetooth wireless keyboards, wireless solar keyboards, and even rollup silicone keyboards.

9. **Decide whether you're planning to print.** It's a bear to print from a tablet, especially if your college doesn't have campus-wide WiFi. That's why many students plan to print at the 24/7 Computer Center. But think it out. Are you really going to want to walk over there at two in the morning when it's 20 degrees outside? And what happens the day before the due date for

your paper (and 5,000 other students' papers) when there's a line around the student union just to get in? (On the other hand, if your school requires all papers to be submitted electronically—well, then, you may not need a printer, in which case a tablet is just fine.)

10. **Find out what your school is using.** If you're planning to take any online courses, to use the university's course management system (Blackboard, for instance), or to access the e-periodicals at the library, check out what programs are needed. Sometimes a tablet, either on its own or with a university-provided app, will work just fine, but in other cases special proprietary software is needed to connect up—in which case a laptop will work much, much better.

 ON THE WEB. If you're still unsure what to buy—or even if you think you are sure—it's more than worth your while to check the reviews of the latest models. Sites we like include: WWW.REVIEWS.CNET.COM, WWW.PCMAG.COM/REVIEWS, WWW.PCWORLD.COM/REVIEWS, HTTP://GDGT.COM/REVIEWS/, WWW.APPLEINSIDER.COM/REVIEWS, and **Walt Mossberg and Kara Swisher** at HTTP://ALLTHINGSD.COM.

Do's and Don'ts for Picking Your Courses

One of the first orders of business in any new semester is picking—and getting settled into—your courses. The job can be both incredibly exciting and, especially if it's your first time, incredibly intimidating. It can seem like there are more choices than stars in the universe. And who really knows what goes on in anthropology, linguistics, or communication studies—not to mention applied developmental psychology, geospatial information systems, and ichthyology (for the curious, that's the study of fish)? But have no fear. Follow our do's and don'ts, and you're sure to land the very best courses your college has to offer:

Do scour the college online catalogue—and the online course page (when available)—for as much information as possible about what the course involves. In the best case, you'll find not only a detailed course description but also a list of the books to read, the assignments required, and even a course syllabus.

Don't limit yourself to just the courses you know—like American history, English literature, or Spanish—or to those courses recommended by an adviser as the "standard first-year program." One of the main points of going to college is to find out about things—even whole fields of knowledge—that you've never even heard of before or that aren't required. Besides, you're probably tired of those old subjects, anyway, and you'll quickly get tired of all those required subjects, too.

Do haul on over to registration (or, if you're just starting college, orientation) at the very first available time. Though we know you'd rather do just about anything else but face up to new classes, you'll guarantee yourself the best choice of classes and times if you're at the head of the line. Many popular courses—and some required ones—don't have enough places at some colleges, and, hey, it's a first-come, first-served world, especially in a time of overcrowding and cutbacks.

Do take the normal course load, perhaps even one that's a bit lighter than normal, if you can.

Don't load up with a basket of courses that would overwhelm even Hermione Granger and her Time-Turner. There are no prizes for taking overloads, and although you might impress your dorm mates with the biggest course load ever, their admiration might fade as *you* start to fade by midterms.

Do carefully consider which world or foreign language to take—and at what level. Some languages are much harder than others—among the hardest are Arabic, Chinese, Japanese, and Russian (though these do offer better job potential). Once you've picked, in many schools you're stuck with four semesters of the stuff (more than virtually any other college sequence). *Quelle horreur!*

Don't overestimate—or underestimate—your level of knowledge in the language you took back in high school. If you have a good mastery of a language, don't go back to baby talk—the very first courses will bore you to tears. But if the best you can do in the foreign language is count to five—and you're not all that sure about four, come to think of it—you probably do want to sign up for whatever-language-it-is 101.

Do make sure to select the correct level math course for your background and ability. In our experience, more mistakes are made in signing up for math classes than in picking any other courses.

Don't assume that just because you got a 4 or 5 on the AP test that you're ready to take multivariable calculus. College courses—especially more advanced calculus courses—can include advanced theory, which is good deal harder than figuring out areas under curves.

Do be aware that some departments, especially science departments, offer introductory courses designed specifically for majors in the field, and other courses (so-called "service courses") designed for students who'd "just like to learn a little something" (translation: pass the requirement) in that science. If you have a serious interest in a field or are thinking you might major in it, by all means take the intro for majors rather than the sublevel service course that not only will bore you to tears but won't count for the major when you get into it. (You wouldn't want to take two intros, would you?)

Don't take the physics course for majors if you really need to be in the physics course for poets—or drawing for art majors, if paint-by-numbers is all the art you've ever done. Not only are the majors courses going to be too hard, but they're also going to focus on all the boring, technical stuff you'd need in order to major in that field.

Do consider taking an online intro course if you're self-motivated, like to set your own time schedule, or want to learn at your own speed.

Don't sign up for the online version (assuming you have a choice) if you're bad at managing your own learning, need a fixed time for class lectures to actually get you to attend the lectures, or can't face the class unless you have a flesh-and-blood prof pushing you to do the work.

Do balance your program, choosing some courses that are easier, some that are harder, some that interest you, and some that fulfill requirements.

Don't listen to your mother or father telling you to "get all the requirements out of the way first." You'll suck the joy out of college and miss out on chances to take courses you might actually enjoy.

Do check out the first-year experience (FYE) course or freshman seminars (FSs). They're a great place to find out more about your college, polish up your skills, or read a book about globalization and the decline of American culture. And in many cases you'll get a real, breathing faculty member, not some TA or adjunct faculty person your college hired yesterday. (See "10 Tips for the First-Year Experience Course" on p. 146 for more on FYE and FS courses.)

Bonus Do. If you're an upper-class student (a junior, senior, or sixth-year senior), be sure to consult with the undergraduate adviser in your department (rather than a general college adviser). Not only will the undergraduate adviser help you pick courses that'll best suit your program or interests within the field, but he or she may also offer you the dirt on which profs will bore you to tears, which profs barely know their stuff, and which profs are teaching some course only because the chair of the department dumped it on them at the last moment. Your departmental adviser can be your best ally in picking courses.

Top 12 Tips for Picking a Major

For many students, picking a major is one of the first—and most stressful—decisions they'll have to make at college. Especially with the tight job market and the perceived link between choice of major and ultimate job success, declaring a major can be a high-stakes activity—on the very first day of college. No worries. Our dozen best tips will help turn this "major" decision into a no-brainer:

1. **Decide when to decide.** Many students beginning college come under considerable pressure to declare their major right away. It could be due to the orientation or registration process itself, or to your parents wondering how you're going to pay for this college thing in the end, or sometimes it just seems that it's what everyone is doing. Whatever the case, you should consider whether it's really necessary for you to declare a major right away when you're getting started at college. If you're unsure what to choose, it can be a much better idea to take lots of courses, in lots of different fields, before settling on one major.

 REALITY CHECK. In highly structured majors with many requirements that need to be taken in a specific order—for instance, engineering, architecture, pre-med, performing arts, and world languages—it's practically a must to declare in your first year. Proceed accordingly.

2. **Consider all the options.** Especially at large state universities, there are more choices than you can shake a stick at (at last glance at UCLA there were 346 majors, programs, and minors). Sure, you may not really know what it's like to study paleobiol-

ogy, international development studies, ethnomusicology, or civil engineering, but you might really want to go into one of these if only you knew what it was. And don't get roped into some major just because you know what it is from high school or you were good at it then. College offers the chance to expand your intellectual horizons, and you should at least consider taking advantage of this opportunity.

5-STAR TIP. Be sure to consult all of the college resources. Virtually all college websites have lists of the majors offered (and those not offered). And check out the departmental web page or departmental office once you've located a few possibilities that interest you. There you'll find not only a description of what you do in that major, but often handouts covering career information, actual course schedules, lists of requirements, and schedules of departmental activities.

3. **Take some upper-division (or advanced or 4000-level) courses.** When possible, it's a good idea to select your major only after you've taken two or three advanced courses in the area. That's because the introductory courses in a field— especially if they are "service courses" designed to appeal to the university population as a whole—can be very watered-down versions of what's really done in the field (and studied in the major). In some fields it can be a surprisingly short step from "That course was kinda interesting" to "Boy, I'm in way over my head."

4. **Pick something you're good at.** You'd be amazed at how often students major in a field they aren't very good at or don't have the skills for. Try to pick a major that you're doing well in, and avoid choices in which you're falling flat on your face.

RULE OF THUMB. Getting lots of A's in a field = Good choice of major

Some A's and some B's = Not a bad choice

All B's = There could be a better choice

Lots of C's = Fuggedaboutit

5. **Pick something you like.** You're going to have to take 10 or 12 courses in your major, so it'll make your life a lot nicer if you actually like the field. It would be especially nice if you have a passion for the discipline, but a lack of burning desire doesn't have to be a deal-breaker as long as you have at least an academic interest in the field.

5-STAR TIP. Never pick a major just to please someone else. Just because your parents want you to be an electrical engineer doesn't mean you should sign up for that major, particularly if you find engineering courses more sleep-inducing than Lunesta.

6. **Don't pick a major just because it's easy or has few requirements.** What good is a major in which you learn nothing and that lets you do whatever you want whenever you want? 'Nuff said.

7. **Pick a strong—or at least decent—department.** All colleges have strengths and weaknesses: that's because money and faculty talent aren't distributed equally across departments. It's fantastic if you can select a major in which your college has special distinction: you'll get the best faculty and most up-to-date resources. But you shouldn't feel obligated to major in the college's most famous departments if you have no interest in those areas.

EXTRA POINTER. If you find that your college is unusually weak in some field, you should consider taking something else. Warning signs include only two or three faculty in the area (you'll have to take four or five courses with each), a college-wide reputation for bad teaching (sometimes the "grapevine" speaks the truth), and labs and computers that date from before you were born (it's hard to do good research with Stone Age facilities).

BEST-KEPT SECRET. If you find there's just no way to make a major work given the puny offerings at your school, you might consider consortiums of schools or other colleges in the same city for which your school allows cross-registration (for instance, the Five College Consortium in Amherst, Massachusetts, or the exchange program between Columbia University and either Juilliard or the Manhattan School of Music). And if all else fails, consider transferring to a college that has what you want. Lack of a major is considered by admissions officers as one of the best reasons for trading your little college for their ginormous university.

8. **Match your major to a career you want.** In today's tight economy—and with the high costs of college tuition—many students are selecting their majors with an eye to the eventual career prospects. Unfortunately, quite a few students do not take enough time to consider whether they actually want to pursue the career they're planning for. Often it's only when they are a short step from graduation (or even just graduated) that the true moment of horror and dread sets in: they've been studying to be a dentist for four or five years, and they realize that the last thing they ever want to see is a tooth, much less gums with gingivitis.

9. **Match the *right* major to the career you want.** There's not always a simple linear connection between majors and careers. For many professions—such as law, medicine, teaching, and business—there is a wide variety of majors you can take, especially ones that teach good analytical skills (think: philosophy, math, political science, economics, physics). Conversely, a single major can lead to a whole variety of careers. Your degree in accounting needn't force you to become a CPA; you could just as easily become a management accountant or a forensic accountant or even work for the CIA in the Middle East.

 REALITY CHECK. If you're picking a major because you think there's a straight path from that major to your intended career, make sure you're right. We've recently seen a student wanting to teach on the college level but taking an education degree intended for elementary school teachers, and a would-be missionary planning to major in anthropology (a field in which missionizing is completely verboten).

10. **Don't pick "(e) All of the above."** It's quite the rage these days for students to amass as many majors as they can—sometimes double and even triple majoring (while throwing in a minor or two). It can be helpful to have a double major if the two fields enhance your skills for a particular line of work—for example, Arabic and international relations, or economics and environmental science, or business and psychology, or criminal justice and sociology. But avoid double majoring just because you can't decide or because you have two (totally unrelated) interests.

IOHO. If you're thinking of taking a minor just because it interests you, you might do better just signing up for four or five courses that interest you rather than picking the official, prepackaged minor that typically includes many unrelated courses in the field. It's always better if you can have it your way.

11. **Ask someone who's been there.** Whatever your choice of majors, you should consult with someone who is actually doing, or has done, that major. No matter how complete the web description is, or how much information the major adviser dishes up, you'll get a different—and in many cases better-informed—picture of the major from someone who has taken the classes, worked with the professors, and slogged his or her way through the requirements. And if you know someone in the community who's in the career you're aiming to join, be sure to consult with him or her about what the profession is actually like. Nothing beats advice from someone who has been where you're trying to go.

12. **Stay calm.** Don't drive yourself crazy thinking that your whole life depends on which box you check on the "declaration of major" form. You major does not freeze your future or put you on a career path from which there is no escape. Bureau of Labor statistics show that the average U.S. worker changes careers three to five times in a lifetime. So relax. Make your best pick, and enjoy where college—and life—takes you.

Top 10 Secrets of the Syllabus

Students often view the course syllabus as something to glance at on the first day of classes, then toss in their backpacks never to be seen again. In reality, the syllabus is a treasure trove of information, one of the few places in the course where the professor reveals his or her conception of the course and tells you what you need to do to excel in it. The trouble is, very few students know how read the syllabus and unearth the important clues that are often found there. You're guaranteed to do a bang-up job in each of your courses if you pay attention to the 10 secrets of the syllabus:

1. **What this course is really going to be about.** Often your only advance information is from the course catalogue, departmental information sheet, or undergraduate adviser, or just general gossip from around campus—and it isn't likely to be 100-percent accurate. That's because different professors teach the same course and can focus on different topics and skills—in that same course. *Physics 286 University Physics, Part Two* can mean very different things to different teachers, so it's worth your while to pay careful attention to the syllabus to see what your particular prof has in mind.

2. **How tough the professor is going to be.** Professors are usually required to put all their course policies in writing on the syllabus. That's because universities view the syllabus as a sort of contract. So the syllabus should tell you more than you ever wanted to know about your professor's policies about everything from attendance, to late papers, to missing tests, to eating in class. Some students like really tough profs, some like softies. Pick accordingly.

BEST-KEPT SECRET. Sometimes professors use the syllabus to make their bark sound worse than their bite. You can detect this common phenomenon when your professor or TA goes over the syllabus orally and immediately starts relaxing the rules. Things aren't always quite as bad as they seem.

3. **What the structure of the class will be.** Any halfway decent class has a *plot:* an ordered sequence of lectures that, taken together, have some point. It's always easier to learn the material if you know the plot and track where in that plot you are at each point in the semester. Look over the syllabus to see if it provides a week-by-week—and sometimes even meeting-by-meeting—schedule of the topics to be covered. Also, see if the course appears to stay on the same level of difficulty throughout the semester, or if it takes a jump off the deep end right after midterms. Forewarned is forearmed.

4. **What's going to be on the tests.** You might not think that the prof is going to tell you on day one what's going to be on the tests. And, in a way, you're right. But the section of the syllabus called "course description" or "course goals" sometimes tips the professor's hand about what he or she thinks are the most important issues in the course—and what's likely to come up on the tests and/or papers.

5. **How much the tests and papers are really going to count.** One standard element of every syllabus is the list of requirements and how much they're going to count. Students often forget to consult these breakdowns as the course progresses; they end up tearing out their hair about quizzes that count .05 percent of the final grade, while blowing off the research paper that counts 30 percent.

6. **Whether you really need to do the reading or not.** Any syllabus worth its salt will tell you not only what to read but when and how to read it: before or after class, in detail or

more superficially, together with study questions or on your own. Plus, the syllabus can give you a pretty good idea of how important it is that you actually do the reading. Some profs assign weekly quizzes—with plot or character details not contained in the Cliff's Notes or Wikipedia article. Hint? Probably a good idea to do it. Other professors say on the syllabus that the reading merely provides "background material" that might be helpful in understanding the lectures. Decoded? Maybe the once-over-lightly will do the trick.

7. **Where you can find key resources to help you in the course.** Many syllabuses point to course resources and other campus facilities that can be of use as the course progresses. Lots of classes now have a course web page (either on Blackboard, at the university website, or elsewhere in the cloud) where the professor may put up handouts and lecture notes, assignments and supplemental readings, PowerPoint presentations and weekly reviews, and sometimes even sample exams or study questions for the midterm and final). Be sure to check this out as soon as you can and refer back to it often. Sometimes the syllabus will also mention campus resources such as the writing center, math or language lab, and tutoring center that could be of help to you later in the course. Familiarize yourself with these, too.

5-STAR TIP. Make a special mental note of when and where your professor and/or TA is holding office hours. Those will be the time for one-on-one help with your assignments. (See "The 14 Secrets of Going to See the Professor," p. 212, for our best tips on making use of the office hours.)

---

8. **Whether you're going to have to "perform."** Some courses require you to do some share of the heavy lifting, by either answering questions in section, leading a class discussion, or giving a seminar presentation. If you're one of those students who'd rather die than talk in front of a group, it'd be good to know in advance what the course has in store for you. (Of course, because learning to think and talk on your feet is one of the most important skills in some fields, it wouldn't be half-bad to stare down your fears and join the ranks of public speakers.)

9. **Whether you're really up to taking this course.** Sometimes courses have prerequisites, which are courses you need to have taken previously, or corequisites, which are courses you need to be taking concurrently. (Both of these are usually listed on the syllabus.) Pay careful attention to what these are and how important the professor says they are. For example, if your Economics 452 Game Theory professor says it *"might be useful,* but is *not strictly necessary,* for you to have taken the intro econ. course," you might give the course a try if you're reasonably smart but haven't taken this suggested prerequisite. However, if the prof says "every homework will require an A-1 knowledge of two-variable calculus"—and you're still taking college algebra—well, maybe you should forget about Nash equilibrium and stick to Angry Birds.

10. **Whether this really is the right course for you.** Ultimately, as a student, you're a consumer, and you should view the information on the syllabus just like the information on the side of the box of a product you're thinking of buying. Careful reading of the syllabus should help you decide whether the course covers the kind of material you want to learn and teaches you the skills you want to develop. Hey, you're paying good money for these courses. Why not take the right ones?

10 Questions to Ask Yourself the First Week of Classes

You may have thought that once you've picked your classes, you're over and done with the process. The die is cast, now just settle in and enjoy your semester. But a far better idea is to size up the professor yourself, by attending the first few lectures and then making your own judgment. After the very first class (or first couple of classes, if the first class is just an intro), ask yourself these ten questions about what you've just observed:

1. **Is the teacher good?** Even after the first class or two, you should be able to tell whether the prof knows his or her stuff and can present the material in a clear, organized, and coherent manner—and whether the lecture has a point. A good teacher will construct each class around one or two main issues and make logical and clear transitions from point to point.

2. **Is the teacher interesting?** Look, college isn't Second City, so don't expect your molecular biology professor to have you rolling in the aisles with laughter. Still, your teacher should run the class in a way that holds your attention (at least most of the time), makes the material real (or at least sort of relevant), and displays some enthusiasm (or at least a few signs of life). Bonuses here could be an interesting use of media in the class, stimulating readings and assignments, and provocative discussion sessions.

3. **Does the teacher care that the students learn?** Signs that the professor cares include a willingness to take questions, an awareness of how the students are receiving the material, and the professor's showing respect when addressing students.

4. **Is the course too hard (or too easy)?** Sure, most college courses, especially first-year courses, are designed to introduce students to new subjects and different ways of thinking. But if you can't understand anything that's going on in the first few classes, this is a sign that you are in over your head—a situation that's only going to get worse as the class gets deeper into the material. (On the other hand, if you've already had the material in some other class—or if the course is such a joke that even Bozo would be at the head of the class—well, why waste your time?)

5. **Does the course presuppose stuff you don't know?** Pay close attention if the professor or the course syllabus announces that you must have a particular skill (such as knowing statistics or being able to use AutoCAD) or have taken some prerequisite (for example, two semesters of university chemistry) before taking this course. Students who lack the skills or haven't taken the prereqs are likely to find themselves playing catch-up from day one, without ever really succeeding.

6. **Does the course require too much work?** The course syllabus should give you a pretty clear sense of how much reading, writing, and testing the course requires. There's nothing wrong with courses that are challenging, and learning to write well is one of the most important things you can accomplish in college. But you need to balance the requirements of this course with all your other commitments. If one course's requirements are so excessive that they eat up all your waking hours, then unless that course is ultra important for your major or your lifelong dream, you should drop it and look elsewhere.

7. **Would another course be a better choice for this requirement—or this major?** Colleges often give a wide variety of choices for the Gen Ed requirement. Don't feel obligated to take the most popular choices or only the courses you've heard of. So too for the requirements for your major. Often there is a different—and better—professor teaching the same required course that same semester or at least in the next semester.

8. **Do you really want to be learning this stuff at all?** Sometimes after looking over the syllabus and hearing the professor describe what he or she plans to do in the course, it's pretty clear that this isn't what you bargained for when you signed up. You don't want to end up like one former student of ours who signed up for critical reasoning, thinking she'd finally stop falling for her boyfriend's lines, and instead found herself doing truth tables and working to master *modus tollendo ponens* all semester long.

9. **Do you feel you can learn from this professor?** Every professor has a different teaching style, and some approaches may suit you better than others. Even if the professor has a great reputation and all your friends loved the course, it may still be taught in a way that doesn't fit your learning style. Don't be a lemming.

10. **Do you like the class?** In a good class, you should have some feeling of intellectual excitement and, yes, some enjoyment from the very beginning. If this feeling is absent at the start, it'll only get worse by the thirtieth lecture. Don't disregard your initial impression. If you don't like what you're seeing, drop the class and add another (well worth the $20 drop/add fee).

The 13 Warning Signs of a Bad Professor

Here are thirteen surefire signs that your prof's a dud—and that you should get out while there's still time:

1. **The professor is deadly boring.** Even in the very first classes, you can tell when it's a struggle to stay minimally conscious for the whole lecture. If you're bored to tears and need to text message nonstop, down a six-pack of Red Bull, or pinch yourself—hard—just to stay awake, you know something's not right here. (Hint: it's the professor.)

2. **The professor is bummed out.** If a professor comes in on the first day of classes already grumbling about how much he or she hates teaching this course, how much he or she would like to be teaching at a better college, or how teaching is a waste of his or her time (because research is where it's at), don't expect things to get any better as the course progresses.

👍 **RULE OF THUMB.** Bummed out to start = three times as bummed out by the tenth meeting.

---

3. **The professor is condescending, combative, or full of him- or herself.** Do you really want a professor who treats you like a five-year-old? Or who thinks that students are the enemy, to be defeated in the pitched battle that is the course? Or that he or she is God's gift to student-kind? Probably not.

4. **The professor shows favoritism.** Maybe he or she doesn't like students who have experience in the field (because they've

already been corrupted or learned bad habits) or prefers majors or upperclass students (even though the course has no prerequisites). Or perhaps the professor has a cadre of students who keep taking his or her courses, so there's an in crowd and an out crowd before the class even starts. College courses aren't rock concerts; so groupies shouldn't be part of the scene.

5. **The professor doesn't give out a syllabus—or gives out a one-paragraph syllabus that is just the course description from the Web.** Some professors say they want to let the course evolve, making careful adjustments based on the pace of the lectures, the speed at which students are doing the work, or the general ebb and flow of the semester. Right. It's more likely that the professor who doesn't distribute a detailed syllabus doesn't actually know what he or she is going to be doing in the class this semester. Students in this course could well be buying a pig in a poke, which of course is not recommended.

6. **The professor isn't clear about the requirements and how much they count.** Professors who don't have a clear and easily expressible idea about how the grading will be handled can end up springing up all sorts of wacky systems or inconsistent grading schemes on the students as the semester progresses. Often students in this sort of class never know how they're doing during the semester and experience unpleasant surprises at the end.

7. **The professor has incredibly petty rules.** Bail out if you encounter a syllabus with page upon page of rules dealing with everything from the use of cell phones to whether you can wear caps to an exam; how to address the professor and when to ask questions; when you can enter the room and when you can leave; policies about eating, drinking, and using the bathroom; twenty-five acceptable reasons for an extension and fifty-three unacceptable reasons; grade penalties for lateness timed to the half hour; and so on. Sure, some rules are

required by the school (due dates, grading policy, and, in cold climes, even snow policy), but the prof's supposed to be teaching a course, not rewriting the tax code.

IOHO. Some professors will tell you the syllabus is a contract and that they have to protect themselves against every possible case that can come up. But the atmosphere they create by doing this is so combative that a shared learning experience is unlikely to emerge.

8. **The professor can't fill the whole class period.** Lots of professors hold a short class the first day of classes: they introduce themselves, go over the syllabus, and call it a day. But if class is let out early the whole first week, you can be pretty sure that the professor is either inexperienced or a bad planner or, worst of all, doesn't really give a damn about the course. Sure, you'd like to blow it off early every day. But why cheat yourself out of the education you've paid for?

9. **The professor seems unsure about the material.** Professors who present their lectures in a halting or tentative way could well be professors who aren't on top of the course content. You might think that colleges would hire only people who really know the material backward and forward, but you'd be wrong. It's not at all uncommon for faculty to be saddled with a course in which they have no expertise. Why should you be saddled with it too, when you've got a choice?

IOHO. If the professor says he or she is going to "learn the material with you," get out as fast as you can. That's professor-speak for "I don't know my a** from my elbow about this stuff."

10. **The professor presents the material in a confused or obscure way.** If your professor's lectures wander aimlessly through lots of unrelated details—or if the professor seems to be just dumping everything he or she knows about the topic without making any of it clear or understandable—something is definitely wrong. Like, the professor is unable to explain the stuff in a way the students can understand—or in street language: meaning he or she can't teach.

11. **The professor uses the class as a political platform.** Even if the class is a political science or government course, the professor should not be using the lecture to spout off on his or her own political views. If your prof wants to be a politico, let him or her go on Politico.

12. **The professor never involves the students.** If a professor attends only to his or her notes and never even looks at the students—or never pauses to accept or invite questions—it's not a good thing. A good class is a dynamic class, and a good professor engages with the students.

13. **The professor has no passion for the subject.** If the professor is just slogging through the material with no apparent enthusiasm for anything he or she has to say—well, how are you supposed to get excited (or even at all interested) in what's yet to come? Find a prof who's engaged in the material—and in teaching it to you.

Tips and Tricks for Improving Your Course Schedule

If you're like most students, by the time the semester gets under way you've preregistered for classes and are 100-percent happy with your schedule. Or maybe not. Perhaps you were closed out of a course, got stuck with a cruddy professor, fell prey to a time or work conflict, or found that the course you wanted or needed is simply not offered this semester. Not to worry. You'll see immediate improvement if you follow our 10 best tips for sprucing up your course schedule:

1. **Wait it out.** If you didn't get into a class you really wanted because the class was closed, get on the wait list (if available). Spaces often clear in the first week, once students realize how hard or boring the class is. If you're patient and sit tight—especially if you can hang on for a week or two into the semester—you could actually end up with a place in the class of your dreams—or at least an upgrade from what you're presently holding.

   RULE OF THUMB. **Top 5 percent on the wait list (position relative to total spaces in the class) = Pretty good shot, definitely worth the wait**
   5-10 percent = Some chance, but worth making contingency plans if you don't get in
   10 percent or worse = Fuggedaboutit (unless you want to sit on the rafters)

2. **Make a personal appeal.** In some cases, you can leap ahead of a wait list by asking for an "override" from either the professor or the departmental office. Make sure you present a

compelling reason for needing the course—like that you're a graduating senior, need the course to qualify for what's offered in the Fall, or are going abroad next year and need to have mastered a language by then. And be sure to ask super, super nicely. Professors (or departmental advisers or secretaries) have significant discretion in which students they let in, so a nice appeal will work better than a demanding one.

3. **Seek out a substitution.** Make sure that you're aware of the full range of possibilities for any requirements that you are trying to fulfill. Sometimes there are courses you would enjoy a lot more—or could get into a lot more easily—than the "standard" courses taken for a certain requirement. Be sure to check out alternatives in the online list of requirements. Also, in some cases departments will allow you "unofficial" substitutions in cases where you have particular interests or where a course conflict screws up your schedule. Ask the undergraduate adviser.

 5-STAR TIP. Sometimes the very same course is cross-listed in two different departments (or programs) under different numbers—with different numbers of places (some still open) apportioned to each listing. Check to see whether spaces are available under a different listing for the same course.

4. **Try off-peak times.** Sure, no one willingly takes classes at 7:30 a.m. or ones that meet on (eek!) Fridays. Nevertheless, you may find that you can really improve your schedule by switching to less popular times. Colleges now are trying to maximize the use of precious classroom space and to provide options for nontraditional and for working students. So you can find classes being offered in a very wide range of time-slots, and you should seriously consider them all if you want to find better courses.

5. **Think "online."** These days, universities are falling all over themselves to build up their offerings of online courses. This means that many of the most popular and required courses—especially intro, skills-based courses—are now offered by the same professors you'd find in the brick-and-mortar classrooms. Switching to an online version might help you avoid course conflicts or give you a more workable time schedule. For more details about online courses, see "10 Tips for Online Courses (and MOOCs)," on p. 154.

6. **Look next door.** Many state universities and even private colleges are near community colleges where you can take courses that'll count for a requirement or a major—and that have open spaces. And many universities have express agreements ("articulation agreements") in place that'll automatically count what the community college has to offer for just what you need. If you are closed out of your college's courses, ask your adviser for details on these options.

EXTRA POINTER. It's often easier to get into the summer school version of the courses you're closed out of. So if you're really stuck, it may be best to just wait it out.

7. **Take 'em out of order.** Don't assume that you have to take the two parts of a two-course sequence (for example, a foreign language, a math sequence, or a two-semester science course) in fall-spring order. Sometimes colleges offer part one in both semesters—and part one is less subscribed in the spring than in the fall. Alternatively, in a little-known but sometimes elegant move, you can take part two first and then go back and pick up part one the following fall—but *only* if part two does not depend on part one (for example, Renaissance to Modern Art History might plausibly be taken before Ancient to Medieval Art History, but only a bonehead would attempt Design, Synthesis, and Applications of Nanomaterials, before General Chemistry).

8. **Upgrade your prof.** Ultimately, your classes are going to be only as good as the teacher is, so switching to another course or section with a better prof could significantly improve your semester. In addition to asking students enrolled in the course, you might check your profs out on online sources such as WWW.RATEMYPROFESSORS.COM. Keep in mind, though, that (as with any internet-rating site) not all the ratings are fully accurate; you can get a more balanced sense of the quality of the professor by ignoring both the most admiring and the most insulting reviews and by focusing on what the majority of students have to say.

EXTRA POINTER. If you're serious about your studies (and you wouldn't be reading this if you weren't), it's best to ignore such extraneous metrics as how easy the class is and whether the professor received a "chili pepper" rating online. You want a challenging and worthwhile course; although eye candy may be enjoyable, it won't help your intellectual growth any.

---

9. **Face down the prereqs.** Sometimes what's mucking up your schedule or blocking you from getting into what you really want is that you haven't fulfilled some requirement or prerequisite that you'd rather eat glass than take (think: statistics, the lab science requirement, macroeconomics). Make sure you don't perpetually put off requirements or prerequisites for other courses that don't appeal to you. Adjust your schedule to provide the right balance of progress on all three fronts: Gen Ed (or distribution) requirements, major requirements, and electives.

10. **Add something you're passionate about.** The most unpleasant schedules are ones filled with only stuff you *have* to take and completely devoid of anything you actually *want* to take. A good

schedule includes at least a course or two that really, really interests you and keeps you excited about being at college. And casting your net more broadly—to include child psychology, nanotechnology, Russian literature, broadcast journalism, or whatever else you have a passion for but that would never fit your major program—not only will make your semester more enjoyable but also will make it easier to enhance the less-than-stellar course schedule you're now staring down.

3

SKILLS 3.0

Being successful at college requires a full array of skills. Some come into play at key moments in the semester, like when you're facing major tests and papers (more on these in Chapter Five). Others are needed throughout the term. Let's face it, on most days you have to go to class, do the assigned reading, and/or study for some weekly quiz. That's why it's important to have the skills of college down cold. Part of the day-to-day routine of your life.

For many college students, this is more of a dream than a reality. Sure, they've learned Skills 1.0—the first-generation level of studying, managing their time, and taking tests that everyone learns in high school. Some have even mastered Skills 2.0, the second-generation level of skills that, with any luck, you've perfected in your first year of college. But do you know what it'd be like to have third-generation skills—fully polished, professional-level abilities that'll drive you to the top of your college class and lead to a great career?

In this chapter you'll learn:

- ▶ Top 10 Time-Management Tips
- ▶ Top 10 Reasons Never to Procrastinate
- ▶ How *Not* to Study
- ▶ 10 Secrets of Taking Excellent Lecture Notes
- ▶ 15 Ways to Read Like a Pro
- ▶ 15 Strategies for Painless Presentations
- ▶ How to Build Your Confidence

Top 10 Time-Management Tips

College is like juggling: five balls in the air, trying not to let any of them drop. Between going to class, doing the homework, taking the tests, perhaps holding down a job or raising a family—well, how's a mere mortal supposed to do all this stuff? It boils down to managing your time: figuring out where each commitment is supposed to go, deciding how much time to apportion to each, and, most important of all, staying on track for the whole 15-week semester. But how are you supposed to do all that? Have a look at our top 10 tips for managing your jam-packed schedule:

1. **Block your courses.** Many students think they'll learn better if they scatter their courses throughout the day with frequent downtime. Wrong. Usually, if you have a gap of 50 minutes between classes, it's much more likely to end up as Twitter or Facebook time than as study time. If you take your courses back-to-back as much as possible, you'll have larger blocks of time to devote to concerted bouts of studying. And if you can group your classes on only two or three days, it will free whole days for studying.

2. **Make a plan.** It's never too early to start figuring out how you'll do all the work in each of your four or five classes. In fact, the very first day of classes is the right time. Enter all the assignments—including weekly assignments, quizzes, and exercises or short papers—into your electronic or print calendar. Then develop an overall plan for both your run-of-the-mill weekly studying and the mondo research paper or killer final. Enter it all in or write it all out; you can't juggle in your head.

3. **Aim to make all the classes.** Going to classes is one of the most time-efficient things you can do. When you miss class, it takes three times as long to learn the material on your own as it would have taken to go to the lecture. And you never really

learn it as well. Who could, getting notes from that classmate who writes illegibly and didn't really understand the lecture anyway?

4. **Determine whether you're an owl or a rooster.** Schedule your studying for times when you can seriously engage with the material. Depending on their biochronology, some students find 11 p.m. the perfect time to focus; others like 6 a.m. Just because your classmate prefers to study at a particular time doesn't mean it will work for you.

EXTRA POINTER. Be sure to schedule time for sleep. Whether you study in the depths of night or at the crack of dawn, you'll need seven or eight hours of sleep. What good is managing your waking time if you're so wrecked that you can't concentrate on what you're doing?

5. **Set up "zones."** Many students have a lot of things on their plate other than college—a part-time (or full-time) job, a few kids to take care of, responsibilities at church. It's a good idea to divide up your week, and your day, into different and nonoverlapping time blocks. If you work at your job in the morning, then be sure to schedule all your courses and study time in the afternoons and evenings. Tuesday and Thursday are your child care days? Don't try to prepare for your Friday test in those time blocks. The key to success when you have multiple commitments is compartmentalization: keeping each activity separate, and not letting one zone bleed into another.

5-STAR TIP. Learn to say no. If you're in your study zone and your boss calls, or your kid needs help with his or her homework, or your rabbi asks you for help with the pancake breakfast, tell them you'll get back to them later. Hey, your work should be at least as important as filling in for the sick worker, overseeing fifth-grade social studies, or arranging the syrup dispensers.

6. **Keep a daily log.** Especially at the beginning of the semester, you should track how long it takes you to do the homework in each of your classes, to prepare for quizzes and tests, and to write short papers. Knowing this can help you estimate the time frame for future course assignments. Also, writing it down will prevent you from overestimating how long you're really studying (at least if you're recording honestly).

 5-STAR TIP. Adjust your study plan dynamically as the semester progresses. Typically, you'll find that some courses get harder as they go, some projects take longer than you planned, and in some courses the workload is divided unevenly over the semester. The more flexible—and the more open-minded—you are about time management, the more successful you will be. Take stock each week: for many students, Sunday night, just as you're looking forward to the next week, is best.

7. **Do your homework on time.** Even though there's no parent or teacher standing over you, be sure you're doing the outside-of-class work when it's assigned. Doing the reading in advance of the lecture, studying for each quiz as it comes along, and memorizing what needs to be memorized on a week-by-week basis are all strategies that will increase your efficiency and cut down on your overall study time. Sure, it's tempting to blow off the homework when there's no test looming or when the prof doesn't bother to call on anyone in class. But the fun will quickly diminish when you have five hundred pages of reading to catch up on two days before the test.

8. **Prioritize your study time.** Every professor thinks that his or her course is the most important thing in the universe. Learn to *triage* your courses—that is, to spend different amounts of time on each course depending on how important or difficult that course is. Do not spend all your time on the course you find most enjoyable or easiest to do. And if you find you're spending every waking hour on one of your courses, cut back. Keep in mind that you've signed up for four or five courses, each of which will count toward only 20 to 25 percent of your overall GPA.

9. **Plan to do each task once.** It's very time-inefficient to do things twice. Some students think they'll learn better by copying over their notes (more neatly this time), listening to the same lecture twice (once in person, once on their iPod), or doing the reading three times (once to get the general idea, once to focus in on the plot and characters, and once to take notes). Fuggedaboutit! All of these are incredible time wasters. And it's not likely that you'll be able to focus or understand better the second time around.

 REALITY CHECK. At the end of the second week, assess whether you've had any do-overs—that is, done any task twice. If you find that you have, diagnose your problem and devise a strategy for doing each task once for the balance of the semester.

10. **Divide and conquer.** Break up larger projects such as research papers, field studies, and studying for cumulative exams into manageable chunks. And spread the stages over a reasonable number of days. Always add some extra time to what you think you'll need, because usually there's a major crunch or crisis toward the end. It's better to finish a little early than to find yourself running around in a frantic state when your computer crashes at 4 a.m. the morning that a paper is due.

Top 10 Reasons Never to Procrastinate

Procrastinate *v.* To put off doing something until a future time [Latin prōcrāstināre "to put forward until tomorrow"].

All human beings put off doing things they think will be unpleasant, painful, or difficult. And college students are no exception. Confronted with a paper, preparation for a test, or even brief review for a quiz, many students' first impulse (and some students' second, third, and fourth impulses) is to delay for as long as they can. But this isn't a good—or in some cases even a rational—strategy. Here's why:

1. **You could run out of time.** Any time there's a hard deadline—which is just about always in college courses—you run the risk of missing the deadline if you keep putting off the work. And with professors unwilling to give extensions except in very special circumstances, you could be setting yourself up for a grade penalty—often as much as one-third to one-half a grade a day—if you're late getting the work in. Big risk.

2. **Ideas take time to jell.** Most college papers require you to come up with an idea, then spend time thinking about it, revising it, and refining it. If you run the clock down to the last minute, you won't have time to go through all the intellectual stages for fully-considered work. And even for tests—if they're essay tests—you'll want to allow sufficient time to think through the issues in some detail, rather than dishing up some half-baked answer you prepared the night before.

BEST-KEPT SECRET. When professors give out paper assignments, say, a week and a half before they're due, they're expecting that you'll pick a topic, think about it, and, if appropriate, research the issues throughout the 10-day period. The idea is *not* (as some students think) that you'll work for two days on the paper, with a choice of Thursday and Friday, or Friday and Saturday, or Saturday and Sunday, and so on.

3. **You could be misestimating the difficulty of the task.** In many cases, it's hard to gauge at the outset exactly how much time it'll take to do the assignment—especially if the work is on unfamiliar terrain or involves many different problems, pieces, or parts. If you procrastinate too long, you may not have enough time to do all the tasks (or do them all well).

4. **You could be misestimating the pain.** One of the main reasons all of us procrastinate is to avoid the pain of actually doing the work. But in many cases students *overestimate* the pain they'll actually be feeling. It's easy to do: when staring down a 10-page paper, a 20-problem problem set, or 400 pages of reading, you feel the task is insurmountable and the very thought of it fills you with dread. But in most cases, when you get started you find that the task isn't as difficult as you anticipated, especially if you break it up into manageable pieces over an extended period of time.

5-STAR TIP. As you whittle down the amount of stuff to be done, the pain will go down. So the amount of pain and resistance that you feel before you start is the *maximum*. Things are guaranteed—100 percent—to get better as you work your way in.

5. **S*** happens.** Any time you have a project that extends over some period of time or that involves some complexity there's the possibility that something unexpected could come up, thus slowing down your work. It could be something bad: you could be sick as a dog for three days, another professor could spring a quiz on you that requires emergency preparation, or some unrefusable work or family commitment could arise out of nowhere. It could also be something good: a new discovery in your research, an unexpected find in a journal, a deeper strand of analysis in your thinking about the issue. All of these could require further thinking *and more time* than you had planned. Whatever the unforeseen event, not running the clock down to the last second will allow you to deal with it.

6. **You blow off your chance for help.** Especially if the assignment is challenging, many students will want to enlist the help of the professor or TA, either in office hours, by email, or at some schools by Skype. But the professor is likely to have office hours only for a couple of times a week; and not every TA is jumping to IM answers back to students. Don't put off the assignment so long that you won't have a chance to consult with the prof or TA in case of difficulty—and to then have ample time to implement his or her suggestions for revising your work.

7. **No one works well under time pressure.** If you put off your work 'til the day (or worse, the night) before it's due, you'll have to work in an incredible rush and under crazy pressure. And, contrary to popular myths, virtually nobody works well under such conditions. It's even worse than that. The acute panic of the night before it's due (the "OMG, how am I ever going to get this done in time?" moment) combined with the guilt of having put off the work for the nine days before (the "Why didn't I get off my a** a week ago?" realization) is not the best combination for doing one's most distinguished work.

8. **You might not have time to polish up your work.** One of the main differences between fair-to-good and really excellent work

is that the really excellent work has gone through a series of drafts (if a paper) or a series of reviews (if it's a problem set). When you're down to the wire, you often skip steps and hand in a less-than-fully-crafted paper or a less-than-fully-checked-over problem set. The prof is sure to notice the rushed quality of the work when he or she pulls your paper or problem set out of the stack.

9. **You put yourself at a strategic disadvantage.** While you're busy cooking up reasons for putting off your work for another day, some of your cohorts are rushing out of the starting gate to do the work (even your duplicitous "friends" who tell you they're going to wait and then pull an all-nighter). These classmates could wind up making you look bad, especially if the professor curves the grades or at least compares the handed-in assignments to each other.

10. **The task isn't going to change.** Deep down—and irrationally—some students think that somehow the task is going to get easier if it gets addressed in the distant future. Of course, this isn't so; the assignment is fixed when it is handed out (that's why the belief is irrational). So grab the bull by the horns, start the work when the assignment is given, and—who knows?—you may actually enjoy doing the work.

FLASH! For an interesting dissenting opinion about procrastination, take a look at a piece by John Perry, a professor of philosophy at Stanford University, at WWW .STRUCTUREDPROCRASTINATION.COM.

The How *Not* to Study Guide

For many students, the biggest difference between college and high school is studying. In college you're supposed to do it, whereas in high school—well, you know, not really. But by the time they've gotten to college, many students have developed study habits and strategies that not only don't help them get ahead at college, they actually thwart their progress. For them—and perhaps even for you—we offer our 15 best ideas for how *not* to study:

1. **Don't spend too much time looking for the perfect environment.** Many students think that if only they could find the perfect place to study, it would all be a cakewalk. So they spend inordinate amounts of time scouting and trying out various locales—first their dorm room, then the coffee shop, then the library, then the lawn, and so on. Such elaborate setup time can be a major time-waster, and, even worse, can make you feel that you can't study unless you are in your ideal study spot. Better idea? Find a reasonably quiet place and just get started. You'll get more comfortable with your surroundings as you get going.

2. **Don't multitask.** Believe it or not, some students study for *all* their courses at one session: fifteen minutes on this subject, fifteen minutes on another, fifteen minutes on a third—you get the picture. It's a far better idea to devote your entire study session to a single subject. That way, you'll build up speed, and the more engaged you get, the easier the studying will become. Worst of all is to intersperse one subject with another—do ten minutes of math, then give up and do ten minutes of freshman comp, then back to the math. That's a recipe for guaranteed confusion.

3. **Don't count busywork as studying.** Some students do a lot of preparing or getting organized for studying, but they never get

down to the actual studying. Don't give yourself credit for studying when you're actually just cleaning your desk, getting together the readings, or reorganizing the files on your laptop.

4. **Don't start with the no-brainers.** Some students think that starting with the easiest tasks—or the ones they're best at—will ease them into the material. Trouble is, when you get to the harder tasks, you still have the leap to make—and you're more tired, too. Suggestion: start with the hardest or most challenging task, then ease into the easier ones.

5. **Don't discard the clues.** Many professors give study questions, or at least say in class or on the syllabus what will be most important in the reading. Be sure to consider these all-important (and time-saving) suggestions before you start studying. If yours is a class with math problems or proofs, be sure to consult the problems done in lecture or section before taking off on the new ones. Often the homework problems are variants or extensions of the work already done.

6. **Don't just memorize.** It's useless to just shovel stuff into your mind that you don't understand. If you really are understanding what you're studying, you ought to able to explain the main ideas, in your own words, to someone who hasn't done the studying. Take the time to think about and digest what you're studying, instead of just preparing to parrot it back on some upcoming exam.

7. **Don't microfocus.** Some students think the best studying is slow studying: reading every word, one by one; writing every word of the paper, one by one; preparing a presentation, one word at a time. But like any cognitive activity, studying is a process that takes place over time and gains strength by building up speed. If you focus too narrowly on the individual elements of what you're doing, you suck the life out of the learning and disrupt the intellectual growth that's possible, even in studying.

EXTRA POINTER. Many students don't bother taking reading notes—or indeed any notes—thinking they'll remember what they studied come test time. Can't be done. Especially when you're taking four or five other courses. Tip: write down notes as you read—and on a clean sheet of paper, *not* in the margins of the book, where you'll never be able to read them. Be sure to leave space for additional comments that you'll add when you go over your notes later in the semester.

5-STAR TIP. If you've invested in e-books and an e-reader that has note-taking and highlighting capabilities, it might be a good idea to take notes in the (electronic) margins. Those will be neat, and revisable too, should you want to alter what you've written come study time.

8. **Adjust your attention span.** You're used to getting your content in 140-character units, in 20-second bursts, or with lots of video to go with it. But college is not Twitter, YouTube, or Hulu. When studying in college, sustained attention is needed. Learn to focus—without breaks and without additional stimulation—for 15- to 20-minute periods. Look, we know it's hard to reprogram your brain. But doing so will prevent your having to start focusing again—and overcoming your resistance—50 times an hour.

EXTRA POINTER. Be sure you do take breaks from time to time. Giving your mind time to rest will keep up your stamina and also give ideas time to sink in.

RULE OF THUMB. For every 45 to 50 minutes of studying, allow a 10- to 15-minute break (tough, isn't it?).

9. **Don't count "study" time as study time.** Some students keep three e-windows open while they read their e-textbook: one for the book, another for Facebook, and the third for Twitter (Windows 7 makes this easy). And then they flit back and forth from screen to screen, counting all the time as study time. When you're counting up your study time, count only the time you actually engaged with the material, not just the time you sat at your study place. If you can't do this honestly in your head, write it down. The pencil never lies.

10. **Don't count a "study" group as a study group.** Many classes have either required or optional study groups in which you get together with other students from the same course to go over the material. If you're participating in one of these, make sure you and your friends are actually studying the material, not just each other. If, for whatever reason, you're not studying the material, have a nice time—just don't count the time as study time.

11. **Don't be too hard on yourself.** Many students set elaborate study schedules—nothing wrong with that—and then beat themselves up when things don't go exactly according to plan. Maybe some task took longer than anticipated, maybe some additional materials were needed to complete the task, or maybe you were just tired or distracted that day. Don't be too hard on yourself when you haven't stuck 100 percent to your plan. Keep in mind that you'll have many study sessions and that remaining in a positive mood about your schoolwork is much more important than how any one study session—or indeed series of sessions—goes.

12. **Don't go it alone.** If in spite of your very best efforts you find yourself spending enormous amounts of time preparing for one class, or are always hopelessly behind in your studying for that class, go see the prof or TA. They've had loads of experience with students just like you, and they can make practical suggestions about how you can get on the right track. (For some tips on how to approach the professor, see "The 14 Secrets of Going to See the Professor" on p. 212.)

13. **Never blow off two days in a row.** Though nobody openly tells you this (OK, now we are!), you're supposed to be studying every day of the week at college. If each professor expects you to be preparing a couple of hours for each lecture hour, and if you're taking 15 hours of lecture a week, you're supposed to be preparing for 30 hours a week. It's hard to fit 30 hours of studying into only three days a week, especially if you have lectures on those days.

14. **Don't cheat yourself.** To get the true value out of college, you'll have to be doing a lot of work on your own. If you don't study—or if you don't study well—you're only cheating yourself. Why do that?

10 Secrets of Taking Excellent Lecture Notes

Taking really good lecture notes is one of the most important skills for college success. Not only will constant writing help you stay awake and focused on the main points of the lecture, but your lecture notes can become quite important come midterm or finals time. Most college students think they're pretty good at note taking. Only one in ten is. Wonder how you can become that one? Have a look at the 10 secrets of excellent note taking, all from the professors' perspective:

1. **Write more, not less.** You should be writing for most of the lecture. Sure, it's a question of balance and emphasis—getting enough down so that you've captured most of the detail, while at the same time highlighting the main points so you can see how the lecture is structured. But in our experience, it's far more common for students to write down not nearly enough than to write down far too much.

    RULE OF THUMB. **15 minutes of lecture = 1 page of notes (or in other words, three to four pages of notes for a typical hour of lecture).**

2. **Use any advance information.** If the professor has given a title to each lecture on the syllabus or has given out study questions in advance of each lecture, make sure you familiarize yourself with these before coming to class. The more you know about what the main points of the lecture are going to be, the easier it will be to take notes. You'll know what you're looking for.

5-STAR TIP. If the professor hasn't bothered to give each lecture a title, you should title them yourself. That will force you to locate the single most important point of that class.

3. **Write down the professor's ideas, not yours.** Some students lard their notes with their own questions, reflections, opinions, and free associations. But the point of taking notes is to get a good rendition of what the professor is saying. That's what'll be on the test. Leave your own thoughts for afterward or for your personal journal.

4. **Forget about complicated note-taking systems.** Contrary to what they tell you, there's no need to use the Cornell Note-Taking System, Mind Mapping, or the "Five R's of Good Note Taking" (whatever those may be). It's more than enough to simply number the professor's points (and perhaps have a sub number or two). Worrying about systems will only slow you down and can distort the actual shape of the lecture. There's always time to go back later and structure your notes.

EXTRA POINTER. When taking notes, be sure to set off subordinate points (that is, points that contribute to the lecture in some way, but are not on the main path). Also, indent and clearly identify any illustrations, examples, comparisons, and interesting (though not central) asides; in doing so, be sure to note their relation to the main points.

5-STAR TIP. Whenever a professor uses a technical or unfamiliar term, be sure to write down—if possible, word for word—the prof's definition of that term. These terms can play a critical role in later lectures and on the tests and papers.

5. **Don't zone in and out.** From your 20 hours a week of media, you're used to getting your content delivered in rapid-fire, 20-second bursts. But the professor is used to dishing up his or her ideas in 15- to 20-minute segments. Train yourself to focus—and to write—for longer intervals. The very act of writing (with the thinking and processing that goes with it) will help condition you to maintain your focus. Above all, don't be distracted by other activities that may be going on around you in the lecture hall—or on your iPhone, iPad, or Game Boy.

6. **Pay special attention to the beginning and the end.** Often the most important parts of the lecture are the first two minutes and the last two minutes, right when many students are shuffling in their seats or packing their bags. Many professors start their lectures by reviewing the key points of the last lecture and listing the main points they're going to cover in this lecture. And they conclude the class with a summary of the main points they have covered and sometimes an indication of what they'll do next time. Be sure to take careful notes during these high-value moments.

EXTRA POINTER. In many cases, if the professor is running behind he or she will compress many important points into the last five minutes of the lecture. Be sure to write extra fast during this key time.

7. **Look for verbal clues.** Professors often try to flag the most important points in the lecture with phrases like "the key point is . . . ," "it's especially important to note that . . . ," and "one should keep in mind that . . .". Look for these indicators of the cornerstones of the lecture. And try to write down—word for word, if you can—the material that follows them.

5-STAR TIP. Be especially alert to any questions the professor poses. Those often come at key turning points in the lecture and often introduce important issues that are going to be talked about at great length (and may appear later on a test or paper).

8. **Focus on the structure.** Every lecture has a plot: a central point with a series of steps that build up this point. Keep focused on the plot—and its subplots—and try to capture them in your notes. Continually ask yourself: *What is the overall point of the lecture? How does each individual point contribute to the overall plot? Why did the professor choose to make these points rather than others?*

9. **Beware of PowerPoints.** PowerPoint presentations (and items written on the board) are usually quite sketchy outlines—reminders to the professors of what to say, rather than fleshed-out treatments of the key points. Make sure you write down the *explanations* of these outlines in your notes, not just the outlines themselves. Come test time, you'll be behind the eight ball if all you have in your notes are these prompts the professor uses.

EXTRA POINTER. Take notes at all class activities—discussion sections, field trips, visits to the museum, review sessions, individual meetings in office hours—not just lectures. You never know what might come in handy when the test or paper comes around.

10. **Always do it yourself.** Don't outsource your note taking to your friend, to professional "lecture notes" (sold at the campus store), or to your note-taking group. Taking notes for yourself is the single best way to engage in—and remember—the lecture. Not to mention getting you to go the lecture, which is an achievement in itself.

15 Ways to Read Like a Pro

One of the main skills to be mastered at college is college-level reading. Sure, you've been reading since you were five years old, but do you read fast enough for college? Do you not only get the plot but also analyze the characters and themes as you read? And for scientific and technical reading, are you really following—and evaluating—the theories, methods, and techniques the author is using, as well as the conclusions he or she is reaching? Maybe not? Here are our 15 best tips to get you reading like an A+ student:

1. **Don't think you're the only one.** Don't blow off the reading on the theory that no one else is doing it. Plenty are—and you don't want them carting off all the good grades, do you?

2. **Decide what's required.** Figure out how much the professor is expecting you'll read. Usually, when there are exact pages specified, the prof is thinking you'll read them all. But when dozens of books are listed for a single week, the professor may be thinking you'll read "in" those books or select from among them. Don't do more—or less—than you need to do.

IOHO. Pay special attention to the distinction between *required* reading and *recommended* (or supplemental) reading—that is, between what you absolutely, positively, 100 percent have to read, and what would be nice to read if only you had the time. We suggest that you stick to the required reading unless there's some special reason for doing the recommended reading (for instance, when it's relevant to your paper topic or you just happen to be interested in that issue—hey, it could happen).

3. **Figure out the point of the reading.** You'll understand the reading a whole lot better and enjoy it more when you know its purpose: Is the reading just general background? Is it the object to be studied in the lecture? Or does it go beyond what the professor is talking about, filling in gaps in the lecture? Figure out what the reading's supposed to be doing, and you'll know better how to do it.

4. **Always read *before* the class.** In most classes, it works best if you do the reading before you go to lecture. That's because most often the professor is expecting you to have done the legwork before he or she does the heavy lifting. And when the task of the lecture is to actually analyze the reading, it's particularly helpful to have read what's going to be analyzed. (Of course, if your professor tells you to read only *after* the lecture, follow his or her advice.)

5. **Let the professor be your guide.** Before starting the reading assignment, make sure you've checked out all the clues the professor has given about what you're supposed to be looking for in the reading. Study questions, comments in the previous lecture, handouts, things the TA says in section—all of these can contain hints that will make you a more probing reader. Also, be sure to pay special attention to any clues the *author* offers about what the key issues are. Titles, section headings, summaries, and any big proclamations ("In this section, I will show that . . .") can be enormously helpful in locating the points that the author thinks you should be focusing on.

6. **Think about it right.** Different kinds of reading materials require different kinds of reading. When you are reading a textbook, the main idea might be to get a general overview of the material and take in some basic facts. When you are reading an article, the point might be to study and evaluate the claims made by the author. When reading a novel or epic, you might be expected to analyze the character of the hero or assess the importance of various events. Look at how the

professor is treating the reading in lecture, and try to mimic his or her methodology in your own reading.

7. **Track the developments.** In any reading—be it a textbook, scholarly article, novel, or a play—there's some building up of what the author has to say. As you read through the material, ask yourself: *How is the argument (or plot or story) developing? Why does this point follow the one that precedes? What work is it doing?* The more you can see why the ideas are ordered in the way they are, the easier it'll be for you to understand the point of it all.

8. **Stop and think.** If you come to something you don't understand (especially if it seems important), don't just put your head down and charge forward. Stop and puzzle it out. In many college readings, what comes after depends on what comes before. If you don't understand what comes before, you won't understand what comes after.

9. **Use a dictionary.** Missing a key term—especially when it's a technical term or a strategically located word—can cause you to not understand what's said from that point on. Always have a dictionary of some sort (whether print, online, or a cell phone app) when you sit down to read. And use it whenever you come to a word you don't know—or sorta know, but, now that you think of it, not really.

10. **Work the problems.** If yours is a math, science, or logic book, you should do the problems in your head as you're reading them. That way you won't just be passively absorbing what the author is saying, but exercising your mind and applying the concepts to the material on your own. Just like you'll have to do on the test.

11. **Maintain the right pace.** Although different kinds of reading go at different speeds, it's important to neither adopt the pace of the snail or go at it like a bat out of hell. A good pace is one slow enough to really understand what's being said, but not so slow that you've squeezed any life out of what you're reading or totally lost any overall sense of what's going on.

12. **Never subvocalize.** Contrary to what they might have taught you in first grade, reading out loud to yourself is a surefire way to slow yourself down. You're supposed to move directly from reading to understanding, not through an intermediate stage of saying each word to yourself.

IOHO. Avoid methods like the SQ3R strategy that encourage you to do an activity out loud in your head. When you're reading fluidly, understanding should be automatic, not subvocalized.

13. **Read the extras.** Be sure to look at sidebars, illustrations, and problems solved in the reading. Even if they look pretty, they still count as content to master. And if the author has included "questions for thought" at the end of the chapter (especially in a textbook), you'd be a fool not to try to answer them, at least in your head.

14. **Keep a record.** Though we're not dead set against highlighting or writing code words in the margins, we think it's best to keep reading notes in a separate notebook or computer folder. Come the test, it's three times as easy to study from a complete document than it is to scan a highlighted textbook that looks more like a Christmas tree than a summary of the reading.

BEST-KEPT SECRET. If you take notes electronically, you'll be able to search them for key terms and concepts when working on your paper or studying for tests. Hey, you do everything else on your laptop or tablet; why not extend your e-time to note taking on your reading?

15. **Keep it in perspective.** Don't have a cow if the reading is not coming easily. Reading is a skill, and in many courses—especially ones in which you're new to the subject—you'll build up your comprehension and speed as the semester goes on. Keep at it, don't get depressed, and pretty soon you'll be reading as if you'd been doing it all your life. Which you have.

15 Strategies for Painless Presentations

Even more than death and taxes, the thing people fear most is speaking in public. Needless to say, college students are not immune from this terror—which, for you psychology hounds, even has a name: *glossophobia.* Unfortunately, it's not always so easy to avoid public speaking. Some schools have required courses in speech, whereas others incorporate reports, presentations, and seminars into a broad variety of courses. Still, there's no need to lose your breakfast (or lunch, dinner, or late-night snack) over your upcoming presentation. Our 15 tips for improving your public speaking will make even a garden-variety speaker into a real Cicero:

1. **Do your homework.** Nobody can give a good presentation without putting in some serious time preparing his or her remarks. Many gifted speakers look like they're just talking off the cuff, saying whatever comes to mind. But in truth they've spent considerable time in advance figuring out what they're going to say. You should, too.

5-STAR TIP. It's always a good idea to try out (at least part of) your presentation on your professor or TA before giving it in class. Office hours work well for this.

---

2. **Play the parts.** Good presentations are structured in sections. Organizing your points into two or three main parts—and telling your audience what these parts are (both at the beginning of the paper and at the start of each section)—can make the difference between a winning presentation and a loser.

3. **Do a dry run.** It's always good to do a run-through (or even a couple of run-throughs) the night before the presentation. This

can help with both your timing and your manner of presentation (be sure to make mental notes if you went on too long or got nervous or stuck). Some people find it useful to have a friend pretend to be the audience. He or she can build up your confidence and maybe even ask a question or two (nothing wrong with trying your luck at interacting with a questioner). And if you have an annoying mannerism (Jeremy used to circle his forehead with his hand when presenting), you friend can point it out—gently, we hope—and, with any luck, you can stop doing it (Jeremy has learned to present with his hands at his sides).

4. **Look presentable.** No need to wear a suit, but it's hard for people to take a presentation seriously when you look like you've just rolled out of bed. Even if you have.

5. **Arrive early.** Even the most experienced speakers can come unglued if they have to rush through their setup—assembling their materials, preparing any handouts or displays, and simply getting into the proper frame of mind for a presentation.

 5-STAR TIP. Be sure to try out all the electronics (computer hookup, PowerPoint, audio, internet connection including videos, microphone) in advance of your talk. And though many speakers don't think about this one, make sure the volume on all the devices is loud enough so that someone at the back of the room can clearly hear what you have to say (have a friend be the "speaker" and you be the "audience" to test it out).

 RULE OF THUMB. Always allow yourself double the time you estimate. Things always go wrong and never get fixed quickly.

6. **Talk, don't read.** Nobody enjoys seeing a speaker burying his or her face in a script, reading stiffly. Try to talk from notes or, if you use a written-out text, try to look down at it only occasionally. Keep in mind that in many cases it's more important that you demonstrate an understanding of your topic than that you capture your prepared text word for word. (Your practice sessions should help you here, as they enable you to better remember what you want to say.)

7. **Take it slow.** The single biggest mistake inexperienced speakers make is going too fast. Remember that your audience is hearing the material for the first time and isn't nearly as familiar with it as you are.

EXTRA POINTER. If you find yourself running out of time, either drop, or briefly summarize, any leftover material. If your presentation includes a discussion period, gesture at the points you haven't fully covered and suggest them as things that could be discussed later.

8. **Use "aids."** For certain sorts of presentations, visual aids—such as PowerPoint decks, handouts, even items written on the board—can help your audience locate and grasp the main points and help *you* remember what they are. Just be sure you fully explain these materials in your presentation: No one is happy to see an outline that he or she can't make heads or tails of.

EXTRA POINTER. Some presenters find the "speaker notes" feature in PowerPoint useful (you see a window with your notes that the audience doesn't see). Sure beats flash cards.

9. **Don't bury the crowd.** Including massive numbers of quotes or unfathomable amounts of data can overwhelm even the most attentive audience. Why would you want to do that?

10. **Be yourself.** As important as the content you present is your authenticity in presenting it. So, play to your strengths, and don't try to be someone you're not—you'll never succeed.

11. **Play it straight.** There's no harm in including a little humor in your presentations, especially if you can carry it off well. But in most college presentations, clowns get C's.

12. **Circle the crowd.** A very important part of public speaking is to make eye contact with people seated in all parts of the room—even those nodding off in the back. This shows people that you're interested in communicating with them—not just getting through this hellish experience ASAP. And it wouldn't hurt to get out from behind the podium or desk and walk around the room a little. Sharing space with the audience can also communicate your interest in sharing your results with them—something you surely want to do.

13. **Appear relaxed.** You don't have to actually be relaxed—few speakers are—but at least try to appear as relaxed as possible. Bring along some water or other beverage, take short breaks from time to time, and get absorbed in the moment. No one enjoys speakers who are trembling and sweating bullets.

14. **Finish strong.** Always be sure to have a satisfying conclusion to your presentation, in which you make clear to the listeners what they now know. This creates a warm feeling in the minds of your listeners and shows them that they've really learned something from your lovely talk.

 IOHO. Welcome interruptions. Some speakers are terrified that someone will interrupt their presentation with a question or comment. Actually, this is one of the best things that can happen: It shows that someone in the audience has engaged with what you're saying, and it can actually lead to genuine progress on the point you were making. And two-way conversation (assuming you're minimally good at it) is always a tension reducer.

---

15. **Know when to stop lecturing.** Certain presentations—
especially in advanced or upper-division classes or seminars—
can require you to present some material, then lead a
discussion. Be sure to attentively listen to any comments or
questions your classmates or professor might raise, before
starting on your answer. In a discussion period, never lecture
(only discuss), and be sure to answer exactly the question
asked (not offer up more canned—but irrelevant—material). In
many classes, how you discuss is as important as how you
present (in some classes, it's even taken into account in the
grade).

How to Build Your Confidence

It's easy to feel a lack of confidence at college. Lectures with hundreds of students can make one feel no bigger than a worm. And even smaller classes can make you feel low when it seems like the student in the front row has all the answers—and the professor's *telling* him or her so. Luckily, like every other skill, confidence can be learned and increased over time, especially if you follow our best practical tips:

1. **Turn off the little voice.** Everyone has an inner critic who from time to time whispers defeating messages: "You're not good enough for college," "Everyone here is more qualified than you," "You'll never pass that mondo midterm." But don't listen. Remind yourself that you've accomplished a lot before getting into this college, and that if you didn't have what it takes to succeed, they wouldn't have admitted you.

2. **Realize you're not alone.** Everyone thinks they're the only one, but a recent study shows that one-third of college students feel inadequate after the very first semester. We can tell you from our own firsthand experience that a majority of students have doubts at one time or another about their ability to do the work. So if you're feeling unsure of yourself, keep in mind that you're in distinguished company: most of your friends are going through (or have gone through) just what you're experiencing now.

3. **Take something you're good at.** Each semester, in spite of the distribution requirements and courses you need for your major, take at least one course you enjoy—and are guaranteed to do well in. Constantly struggling at courses that are very, very challenging saps your strength and can, over time, undermine your confidence.

4. Start small. Try taking a few small risks to help you overcome some of your fears. Maybe you could ask (or answer) a question in the discussion section. Or approach a professor with a question before or after class. Once you've broken the ice, even a little, you'll begin to feel more secure.

EXTRA POINTER. Low-risk activities that are built right into the course provide an excellent opportunity to bolster your confidence. Getting a check-plus on a short homework assignment or a 10 on the weekly quiz can do wonders for your self-esteem.

---

5. Reward achievements. Everyone feels better when they give themselves some recognition for a job well done—even a small accomplishment. Get yourself a slice of pizza—with extras—for that 10 on the quiz. The positive reinforcement will make it easier for you to study for next week's quiz. And the $3 investment will remind you that your achievements, too, are something worth celebrating.

6. Make all the classes. It's hard to feel confident about yourself when you're missing key pieces of the course—pieces that, when missed, prevent you from doing well and, hence, feeling confident. Students who pop into class erratically have much greater trouble understanding and following the lectures they do attend. And they have much more trouble answering questions on tests that depend on material in classes they missed.

7. Take a small class. Even though it might seem less scary to hide in the anonymity of a huge lecture hall, taking a small class can offer a more supportive and nurturing environment for learning. Especially if you strut your stuff by asking or answering a question and receive positive feedback.

8. Get feedback early. Your confidence can soar if you consult with your professor (or TA) early in the semester. Whether it's about a point in the lecture you didn't understand, your initial ideas for a paper, or worries about how to prepare for a test, you will feel immeasurably better after your instructor steers you in the right direction—or assures you that you're already going in the right direction. Many low-confidence students are too scared to talk to their professors. This only makes their problem worse. (For more on seeking out your professor, see "The 14 Secrets of Going to See the Professor" on p. 212.)

9. **Divide big tasks into small pieces.** Many students doubt their ability to write a 15-page research paper or prepare for a comprehensive final. But if they conceived of the paper as three five-page pieces, and the final as five three-week units, the task would suddenly seem a lot more doable. And the feeling of accomplishment generated when one part of the project is completed would help propel them to finish the rest of the work.

10. **Do a trial run.** Many college projects allow you to do a no-risk practice round before the real thing. Taking a practice test at home before the midterm, trying out your oral presentation on the TA before the section meeting, discussing answers to the study guide with your study group before the final—all of these will build your confidence before the actual event. And if your instructor or cohorts say a few kind words about your ideas— and if you believe they mean them—well, that can help, too. Incredibly much, it turns out.

11. **Take comments constructively.** Many students see every mark on their paper as a biting criticism and either get all depressed or ignore them completely. Train yourself to view the comments in a more positive light, as ways the professor is trying to help you do better on the next piece of work (rather than sinking your ship). Learning how to use the comments to improve— even after a not-so-impressive start—can be the best confidence booster of all.

12. **Apply for a prize.** Many departments have various prize competitions for their majors or for all students at the college.

And in many cases the competition isn't as tough as you might think. So give it a whirl. Winning even a $10 gift certificate or a mention on the plaque in the department office can be a real confidence booster.

13. **Look for real-world apps.** A chance to work at an inner-city clinic (if you're in a health care field), at an engineering consultant firm (if you're interested in waste-management systems), or an insurance office (if you're studying marketing) can give you a real shot in the arm. Seeing how what you've learned in college can have real worth in the real world will build your confidence like nothing else. And then, when you return to college next fall, those dull, dreary lectures won't seem quite so meaningless.

14. **Recognize that learning is a process.** If you expect to master a new field right off the bat, or be able to write a bang-up research paper when you've never written one before, you set yourself up for a letdown—and for a crisis of confidence. Be patient with yourself as you start on new tasks or skills. Think back on skills you mastered in the past (whether it's snowboarding, Texas hold 'em, or vegan cooking) and remember what it was like when you first started.

15. **Avoid the bubble bursters.** You know who we mean: the people who, no matter how good your achievement, can always find something wrong. For some students, it's their parents; for others, it's their perfectionist professor or adviser; and for still others, it's the person who shares their loft with them. Adopt a "don't ask, don't tell" policy toward such naysayers: they won't ask how you're doing, you won't tell them about your successes.

4 SPECIALTIES OF THE HOUSE

It's unavoidable. Virtually every college has some basic requirements that everyone has to take, like it or not. They may have the name general education, core, distribution, or lower-division requirements. But whatever you call them, you gotta take them. Think of them as getting your fiber or taking your medicine.

Colleges are requiring this stuff because it really is good for you (or so they think). So what's not to like here? Well, the problem is that some students get so tied up in these must-do courses—getting C's and D's or, worse, failing them, then having to retake them umpteen times—that what was supposed to be a basic skills-developing or area-introducing course turns into a major GPA-buster and impediment to finishing your degree in a finite number of years.

To smooth your way through the gamut of required courses your school might offer—that is, inflict—on you, we offer some tips that will help you easily manage the most common and, for some, the most vexing, required courses.

In this chapter, you'll learn:

▶ 10 Ways to Whip the Freshman Comp Requirement

▶ 10 Tips for Taming the Math Requirement

▶ Top 10 Tips for Mastering the Foreign (or World) Language Requirement

▶ 10 Ideas for Learning to Love the Lab

▶ 10 Tips for the First-Year Experience Course

▶ Facing Up to Remediation: Top 10 Strategies

▶ 10 Tips for Online Courses (and MOOCs)

▶ How to Take Courses on the Web—for Free

10 Ways to Whip the Freshman Comp Requirement

Many students starting out in college encounter something like this:

ENGL 1013 Composition I (Fa, Sp, Su). Required of all first-year students unless exempted by the Department of English. *Prerequisite*: ENGL 0003 or an acceptable score on the English section of the SAT, ACT, or another approved test.

It's that most despised of all college courses: the freshman composition requirement. A one-size-fits-all course designed to teach you, as they say, "writing across the curriculum"—which in ordinary language means the basics of spelling, grammar, and composition that, ideally, you'll be able to carry over to all your other courses. Skeptical? Too bad. You're stuck. So you may as well equip yourself with the 10 best tips from Raina Smith Lyons, assistant director of the program in composition at the University of Arkansas:

1. **Go to class.** Sure, you might think that not much goes on in class. And maybe at your high school or even in your other college courses, it's true. But in freshman comp, a majority of the activities are centered around the class meetings. You may have one-on-one critiques of your papers, "workshopping" (that is, peer discussion of rough drafts), presentation of sources that go beyond the textbook, as well as actual in-class writing. And most instructors take roll and count it toward your grade. Upshot? In freshman comp, in particular, it's best to get yourself to class. Every time.

BEST-KEPT SECRET. Many colleges are experimenting with teaching their freshman writing classes online—not because the faculty wants it this way, but because the administration sees it as a way to save money. According to one recent study, at some schools 15 to 25 percent of freshman comp courses have no in-class component. But what they don't tell you is that in many cases some of the more valuable course components have been dropped: student presentations, individual conferences with the instructor, and group writing projects. Look before you leap.

2. Do all the work assigned. Most freshman comp classes have a graduated series of tasks. You start slow, perhaps just by presenting someone's argument; then as the semester progresses you build up to harder tasks—such as comparing a number of positions, learning to evaluate the argument, and, ultimately, presenting your own reasoned views. Miss a key step or skill, and you're behind for future work.

EXTRA POINTER. Do all the work, even if it doesn't make sense to you. Some instructors assign "free writing" or other assignments just to get the juices flowing and to motivate you to write more.

3. Talk to your teacher. Use e-mail, office hours, or a simple face-to-face conversation after class to make the teacher aware of any problems you're having—for example, not understanding the assignment, trouble getting started, inability to "prewrite," or wanting to hand in a late assignment. Whatever the case, your instructor is happy to help—if you come to him or her while there is still time.

4. **Finish your drafts early.** One of the main things they're trying to teach in these freshman comp courses is the importance of writing drafts of your work and thinking through the issues over a period of time. This process is thwarted when you leave the draft to the last minute—especially if the teacher has given you three or four weeks to do the essay.

 5-STAR TIP Program yourself to think the paper is due one week before it really is. That way, you'll have a full week left to do a series of revisions.

5. **Be sure you understand the assignment.** Freshman comp courses often try to teach you to write a general persuasive or critical essay rather than to use the tools from any particular discipline or major. So they often teach a variety of kinds of papers, each with its own characteristic structure and tasks. Make sure that for each of the four or five paper assignments you know exactly what's being asked of you. If the instructor has gone over an outline in class, as many do, be sure to follow it in your paper.

6. **Offer up a good thesis.** Part of the success of a freshman comp paper is determined by the quality of the thesis: the single sentence, usually at the beginning of the paper, that expresses the one key point you're trying to get across in the paper. Pick too obvious or simplistic a thesis, and your paper is heading for a C. Pick a better or deeper thesis, and your paper is on the express track to an A. If you're not sure what your thesis should be, it's well worth your while to run it by the teacher.

7. **Be sure to prove what you've claimed.** In some of the freshman comp assignments you're asked not only to compare or contrast points of view but also to provide reasons or

arguments for a given claim (whether that of some author or your own). Be sure to do so, if asked.

8. **Go beyond your conclusion.** Usually freshman comp papers ask you to conclude by summing up what you've shown. A really good ending, though, can also go beyond what's been shown in the paper: either pointing out some further dimension of the issue or offering some broader assessment of your results. Sure, a conclusion is meant to point back. But it can also point forward.

9. **Imaginatively use campus resources.** The writing center, in which you can receive up to an hour's worth of individualized help from a trained writing expert (often an English graduate student), can beat the 10 or 15 minutes you might get from a TA or lecturer. The reference librarian can help you use electronic databases that'll provide strong sources for your paper, if sources are needed. (See "14 Techniques for Doing Research Like a Professor" on p. 190 and "Top 10 Tips for Doing E-Research" on p. 196 for more on this.)

EXTRA POINTER. Did you know that your campus has experts in the faculty of many departments? Your paper "What effects do media have on young children?" could be strengthened by a chat with a professor of cognitive science or child development who actually does research on living, breathing children.

10. **Present good-looking work.** Be sure to proofread your paper manually after you've run the electronic spell-check. Even the best spell-check won't catch homonyms or a wrong word spelled correctly. Also, be sure to take out any sentences that don't do any work or that aren't directly relevant to the task asked: in other words, put yourself in the place of the reader

and trim out any fluff. In a composition course, the presentation of the ideas can be as important as the ideas themselves.

 BONUS TIP. Play to your interests. You'll enjoy your required freshman comp course more if, when given a choice, you pick topics that get you excited.

10 Tips for Taming the Math Requirement

For many college students, the math requirement is the single biggest obstacle standing between them and their cap and gown. Believe it or not, some students take the same math course two or three times and at the end of their ordeal have just barely passed. Doesn't have to be this way. College math is easily manageable, and might even turn out to be fun, if you follow our 10-step plan for acing the math requirement:

1. **Get in—and stay in—the right level.** Colleges often have several levels of calculus and up to five versions of algebra. Select carefully to avoid taking classes that are too hard—or too easy—for your level of ability and training. Double-check after the first test, and switch classes if necessary. Why torture yourself if you're never going to be able to master delta-epsilon proofs?

2. **Take the credit.** If you have AP math credits, use 'em. Your first-year adviser or a representative from the math department can tell you what college credit(s) you've earned and what course you should enroll in if you want to continue your study of math.

> **BEST-KEPT SECRET.** Be sure to figure out whether you've taken the Calculus AB or the Calculus BC course. And if you're lucky enough to have taken the new AP Statistics course, be sure to put in a claim for that, too.

3. **Do every single homework problem.** In other subjects, homework may not be so critical; if you do it, that's great, and if you blow it off, well, that's OK, too (you'll do some extra cramming come test time). But in math it's supercritical to keep up with the homework. Doing the homework problems is the way you learn math. Not to mention the way you learn how

to do the various kinds of problems that will be on the tests. Also you'll understand the lecture better if you do the problems when they're assigned.

4. **Always have a strategy.** Never go at math problems with a sledgehammer. Start by figuring out what type of problem you're dealing with, and consider various strategies for solving this sort of problem. Then select the strategy you think most appropriate or promising. Never lunge wildly with a strategy that's totally inappropriate for the task at hand. You can waste tremendous amounts of time going down blind alleys if you don't think before you plunge in.

5. **Be ultraneat.** In all your math work—whether your class notes, homework, or tests—be obsessive about neatness. A 5 that looks like a 6, an *x* that looks like a *z*, or a + that looks like a − will mess you up like you wouldn't believe.

6. **Get down the intermediate steps.** Some instructors are careful to write down every step of a problem as they are doing it in class; other professors (like the ones who are teaching this course for the hundred-and-eighth time) aren't so fastidious. In either case, you should be sure to write down what the professor puts up; then, when you get home, fill in whatever steps have been omitted (if any).

IOHO. Many students complain that they can't understand what their non-native-English-speaking TA is saying. Many of these complaints are unfounded. But if you really can't understand your TAs or your professor's English, we recommend you go to an office hour and engage him or her in basic conversation (not technical math talk). Often, once you've had an ordinary conversation, you'll get used to your teacher's accent, which will make the classes go a whole lot easier. But if after all that you still can't understand your TAs English, change to another section. You can't learn if you can't understand.

7. **Pinpoint your sticking points.** When you get stuck on a problem, don't just throw up your hands in disgust and

announce you're clueless. Figure out exactly where you got stuck—and for what reason (Was there a theorem you didn't know? Were you missing a concept? Did you fail to consider an alternative?). Then go for help. The help will be much more effective, and the helper more motivated to give it, if you can pinpoint your exact problem, rather than just reporting your veil of confusion. (For some tips on seeking help, see "The 14 Secrets of Going to See the Professor" on p. 212.)

8. **Join a group.** Study groups (once or twice a week) are especially valuable in problem-solving courses like math. Even if you're a math whiz, you can benefit from teaching your less-gifted friends how to do the problems or proofs. Making challenging material clear to others is one of the best ways of getting your mind around difficult concepts and strategies.

EXTRA POINTER. If your TA is holding a group office hour or review session before a test, make it your business to go. When the TA has the test questions in mind, he or she is most likely to drop hints about what's going to be asked.

---

9. **Test yourself.** By far the best way to study for math tests is to prepare a test for yourself and do the problems. You'll see very quickly what you know—and what you don't.

5-STAR TIP. Most textbooks have extra problems in the back, with answers provided for at least half of them, usually the odd-numbered ones. These make great choices for your practice tests. Also, some professors give out sample problems or copies of previous tests before the exam: don't squander this important resource by taking "just a quick peek" at the questions as you put the handout into your backpack. And if all else fails, make up your own problems: construct variants—preferably harder variants—of the ones you did in class or on the homework.

---

10. **Think about tutoring.** If you're really having difficulty in your math class, you might want to find a tutor. Sometimes a TA who has previously taught the course is available, sometimes a junior or senior can help you out, and sometimes the on-campus learning center or math lab has trained people available to help you. Just make sure the tutor is both good at math and familiar with the particular course you're taking (and ideally its instructor too). And be sure to bring the textbook, your class notes, the problems you've done, and most important, any info about the tests, to each of the meetings with your tutor. That way he or she can tailor the tutoring sessions to your exact needs.

BONUS TIP. Adopt a can-do attitude. Don't let some label that your third-grade teacher pinned on you rule your life today. If you tell yourself "I'm just not good at math" or "I'm intuitive, not logical" or "Girls just can't do math as well as boys," you've defeated yourself before you even start. Why do that?

Top 10 Tips for Mastering the Foreign (or World) Language Requirement

Fala português? Puhutko suomea? Sen söyle türk? Spreekt u nederlands? Kana (or *Kina*, as the case may be) *Hausa*? All of these are ways of asking whether you speak some language: Portuguese, Finnish, Turkish, Dutch, and Hausa (one of Africa's most common languages), respectively. You too would know this if you had completed your foreign language requirement in one of these tongues. Or at least you'd know what *¿Habla usted español?* or *Parlez-vous français?* means (not telling you these).

To help you get through your foreign language requirement—a four-course sequence at most four-year colleges—here are our ten best strategies:

1. **Pick for a reason.** The foreign language requirement is one of the very few two-year requirements at many colleges. Select your language for a reason. Good reason: Pashto will be useful in your career at the state department in Pakistan or Afghanistan. Less good reason: I took Spanish in high school and kinda, sorta—well, now that I think of it—didn't really like it all that much.

2. **Attend all the classes.** The foreign language class is one of the few classes that is truly cumulative: every lesson includes some content that, together with the other classes, builds your knowledge of the language. Your usual "cutting allowance" won't cut it in foreign language courses.

3. **Learn the conjugations—both ways.** The secret to learning languages is mastering the verbs, not the nouns. So practice the verb conjugations (you know: *I am, you are, he is* . . .) in both directions—that is, from the foreign language into English and from English into the foreign language. In some courses,

the tests could ask you to go both ways. And even if that's not required, you'll learn the forms really well only if you practice both ways (flash cards, especially the new electronic flash cards put out by WWW.STUDYBLUE.COM, are especially helpful here).

4. **Learn all the "moods."** No, not your moods (you know those already), but the verb moods. Subjunctive, conditional, aorist—each language has its own (Czech reportedly has ten tenses, voices, moods, and aspects). As you move past the first year in your study of the language, these unusual-to-English-speaker moods become increasingly important.

5. **Pay attention to sentence structure.** Though English usually is arranged in subject-verb-predicate order, many other languages don't follow this pattern. Master the way your new language structures and constructs the sentence—to the point that you can anticipate what's coming next as the sentence unfolds (which will help get you away from word-by-word translation or sentence construction—an achievement in itself).

6. **Learn how it sounds.** Americans are really bad at vowels. But foreign languages often have many grades of vowels and many vowels that sound different from English. Learn the proper pronunciation—and the length—of vowels.

7. **Memorize in bite-size pieces.** Every language requires memorizing vocabulary. You'll have a much easier time if you memorize a few words each day, rather than leave 484 words 'til the midterm.

8. **Beware of "false friends."** In every language there are words that sound a lot like an English word, but mean something else entirely. For example, in virtually every language but English, a "preservative" is something you might need on a date but wouldn't want to find in your peanut butter. Check out this false friend and gazillions of others at HTTP://EN.WIKIPEDIA.ORG /WIKI/FALSE_FRIENDS.

9. **"Friend" a foreign student.** The only really good way to learn a language is by talking with a native speaker. So find an

international friend (or hire a native speaker) and have ordinary conversations with him or her. That way, you'll learn not only the language in context but also all the words you really need to know (but somehow never learned in Portuguese 102). Failing that, try going to a language lab or language table to practice your conversation.

BEST-KEPT SECRET. There are many opportunities on the Web to practice your language with native speakers in exotic locales. These include WWW.LIVEMOCHA.COM, at which you can chat for free with over a million native speakers in twelve languages. (What a deal—foreign language plus social networking!) And for students who'd like to subscribe (and pay a small monthly fee), check out WWW.CHINESEPOD.COM and its sister sites WWW.FRENCHPOD.COM, WWW.SPANISHPOD.COM, and WWW .ITALIANPOD.COM; you'll find over a thousand podcasts, along with practice, review, and reinforcement. Another very good site (recommended by one of our students) is WWW .RADIOLINGUA.COM; here you'll find the very popular CoffeeBreakSpanish and CoffeeBreakFrench podcasts, as well as the One-Minute podcasts in, among other languages, Irish, Polish, Russian, and even Luxembourgish.

5-STAR TIP. It's always fun to listen to the evening news in the language you're studying (you'll learn interesting things about the culture, too). Check out your TV, YouTube, and other web content areas for broadcasts and recordings. If you're studying Spanish, check out the new Spanish Immersion TV site at HTTP://LOMASTV.COM. Also, many foreign films can be streamed from Netflix, Amazon, and other sites. Just be sure either to not look at the subtitles or to set them to some language other than English.

10. **Entertain your prof (or TA) in the language.** If you visit your teacher in an office hour, or talk with him or her after class, be sure to converse in the foreign language—100 percent of the time. That'll not only give you some spontaneous practice in talking the stuff, but earn you some brownie points for trying really hard.

BONUS TIP. Make peace with your lot. For better or worse, many schools require four courses in one foreign language. Try to do well in them, and don't fall behind. Most of all, stick with the one you started. We've seen countless students take a semester of French, then switch to German, only to try Italian. False starts in foreign languages are one of the main reasons college can drag on for more than four years.

10 Ideas for Learning to Love the Lab

Many schools have a lab requirement. And many students hate the lab requirement almost as much as they hate the freshman comp, math, and world language requirements. Too boring, too hard, too stupid: these are common complaints students have. But it doesn't have to be this way. Especially if you follow our ten best tips for conquering the lab requirement:

1. **Know what you're picking.** At many schools, there's a broad variety of courses that satisfy the lab requirement. You might be surprised to know that in addition to "hard" sciences such as chemistry, physics, and biology, in many schools astronomy, geology, anthropology, environmental science, and psychology can count toward the lab requirement. Suggestion: pick something that you like and that you wouldn't ordinarily have a chance to take. This is one of your best opportunities at college to turn a requirement into an elective—something you *choose* to take because you like it.

2. **Know which courses count for a science major.** Sometimes you'll want to take a course that will both satisfy the distribution requirement and count toward a major. Be sure in such a case that the course you select will in fact do double duty. Some courses—for example, physics for humanities majors or the biology of everyday life—are specifically *excluded* from the major. They're geared to the general university population and hence considered too easy for serious scientists (or even for majors).

EXTRA POINTER. Be sure to figure out when your lab meets. An astronomy course could involve night trips to the observatory; an earth sciences course might go out on field trips to look at rock formations.

3. **Attend to the "requisites."** Some lab courses, especially ones that can count for the major, have prerequisites and/or corequisites: courses you must complete before—or at the same time as—the lab you're taking. Especially important in physics, chemistry, and sometimes biology is the amount of math that's required. Some courses are algebra-based (or, in street language, assume you've taken high school math), while others are non-algebra-based (that is, require calculus and often involve a good amount of theory).

EXTRA POINTER. Often the course description isn't fully explicit about the prerequisites, or the professor is implicitly assuming some level of math training. If in doubt, ask.

4. **Take it on time.** It's always good to polish off the lab requirement in one of your first two years of college. And if the information from the courses is needed for some upcoming professional exam—the MCAT, DAT, GRE, or GMAT, for instance—it's an especially good idea not to run this requirement down to the wire.

5-STAR TIP. You'll want to take the lab in the same semester as you're taking the lecture. Believe it or not, some students take the course and leave the unpleasant-for-them lab for another semester—by which time they've forgotten all the material.

5. **Do the pre- and post-work.** Many lab courses have an in-class and an out-of-class component. In advance of the lab, you might be asked to read the lab manual and write out answers to some questions; after some labs, you might have to write up a two- to three-page lab report summing up your methods, reporting your results, and drawing some conclusions. Be sure to do all this assigned work. It'll help you understand the

lectures in the course, and the demonstrations in the lab, and, in some courses, will count toward the grade and could even appear on the tests. Why row with only one oar in the water?

6. **Connect it.** Many students consider the lab as a self-contained activity, not as something connected to other parts of the course. (This view is reinforced by the fact that at many schools you sign up for a one-credit lab course under a number different from the science lecture number.) You'll understand the lab better if you ask yourself, *How is this lab supposed to reinforce the concepts of the course? Why is it placed at the point in the course it is? Why are you doing a lab at all?* (Possible answer: *The last lecture drew ray diagrams, and this lab shows the real, physical properties that rays exhibit in different media.*)

7. **Volunteer for demos.** Many labs include a portion where the professor (or TA) calls for volunteers to assist in some demonstration. Be the guinea pig. Not only will you enjoy showing off your erudition to your classmates (and to the professor), but you might actually enjoy doing the stuff. And if you do a really good job in the demonstration—like answering the questions with the key concepts from the class—you might get a few extra points when the prof calculates the grade.

8. **Play all the parts.** In many labs, the students are divided into groups of three or four, with various tasks assigned to each. There could be the "do-er," the "recorder," the "time-manager," and the "question asker" (YRMV, depending on the lab). Take your turn in each of the roles. Not only will this make the lab more interesting, but you'll learn (and remember) the material better if sometimes you're actually mixing the chemicals, dissecting the amoeba, or rolling the ball down the plane—not just taking the notes, watching the stopwatch, or asking some super-obvious question.

9. **Think abstractly.** It's an important part of every lab to observe the experiment and record what you see. But it's also important to apply the theories, principles, and constructs of

the course to what you've seen (look to the lectures and readings for these). The professor doesn't only want you to say that the ball started rolling faster as it got to the bottom of the hill; he or she wants you to apply the concepts of kinetic and potential energy, acceleration, and gravity to the case. (Hey, this isn't your seventh-grade science fair.)

10. **Use the office hours.** It's a good idea to seek out your professor, TA, or lab instructor when writing up the lab report, especially if it counts toward the grade. (If you have a week to write the report, go early in the week.) You'll be able to make sure you've understood the science and captured the key concepts—not just parroted the purpose and procedures of the experiment straight out of the lab manual. And be sure to make the corrections that the instructor suggests. Even if it's a pain to go back and fix up the report you thought was finished, you'll get a better result. And who knows? You might actually learn something, if you take the time to learn from an expert. Didn't expect to do that in what you thought was a cruddy distribution requirement, did you?

10 Tips for the First-Year Experience Course

One of the hottest new things at college is the first-year experience (FYE) course—a one-semester class that matches the very best faculty of the school (or at least well-trained TAs) with an engaging, often relevant, subject of study. All in a small-group, friendly atmosphere. Some schools focus their first-year experience courses on easing the transition from high school to college: these courses emphasize academic skills, personal development, and learning your way around the campus. Other schools adopt a "professor's prerogative" model: here, professors are invited to teach a course on a topic in which they are doing research—or are just plain interested in thinking about. Under this second model—sometimes called a freshman seminar (FS)—you might find courses such as Comic Books and Conflict; Midwives, Healers, and Physicians; and Energy: What We Use and Where It Should Come From (these courtesy of City University of New York; check your college's online catalogue for the options at your campus).

Whatever kind of first-year course your school offers, you'll want to get off to the best possible start—and you will, if you follow these 10 best tips from professor J. Steven Reznick, associate dean for first-year seminars at the University of North Carolina:

1. **Make a list.** Each first-year experience course will be limited to approximately 15 to 25 students, so even at a small school you may not get your first choice of classes. Enrolling in any first-year seminar is better than enrolling in no first-year seminar, so be strategic: look at the first-year seminar offerings at your school and come up with a list of seminars that would be of interest to you.

EXTRA POINTER. If you'd like to see what an elaborate FYE program looks like, take a look at UCLA's (WWW.COLLEGE.UCLA .EDU/FIATLUX) or UNC's (HTTP://FYS.UNC.EDU/).

2. **Play to your strengths.** Some first-year seminars emphasize in-class discussion; others emphasize hands-on activities, social interactions, creativity, or community service. When putting together your list of seminars, pick a class that is not only on a topic you're interested in, but is also built on a type of activity that you enjoy.

3. **Avoid your major.** Some students enter school with leanings toward a specific major, and think it would be natural to look for seminars in that major. Not generally a good idea. When you do get into your major, you'll have lots of advanced courses on interesting topics in that field. Think of your first-year experience course as an opportunity to explore completely new territory: something that just sounds interesting or that you've always wanted to learn about.

4. **Speak up.** If your seminar encourages discussion, open your mouth (even if public speaking makes you a little uncomfortable). A first-year seminar is a great context for you to get beyond your high school timidity and find your college voice.

5. **Add some spice to the stew.** Even if your seminar is not focused on discussion, it is supposed to be interesting, and instructors are always glad to have student participation. You can help by asking questions, introducing new ideas, and steering the course toward interesting topics.

6. **Show up.** Class attendance is always the right thing to do (not only because it is the key to getting a good education, but also because you're paying for the classes). But in a first-year seminar—with only 15 to 25 students—your absence from class will really be noticeable. More important, first-year

seminars are often an ongoing conversation or debate built on previous presentations and discussions. So if you aren't in class, you aren't in the dialogue.

7. **Keep in mind that first-year experience courses are still courses.** Don't lose sight of the fact that, although your first-year seminar has some qualities that make it different from traditional courses, it's still a regular course that might count as credit hours, might meet your school's Gen Ed requirements, and might be graded. Have fun in your first-year seminar, but don't forget to get the job done.

8. **Make friends.** One important aspect of first-year seminars is the opportunity to make new friendships. The word "make" is an active verb: sitting back and waiting for friendships to happen is generally not an effective strategy. You can play an active role in helping make friendships happen by starting conversations, issuing invitations, and organizing events.

9. **Build a relationship with your instructor.** If most of your other first-year courses are huge, the instructor in your first-year seminar could be the faculty member you know best and who knows you best. Getting off to a good start with one prof can be helpful in many ways: for picking future courses, getting academic advice, and ultimately obtaining a letter of recommendation. Your first-year seminar offers a great opportunity to make this connection.

10. **Spread the word.** Interesting first-year seminar topics can initiate a wave that extends far beyond the classroom. Talk about your seminar with parents, friends, and the stranger sitting beside you on the bus or in the cafeteria. You'll learn more deeply about the focal topic by describing your seminar to others and by thinking about their questions and observations.

Facing Up to Remediation: Top 10 Strategies

They're called "developmental-" or "preparatory-" or "college-prep-" courses—but really they're *remedial* courses, designed to get your skills in math, reading, or writing English up to college level. About 20 percent of college students take them. They don't offer credit toward your degree—but you have to take them in order to take the courses that do count toward the degree. And there can be lots of them; at some colleges as many as six or eight (depending, of course, on each student's educational background and abilities).

Kinda makes you want to scream. On the other hand, how can you expect to take, and succeed at, advanced courses if your basic skills aren't up to snuff? And what kind of career are you really going to have if you can't calculate well, understand documents written by others, or communicate your own ideas in writing, clearly and effectively? So suck it in. Get used to the idea that for the first year or two of college you might have to take a few of these remedial—oh sorry, we meant "developmental"—courses. These must-do courses might not go half-badly if you follow our ten best strategies for facing down the beast:

1. **Take 'em right away.** It's a natural impulse to put off taking remedial classes: *Why should I should have to do pre-college courses—at college—before doing real college courses?* many students wonder. But resist the urge to put them off. Get these courses out of the way ASAP so that you'll be able to move forward in your major or program.

> **EXTRA POINTER.** The one case in which you might consider
> delaying remedial courses is math, *if* English is your second
> language or your understanding of spoken English isn't up to
> college level. Math classes are taught on the assumption that
> you can understand basic English terms such as "greater
> than" or "less than," so if need be, get your English up to
> speed before enrolling in math (hint: the remedial courses in
> writing and reading might be just the thing).

2. **Get in at the right level.** College prep (or developmental or
   remedial) courses are often offered at different levels—some
   more basic, some more advanced. It's important to get into the
   appropriate level, based on your training and abilities. Use
   college-provided placement tests as a guide. But also use your
   own experience and sense: if you get into a class that seems
   way too easy or too hard, consult with an adviser about
   switching up or down a level.

3. **Do the sequences in order.** If you need to take a series of
   courses in a particular area—math, writing, or reading—keep in
   mind that usually these courses are intended to be taken in a
   particular order, with the skills taught in the second course
   presupposing the skills taught in the first course. It usually will
   not work if you try to take them out of order, or take two
   courses (in the same field) at the same time—even if that
   seems more convenient or efficient to you.

4. **Avoid *coursus interruptus*.** Once you start on a remediation-
   sequence, don't interrupt the sequence until you have finished
   it all. For example if you have three math classes to complete
   (say, arithmetic, mathematics, and algebra), plan on taking one
   each semester for three consecutive semesters (including
   summer school, if possible). Studies have shown that students
   who take the courses without a break have better results,
   because when you start, stop, and start again you tend to
   forget what you've learned and lose your momentum.

5. **Make all the classes.** Remedial classes, even more than some other college classes, are cumulative and are designed to build up your skills over the course of the semester. These classes can cover a lot of ground and don't usually include a lot of repetition of—or "going over"—what was done last time. Students taking these courses have consistently reported that missing even one or two classes makes a big difference in their ability to pass the class.

6. **Exercise your mouth.** A lot of students don't feel comfortable asking questions in class if there is something that they don't understand. Maybe they are embarrassed to admit that they aren't grasping a certain concept or they feel that the professor might not welcome questions. But most professors really want to know when students don't understand. And the only way they'll know this is if you speak up.

7. **Do all the homework.** Homework is not busywork (even though you'll be busy doing it). It's your main chance to develop your skills. Just as you can't learn to drive by listening to someone explain how to drive—you have to actually practice driving the car yourself—you can't learn math, writing, or reading without doing the problems, writing the papers, or reading the textbook.

EXTRA POINTER. Take a look back at the problems done in class before starting your homework. Often the problems assigned for home (and later put on the tests) are variants of the ones done in class.

5-STAR TIP. Use some of your homework time to read the textbook *before* the next lecture or to look over the next set of problems before the teacher does them in class. It'll help you understand the class a whole lot better.

8. **Take the tests seriously.** Many remedial classes have very frequent testing (in the form of either quizzes or hourly tests), in order to reduce the failure rate. Don't take the frequency of testing as an excuse to blow off a test or quiz from time to time. Often, each test focuses on a skill needed for other, more advanced skills taught in the course, and you will have trouble down the line if you haven't mastered material from an earlier stage.

5-STAR TIP. After you get back your tests, be sure to read the feedback, and pinpoint any problems you had. Go back and correct your answers and be sure you understand what (if anything) went wrong. Don't just ignore bad results and figure you'll somehow do better next time.

9. **Use all the resources.** Colleges provide a lot of services to foster student success in remedial courses—for instance, support labs, writing centers, special advisers, and tutors. And the instructors themselves hold office hours to assist students. It's all there for you. Don't let it go to waste.

EXTRA POINTER. Ever consider forming a study group? Well, now you can—remotely. Find up to eight friends and set up a Skype video conference once a week (Skype now accommodates up to nine participants, complete with video— for free!). If your computer or tablet doesn't come preloaded with Skype, you (and your friends) can download it, free, from WWW.SKYPE.COM.

10. **Don't plan to fail.** Sadly, statistics show, at some schools a failure rate of 50 to 60 percent among students taking

developmental courses. Don't set out to become a statistic. It's not just demoralizing to fail a course—it's super-inefficient and a complete waste of money. If you view failure as a realistic option, you could create a self-fulfilling prophecy— especially as the semester drags on and the material becomes a little more difficult. Aim to succeed—on your very first try!

10 Tips for Online Courses (and MOOCs)

One of the most important new trends in college is online learning: instead of large, in-person classes at set times, students can take courses on the Web at whatever time suits their personal, work, or family schedule. And in many cases (though not all) it is the very same professor teaching the web course as who is teaching its in-person sibling, with substantially the same assignments required in both versions of the course (though again, not in every instance).

Before making the leap to the twenty-first-century virtual classroom, educate yourself about what's really at stake. Have a look at our 10 best tips for students considering online learning:

1. **Figure out whether it's for you.** Taking an online course requires a special set of skills: self-direction, time management, virtual communication, and, most important, motivation. Be honest with yourself. If you can't manage to take a course without a set time for lecture and a flesh-and-blood professor to "encourage" you to get to class and do the reading, stick to the in-person classes.

 ON THE WEB. You'll find useful—and entertaining—self-assessment tools at a number of major college websites (check to see whether your university has one). Three we especially like are the University of North Carolina's (WWW.UNC.EDU/TLIM/SER/), Penn State's (HTTP://ETS.TLT.PSU.EDU/LEARNINGDESIGN/ASSESSMENT/ONLINECONTENT/ONLINE_READINESS), and Dr. Marcel Kerr's (Texas Wesleyan University) "Test of Online Learning Success (ToOLS)" (HTTP://FACULTY.TXWES.EDU/MSKERR/TOOLS.HTML).

2. **Find out the method(s) of instruction.** With online courses, there's no "one size fits all." Most courses involve formal lectures (just like the face-to-face versions); others may have no lectures but only discussions and projects to be submitted. If there aren't any lectures, or if the lectures are significantly shorter than the usual 50-minute versions, bear in mind that you'll be responsible for more of your learning (good if you're the take-charge sort of student, not so good if you just want to sit there and soak up your professor's pearls of wisdom). Also, be aware that some online offerings are *hybrid* or *blended* courses: you have some web study and also some in-person activities; for example, meetings with TAs, workshops, or labs. If your course includes such real-world activities, make sure your schedule allows for them.

3. **Inquire who the teacher is.** In some cases, the person teaching the web course is the very same person who teaches the regular, face-to-face version. But in other cases, the university hires an adjunct (that is, part-time) professor or an advanced graduate student just to save money. Know what you're getting. Check out the instructor bio of the course web page. Look for his or her degrees (the higher, the better), teaching experience (how many years, at what level), and whether he or she is trained in the field you're going to take. And if the info isn't there, send an email (polite, of course) asking a few questions about the instructor's background. A good instructor should not take offense and should have nothing to hide.

4. **Mine the syllabus.** Even more than in a traditional course, in an online course the syllabus is the controlling document: Not only does it tell you the course goals, the readings and assignments, and how the grading works, but it also may lay out, day by day, what you're supposed to do. (One online professor we know gives out a two-page syllabus in his in-person class but a ten-page syllabus in the web version.) So, be sure to go over each point of the syllabus. And, again, if you're not absolutely, 100-percent clear about something, send

an email. You can't do the course right if you don't know what to do.

5. **Assess your level of comfort.** In some online courses, you'll find that virtual group activities are an essential—and in some cases, graded—part of the course. You may be asked initially to share information about yourself (for example, introducing yourself or providing a photo or bio), and, as the course moves on, to interact in real time with fellow students taking the course. This is not everyone's cup of tea. If this is an environment you don't feel fully comfortable in, you might do better in the traditional, more anonymous course offered in the brick-and-mortar classroom.

6. **Get the equipment.** Depending on whether your course is video or audio, one-way or two-way, and what the subject is, you'll need hardware and software up to the task. If there's some special program being used to run the course (for example, Blackboard, Moodle, Canvas, WebTV, Angel, Sakai), make sure you have whatever browser, plug-ins, and media players are needed to access the site. Then check out the course web page to see what software, if any, is needed for that particular offering. Depending on the course, you might need word processing, spreadsheet, presentation, graphics, image manipulation, calculation, or other software.

EXTRA POINTER. Be sure you have your password well in advance of the first class. You can't get on without it.

7. **Learn the geography of the site.** Take the time to familiarize yourself with the overall layout of the course web page. Pay special attention to any tabs: for example, syllabus, class assignments and readings, homework and problem sets, virtual office hours, and extra resources. In an online course *you're* in charge of running the course. The sooner you know how to do it, the better it'll go.

8. **Set a time.** The single most important thing you can do if you're taking an online course is to commit yourself to a regular time when you positively, absolutely, without fail will listen to each of the lectures—and then stick to it. Especially if you're taking the online course because it better fits with your work and parenting responsibilities than the in-person version, you need to find a time that you can free yourself from these competing demands. Tell the boss to call later, send the kids to a friend's, make your spouse or partner cook the dinner.

9. **Keep up with the pace.** The biggest pitfall with online courses is falling behind. It's the easiest thing in the world to put off that reading or plan to write the paper *next* weekend, when there's no prof and no fellow students to impel you on. And if you're used to cramming from high school, from college courses you've already taken, or from the way you do your work at your job—well, the online learning structure (or lack thereof) will magnify your problems tenfold.

5-STAR TIP. Watch or listen to each lecture as soon as it is put up. That way, you'll have plenty of time to do the associated homework and the reading for the next lecture.

5-STAR TIP. Many online courses include not only quizzes and problem sets but also answers to the quizzes and solutions to the problem sets. Be sure to include these in your class preparation.

10. **Take advantage of the virtual face-to-faces.** Even though there's less immediacy when your online professor isn't breathing on you as he or she lectures, there are many opportunities for personal interaction with the teacher. Be sure you attend all discussion sections, group chats, and question-and-answer sessions. And when you need help—for instance,

in preparing your discussion postings—ask. If the online class is smaller than the 300-person version, you might get even more face time with the professor than you would have gotten in the traditional course. Electronic need not be impersonal.

EXTRA POINTER. In some online courses there are weekly threaded discussions: the instructor (or some student) puts up some question for consideration and the students are expected to respond to the question and to each other's answers (sometimes even for a grade). If your course includes these, be a good citizen and take your turn. Not only do you help create the course community, but you also could conceivably improve your own critical and communication skills. And if you're one of those students who likes to think things out before committing yourself—or if you just like to hide behind the electronic wall—you might find this discussion format even more enjoyable than the traditional in-person discussion section with the TA.

FLASH! One of the newest forms of online education is the massive open online course (or MOOC, for short). Hosted by companies such as Coursera, edX, and Udacity, these are mass-market courses, licensed from big-name universities, that give millions of students worldwide the chance to take—though in most cases not for credit—the same courses as traditional students are taking. Hundreds of thousands of students have signed up for "techie" courses such as Gamification, Artificial Intelligence, Machine Learning, and Building a Web Browser. But lately the offering has broadened out to the humanities and social sciences, so you can now find out about Greek and Roman Mythology, Aboriginal Worldviews and Education, and even A Beginner's Guide to Irrational Behavior. Check it out if your school is short of good courses, if you are eager to learn from a big name professor at a big U, or if you're just interested in broadening your horizons.

ON THE WEB. For more on the advantages—and potential shortcomings—of MOOCs, check out:

WWW.NYTIMES.COM/2012/11/04/EDUCATION/EDLIFE/MASSIVE-OPEN
-ONLINE-COURSES-ARE-MULTIPLYING-AT-A-RAPID-PACE.HTML?PAGEWANTED=4
&HPW&PAGEWANTED=PRINT

HTTP://NATION.TIME.COM/2012/09/04/MOOC-BRIGADE-WILL-MASSIVE
-OPEN-ONLINE-COURSES-REVOLUTIONIZE-HIGHER-EDUCATION/

FLASH! See what the *New York Times* editorial page has to say:

WWW.NYTIMES.COM/2013/02/19/OPINION/THE-TROUBLE-WITH-ONLINE
-COLLEGE.HTML?HP&_R=0

How to Take Courses on the Web— for Free

Once you've polished off your required coursework (or even before), you might want to take a course because you're actually interested in the subject. Trouble is, not every course is offered at every university—especially if yours is a small college and you have a very specialized interest. Luckily, you live in a very special time. Thanks to the generosity of the William and Flora Hewlett Foundation and the Andrew W. Mellon Foundation—and the work of the OpenCourseWare (OCW) initiative of universities worldwide—you can take any of eight thousand courses at the very best universities online—all without paying a dime, and at the time and place of your choice. Sound too good to be true? Here's how it works:

✔ **Find the sites.** Begin by searching either the master list of all courses provided by the OpenCourseWare Consortium WWW.OCWCONSORTIUM.ORG—or else surf on over to one of the sites of the major participating universities:

MIT: WWW.OCW.MIT.EDU

Yale: WWW.OYC.YALE.EDU

Notre Dame: HTTP://OCW.ND.EDU

Carnegie Mellon: WWW.OLI.CMU.EDU

UC Berkeley: HTTP://WEBCAST.BERKELEY.EDU

UC Irvine: HTTP://OCW.UCI.EDU

Tufts: HTTP://OCW.TUFTS.EDU

Stanford: HTTP://ITUNES.STANFORD.EDU

Utah State University: HTTP://OCW.USU.EDU

BEST-KEPT SECRET. A very useful resource (different from those just mentioned) is WWW.OCWFINDER.COM. Here you can search for courses using a wide variety of filters.

FLASH! A new website that describes itself as "a perpetually improving educational ecosystem" gathers some of the best courses from ten leading universities: WWW.ACADEMICEARTH.ORG. Check it out.

✔ **Play to their strengths.** Every college has some fields it's strong in and other fields in which it is less distinguished. You won't be surprised to hear that biology, chemistry, physics, statistics, and math are strong at MIT and Carnegie Mellon; philosophy, religion, and history, at Yale, Notre Dame, and Berkeley; and biological and irrigation engineering, at Utah State. If you have the skills and knowledge needed, try to take the courses you want at the best schools that offer them.

✔ **Take something that interests you.** You'll be more motivated to listen to all the lectures if you pick a subject for which you have a true passion. Some of the ones we like include:

Donald Kagan's *Introduction to Ancient Greek History* (Yale, Classics)

Shelly Kagan's *Death* (Yale, Philosophy)

Amy Hungerford's *American Novel Since 1945* (Yale, English)

Asma Afsaruddin's *Women in Islamic Societies* (Notre Dame, Middle Eastern Studies)

Norman Crowe's *Nature and the Built Environment* (Notre Dame, Architecture)

Gary Merkley's *Sprinkle and Trickle Irrigation* (Utah State, Biological and Irrigation Engineering)

✔ **Pick your modality.** Some of the courses offer full video downloads, others just audio, and still others just print materials. Though we're partial to the video lectures—the closest thing to being there in person—students listening to the class on the freeway or the treadmill will prefer the audio classes. Safer, too.

✔ **Pick your language.** Some of the courses (especially at the MIT site) offer translations into foreign languages, including Spanish, Portuguese, Chinese (traditional and simplified), Persian, and Thai. So if English is not your native language, you may enjoy the top-notch courses in your native tongue. The OCW Consortium website also offers courses at universities in countries ranging from Afghanistan to Vietnam—with special concentrations in France, Iran, Japan, Korea, and Spain.

EXTRA POINTER. Some sites even offer closed captioning— good if you're hearing impaired or if you find it easier to learn with subtitles.

✔ **Get on top of the layout.** Course web pages are usually arranged in the standard order of the college semester. Typically, on the left side of the page you'll find the course description, instructor bio, syllabus, topics and readings for individual lectures, tests and paper assignments, and downloads. On the right side of the page, look for related resources that often provide a wealth of material for additional study on topics of interest.

✔ **Get a hold of the readings.** It's always worthwhile to get your hands on the assigned readings and exercises; they'll make for a richer course experience and better learning.

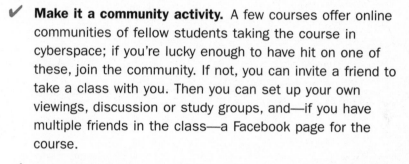

EXTRA POINTER. If your university library doesn't have the assigned readings, check with the interlibrary loan (ILL) department for help getting them.

✔ **Make it a community activity.** A few courses offer online communities of fellow students taking the course in cyberspace; if you're lucky enough to have hit on one of these, join the community. If not, you can invite a friend to take a class with you. Then you can set up your own viewings, discussion or study groups, and—if you have multiple friends in the class—a Facebook page for the course.

✔ **Negotiate credit.** If you're planning to do all the work, see whether you can get credit for the course as a directed or individual studies course. At some universities—especially if your university doesn't offer the course you're taking, or offers only a lower-level version—you'll be able to sign up with a professor at your own school and get course credit.

5-STAR TIP. In making your pitch for credit, be sure to mention that you intend to hand in the papers to your local professor and take the tests under test conditions. And, if your school will accept a petition only if approved by a professor, make sure you have him or her on board before submitting your request.

5 IT'S SHOWTIME!

There are times at college when you have to perform. Not just in some little sideshow, but in a major front-and-center performance. We're talking about tests and papers—the two or three or four moments over the course of the semester that really count. These are the times when large chunks of points, or large percentages of the grade, are up for grabs. It's a very rare student indeed who can waltz into the test or approach the due date on the paper without his or her adrenal glands pumping out some serious cortisol.

Now, we can't promise to eliminate every pre-performance jitter or butterfly, but we can offer you behind-the-scenes tips and techniques that'll give you more power and confidence come the dreaded test and paper times. This advice can help you keep the lid on your limbic system (for you nonbiology majors, that's the so-called emotional brain) as you face down these big moments of college.

In this chapter you'll learn:

► 12 Tips for A+ Test Preparation

► "So What's Going to Be on the Test Anyway?"

► Top 13 Test-Taking Tips

► 10 Tips for Writing the Perfect Paper

► 10 Things Your Professor Won't Tell You about Grading

► How to Turn a B into an A

► 14 Techniques for Doing Research Like a Professor

► Top 10 Tips for Doing E-Research

12 Tips for A+ Test Preparation

It happens every semester. You have to face that much-anticipated test, on which part of this semester's grade now rests. Sorry, we can't turn the test or midterm into a walk in the park. Only your professors can—and we wouldn't be counting on that. But how well you prepare will in no small measure determine how well you do. So here are our dozen best test-prep tips (together with a brief glance into the professor's mind to show why they work):

1. **Spend a week.** Start studying for each exam at least a week before you are due to take it. This will give you time to divide the material into manageable portions that you can digest over a number of study sessions. This is especially important in the case of a test with tons of material. Whatever you do, don't try to swallow the whole elephant—the whole course, that is—in one cram session. (Spending a week works because in most courses the prof is expecting you to have processed and digested the material—something you can't do in one fell swoop.)

2. **Scope out the scope.** Be sure you know what's fair game on the test and what's not. Many times students aren't exactly sure which lectures, readings, sections, and homework are to be covered on the test. (*Does the test include the material that was on the last test? Is the most recent lecture included? Are we responsible for that article discussed in section?*) You can't study right if you don't know what you're supposed to be studying. (Scoping out works because the prof's assuming you've paid attention when he or she said what's going to be covered on the test.)

3. **Do, don't redo.** Preparing for the test is *not* the time to reread all the reading, recopy all your notes, or listen to all the lectures again. Time constraints (like the need to keep up with your other work) just don't allow for this. Instead, concentrate

on working with the materials you have: the reading and lecture notes and what you can remember from having heard the lectures once. (This works because you probably remember, or can recover, more than you think. And even if you can't, you simply don't have time to do it from scratch.)

EXTRA POINTER. If you haven't done some key parts of the reading, you need to assess the relative importance of the reading versus the lecture notes. Time is of the essence now, and atoning for missed readings by reading them now may not be the best strategy.

4. **Discover the plot.** Now that you're up to the test, you are in a position to know how the parts of the course up to that point fit together. Check out your class notes, and have a look back at the syllabus and at any handouts, to figure out the highest points of the course. Then use this understanding to guide your studying for the exam. (This works because in most courses the main plot of the course is what the professor wants you to have learned—and therefore what he or she will ask you about on the exam.)

5. **Figure out the format.** There are many kinds of questions your professor could be asking—multiple choice, short answer, essay, problem solving. Make sure you know which is his or her favorite type of question. (This works because you study better when you know what kind of test you're studying for.)

EXTRA POINTER. In addition to knowing what kinds of questions are likely to be on the test, it would be good to know what percentage of the exam is devoted to each type of question. You wouldn't want to spend 80 percent of your time memorizing for the short answers, only to discover that 80 percent of the test is essays. (See "So What's Going to Be on the Test Anyway?" on p. 171 for some tips on how to do this.)

6. Mark up your class notes. The time for obsessively neat notes is now officially over. Go ahead and mark up your notes—both class notes and, if you have them, reading notes. Highlight the main points or draw arrows or stars at central issues. Make notes in the margins about how the main points interrelate. (This works because forcing yourself to actively process your notes helps you locate the key concepts and the connections among them—just what the prof may be asking about on the test.)

 5-STAR TIP. If you don't have a full set of notes for the class, it'd behoove you to ask someone in your class (preferably someone smarter than you) to lend you his or her notes. And if you've taken your notes on scraps of paper or scattered pages, it wouldn't be a half-bad idea to arrange the pages in lecture order. You'd be amazed how many students can't find the plot of the course or locate relations between points simply because their notes are out of order.

7. Load up your mind. Some classes require that you memorize a certain body of material. Perhaps it's verb conjugations in a German class, theorems in a logic class, or the dates of particular events in U.S. history. Take the time to do this drudgework. (This works because sometimes you'll get many points simply for spitting it all back. And even if just storing the content in your mind isn't directly rewarded, the exam could ask you to perform higher-level tasks that require you to have memorized the items—for example, a translation exercise that requires recognizing the verb forms or a math proof that requires application of a theorem.)

EXTRA POINTER. Use acronyms: words formed from the initial letters of the things to be memorized. Make them as clever as you can (they're easier to remember that way), and then sing them out loud while making faces and flapping your arms (you'll remember the tunes and your bizarro motions).

8. **Capture the concepts.** In many courses, the real studying work is to get your mind around the key concepts and central ideas of the course. This isn't just memorizing some code words (as in the previous Extra Pointer), but really understanding the main points. (This works because in an essay exam what's being graded isn't so much your recall of key points but your ability to explain them clearly enough, and in enough detail, to communicate a real understanding of the idea.)

9. **Construct a pretest.** Before the test, take matters into your own hands and make up your own exam with questions in the same format that you'll see on the test. Then try out your test under "test conditions": writing it out, timing for each part, no breaks, and no peeking at the book or your notes. (This works because if you pretest, you'll know what to expect and have had some practice doing it. And you'll see where you've made mistakes, which, hopefully, can be corrected before the real test.)

5-STAR TIP. Be sure to monitor—and evaluate—your test-taking performance as you go. If you find that you're devoting too much time to one question, or spending too much time thinking rather than writing, or getting so tensed up that you can hardly think straight, make a mental note. Then when you've finished your trial run, think up strategies you can employ so you can avoid the same pitfalls when you take the real test.

10. **Go to office hours.** It's always worthwhile asking the prof (or TA) if he or she will go over the test you've constructed. Ask whether your answers were good ones and whether your questions were the kinds of questions that could come up on the test. (This works because you'll be getting one-to-one, directed feedback on your work, and with any luck the prof or

TA might drop some hints about what's going to be on the actual test.)

11. **Make the review session.** If your professor or TA is holding a review session the night before the test (which sometimes happens in large courses, often before the midterm and/or final)—well, that's a gift from God (or the Fates, depending on what you believe). Most likely the prof or TA will go over the course material to date and emphasize the important points. (This works because this is the time when professors are especially eager to help the students, so they give particularly useful information. And because often they've just made up the exam or are planning to write it that night, they can't help dropping some serious hints about what's going to be on the test.)

12. **Observe the eight-hour rule.** Stop studying for your exam at least eight hours before it begins. The idea here is to keep yourself from walking into your exam like a zombie from lack of sleep (or all wired up from too much Red Bull, Adderall, or who knows what). The eight-hour rule also allows time for the ideas and concepts you've studied to settle into your brain. Trust us. It's been scientifically proven that people who study right up to the last minute perform worse than those who have had a period of relaxation prior to the test. (This works because of a simple equation: lucid, clear thinking = lucid, clear writing = clearly top-notch grades.)

BONUS TIP. The morning of the exam, have an Egg McMuffin or at least a cholesterol-free egg and reduced-fat white cheddar breakfast sandwich. Your brain will work better with carbs and protein (even in reduced dosages). And while you're at it, don't forget to take out a double espresso for the test. Hey, you've studied like a fiend. Why not load up like a fiend?

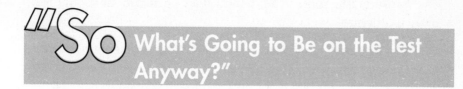

"So What's Going to Be on the Test Anyway?"

For some college students, nothing will match that moment of terror when they look down at their test and find questions they've never thought of staring back at them. But at that very same moment there's usually some student somewhere else in the room feeling smug satisfaction at having sussed out the exact questions in advance. (Lynn even admits to once wasting valuable exam time shooting "I told you so" looks at her BFF and study partner.) How can you figure out in advance what's going to be on the test—and dramatically increase your chances of acing that exam? Here are some clues from behind the curtain:

Clue #1: **Professors test what they talk.** Students often think professors are out to trick them by testing picky, obscure issues. Nothing can be further from the truth. Professors usually try to teach the most important material—and then test it to see whether students have mastered it. Kind of makes sense once you think about it, doesn't it? So look over your notes and see what the prof spent the most time on. That's likely to provide the most fodder for the test.

Clue #2: **Professors ask what interests them.** In many courses, you can detect some issue that really excites the prof so much that he or she brings it up again and again, even as the course moves from topic to topic. It's a good bet that your prof's obsession will pop up on the test in some form or other.

Clue #3: **Professors drop hints.** Much as we try to keep silent, most professors can't help themselves. They have high-value information that throngs of adulating students are eager to get—and that they are eager to give. So take seriously comments in lecture like, "Wow, this would make a really good test question" or "and speaking of . . . [nudge, nudge, wink, wink]." This may all sound like a joke, but it's not.

Clue #4: TAs spill the beans even more than professors. TAs are usually younger and less experienced. And would like to be liked. So they'll usually cave quickly if you ask them a few questions after class or in office hours—or just show up to section meeting. No bribery necessary!

 EXTRA POINTER. Be sure to write down in your notes—ideally, word for word—any hints your prof or TA drops in lecture, discussion, an office hour, or a review session. Come study time, these hints, including their exact phraseology, can prove gold mines of information for what will be on the test.

Clue #5: Professors are lazy. Professors are pretty busy and don't have much time to write entirely new exams. As a result, many times profs will simply reuse—or modify slightly—questions they asked last time around. If you can dig up one of the old exams from a friend who took the same course, from library reserves, from fraternity or sorority files, or (if your stars are aligned) from the prof him- or herself, you can get a pretty good idea of what to expect.

5-STAR TIP. Be sure not to use Dr. O's exam to study for Professor P's upcoming test—even if both teach the same course. Most likely Professor P thinks Dr. O is a loser and would never be caught dead asking such idiotic questions.

Clue #6: Professors tell it up front. The syllabus often lists the educational goals of the course, which can give you pretty good information about the test questions. After the first day of class, you might never think to cast another glance at the syllabus, but it can actually give clues about what the professor thinks is most important—and what he or she's likely to want to test you on. The same applies to the titles for individual lectures or the questions for study (if any) for each meeting.

Clue #7: Professors recycle. Not only questions from previous years, but questions or problems from the homework, quizzes, and problem sets often reappear in slightly different form on the test. Hey, everybody's going green these days.

 5-STAR TIP. If the professor hands out a study guide or "sample" questions—well, that's a no-brainer. Those kinds of questions—or sometimes those very questions or very close variants of them—are bound to appear on the test.

Top 13 Test-Taking Tips

Many college students shudder at the thought of the first test—or any test. *You* shouldn't. Especially if you follow our baker's dozen of best tips for acing the exam:

1. **Bring a beverage.** A nice drink enables you to relax and concentrate on the task at hand. You might even be able to trick yourself into thinking that the next fifty minutes will be a productive and satisfying work hour. At least you won't be thirsty.

2. **Survey the landscape.** When you first get the test, look over the whole thing. Figure out what the tasks are, paying special attention to how many questions you're supposed to answer (be sure to note any choices offered). You'd be amazed at how many students make mistakes about the basic instructions.

3. **Budget your time.** Make a plan for how much time you're going to spend on each question (some professors tell you, in which case you should make sure to follow their instructions). Be sure to devote the most time to the parts of the exam that net the most points—not the ones you like best or know most about. Spending tons of time on questions that don't count much is neither cost- nor grade-effective.

4. **Don't waste time.** Some students begin their exam by writing elaborate outlines or reproducing long lists they've memorized. Don't. If you need to jot down a few notes or a couple of acronyms, that's fine, but you need to spend most of your time writing out the answer, not preparing to write it.

EXTRA POINTER. Another major time waster in cases where a professor offers a choice of topics is to get far into an essay, only to stop and choose another question. It's not uncommon for a professor to find a page—or even several pages—crossed off, followed by an essay on another topic that the student didn't have time to finish. Ouch.

REALITY CHECK. It's never a good idea to answer all the choices on the theory that the prof will read them all, then give you the grade for the best one. The prof, who has only a few minutes to read your exam, will just read the first choice. No prof is going to do triple the work for your indecisiveness—or your attempt to game the system.

5. **Consider the alternatives.** On a multiple-choice test, make sure you've read all the choices before deciding on one answer. Sometimes the correct answer lies in making a small differentiation among a number of very similar answers. And of course, unless they're taking off points for wrong answers (which professors almost never do), always fill in *something* (even if it's all c's.)

EXTRA POINTER. Forget all the high school tricks, like favoring d's and e's (because "the teacher wants you to read all the choices"); never picking answers with the words *all* or *none* ("things are never as categorical as that"); or always varying your choices ("no teacher would pick three c's in a row"). These strategies are unlikely to work at college. Professors haven't been to high school in a long time. And no one has bothered to remind them of these practices.

6. **Size can matter.** When confronting a short-answer question, consider the possibility of writing two or three or four sentences, rather than just a few code words. What seems "short" to you may seem microscopic to the professor and not enough to show your understanding of the issue. Also, in a problem-focused test, be sure to show all your work. Even if you don't get the correct answer, the grader might see that you were on the right track and give you partial credit.

7. **Answer exactly the question asked.** Believe it or not, more points are lost on essay tests by not answering precisely the question asked than by giving wrong answers. Professors devote lots of time to constructing their questions, so you can assume they really mean what they ask.

 5-STAR TIP. Don't be thrown if a question seems to you too narrow or covers only one lecture or reading. Some professors like to test by *sampling*—that is, by asking you about a representative part of the issue, then assuming that you could do just about as well on all the rest. (Other professors like to test by *coverage*—that is, by asking about a very broad swatch of material to see how much you've taken in. In this case, you can expect questions about many of the topics discussed in class.)

---

8. **Explain, don't gesture.** Some students think the answer is so obvious—and the professor knows it, after all—that they only need to wave their hands at the answer (rather than wasting all that ink to spell it out). But the prof is looking for you to demonstrate your knowledge and understanding of the material, which can be done only if you take the time to make explicit your points.

9. **Be specific.** Be sure to bring in examples and illustrations to bolster the points you make. Ideas are much more clear when they're illustrated, not just presented. And be sure to consider

all elements of the course—not just the lectures, but also the assigned readings, the discussion sections (if any), and any out-of-class activities—for possible sources of examples. Some ingenuity here can really strengthen your answer—and impress the professor in the process.

10. **Keep it real.** Write in simple, clear language. You're not going to impress the professor when you use all sorts of words whose meanings you don't really know, or lard your paper with all sorts of jargon that you feel you somehow must get in. And avoid BS or other sorts of fillers, and any irrelevant material. When an instructor is reading seventy essays on the same topic, extra junk that is unrelated to the topic really stands out like a sore thumb. Some graders just ignore it, but others will take off points.

11. **Give 'em a break.** Take pity on your grader, who is facing a huge stack of exams and would prefer scrubbing toilet bowls to wading through the pile. Begin to give your answer in the very first sentence (except if you're specifically instructed otherwise) so your grader doesn't have to excavate to unearth it. Number the question you're answering and label any parts. Divide your essay into paragraphs. Circle your answer to a math or science problem. Don't have arrows pointing to who-knows-what page. And it wouldn't hurt if someone could actually read your writing. A happier grader makes for a happier grade.

12. **Keep your cool.** Some questions are meant to be hard. That's how the prof separates the sheep (the truly outstanding pieces of work) from the goats (the not-all-that-hot tests). Don't panic if something seems to need more mental effort and struggle. It probably does. If you're truly stuck, make a mental (or written) note of what piece you're missing, then go on to the next question. Your mind keeps working while your pen keeps moving, and often you'll have time later to go back and use these "reminders" to fill in the blanks.

13. **Always stay till the bitter end.** If you finish early, go over previous answers. Correcting even one calculational error or

adding even one idea or example can easily add a few points to your score. And you never know when you could use those extra points (like when you get a 79 or an 89 and your school doesn't have pluses and minuses). Don't be psyched out by those people who leave after twenty minutes. Some of them have done so badly they're just throwing in the towel.

BONUS TIP. When you get your test back, be sure to go over your instructor's comments one by one. This is one of the few times in the course you'll get customized feedback on your work. Don't waste this valuable resource by thinking it's too painful to look at the criticism. Who knows? There might even be words of encouragement. (Could happen. You never know.)

10 Tips for Writing the Perfect Paper

Like an architectural masterpiece or a well-crafted symphony, the perfect college paper is carefully constructed—rather than barfed out onto the page at 3 a.m. the night before it is due. Each part is meticulously selected and polished up, then assembled with the others into a coherent and convincing whole. We should know. Between us, we've read tens of thousands of college papers—some perfect, others not so perfect—from which we've gleaned our ten best tips:

1. **Decide what kind of paper you're writing.** There's no one-size-fits-all in college. Some professors assign *research* papers, in which case you'll need to head to the library or resources on the Internet (see "14 Techniques for Doing Research Like a Professor" on p. 190 and "Top 10 Tips for Doing E-Research" on p. 196). Other professors assign *analytical* papers (in which you're asked to analyze or evaluate some object, phenomenon, or text, without seeing what other scholars have thought about it); in this case, you'll have to turn to your head for the answer. Still other professors assign a hybrid of the two, in which case you'll have to divide your labors. Know what type of assignment you're being asked to do before you start working on the paper.

2. **Answer exactly the question(s) asked.** Professors spend unbelievable amounts of time formulating the questions for the paper. Take the time to puzzle out precisely what's being asked. If there is more than one question or part asked, figure out how each question is different from the rest and what materials would be relevant to answering it.

5-STAR TIP. Pay special attention to any verbs used in the paper assignment. *Compare, contrast, discuss, evaluate, explain, consider, formulate a hypothesis, raise an objection, argue for, trace, illustrate, defend,* and *summarize* are all different tasks. Know which one(s) your professor is asking you to do—and what it would take to do it (or them). If you're not 100 percent, positively, absolutely, no doubt about it, sure, ask.

3. **Be sure to fill the space.** When a professor assigns a four- to six-page paper, he or she is usually expecting that the good papers will be more like six pages (whereas the students who don't know what to say will probably manage to fill only three or four pages). Worry more about writing too little than writing too much. (Of course, you should never exceed the page limit. That'll never make the professor happy.)

EXTRA POINTER. If you're not sure whether the professor means single- or double-spaced pages, it'd be a good idea to ask. And skip the 2-inch margins and 16-point type. When professors see those padding techniques, they start the grade clock at a C.

4. **Make sure your paper has a point.** Every paper should have a thesis—that is, a single point that is expressed in a single sentence. Without a thesis, a paper is just a report. And most college professors don't like reports. We think that the thesis sentence should be the very first one in the paper, but some professors like you to write a brief introduction or "setup" paragraph (if you get one of these profs, follow their instructions). In any case, everyone would agree that the thesis sentence should come at least by the beginning of the second paragraph.

BEST-KEPT SECRET. It's not enough to just state a thesis; you have to structure the whole paper around your thesis. Make sure each point you make in your paper supports the thesis you have advanced at the beginning of your paper. If you can't remember your thesis, refer back to it frequently as you write.

REALITY CHECK. If you think a paper question is just a "prompt"—like in high school or on the SAT or ACT—think again. College papers are almost always targeted questions, not occasions for you to spout your own opinions about whatever occurs to you when reading the question.

5. **Give your paper direction.** A good paper moves through a series of steps that are arranged in some logical order. Make sure you have a reason for arranging your points in the order that you do—and that it is clear to the reader what that reason is. And make sure that each step does some work in advancing your argument. For each paragraph—then for each sentence within the paragraph—ask yourself: *Why is this here? How does it advance the overall argument?* And if your answer is "It doesn't," go back and take it out.

EXTRA POINTER. Use "logical indicator" words such as *moreover, therefore, since, consequently, nevertheless, thus, then, now,* and *first (second, third)* to mark turning points in your argument. Not only will such "hinges" help your reader understand where your argument pivots, but they will also help you think out how it's structured.

6. **Write for a reasonably intelligent person—not the professor.** Many students make the mistake of writing for the

professor—someone who already knows the answer and for whom, they think, a code word here or there will be more than enough. Write instead for a smart-enough person who has not already taken the course. Take the time to explain each of your points fully—so that someone could understand what you mean just from what you write.

EXTRA POINTER. Be sure to explain any technical or unusual terms in ordinary language. Don't assume that the reader is a specialist in that field and will know what "etiological considerations" are (they're causal factors, in case you're interested).

---

7. **Avoid vagueness.** Many college papers suffer from being too general. They make many true claims, but express them in such an unspecific way that one can't really form a firm conception of what is being claimed. Be as particular as possible. And use specific and detailed examples—often more than one—to prove your points. Just like on the test.

8. **Have a quote quota.** In an analytical paper, it's usually not necessary to offer up elaborate quotes or sometimes even to quote at all. After all, it's *your* analysis that's being asked for. Even in a research paper, you should not use so many quotes that the paper becomes a mere summary or cataloging of other people's work (see "14 Techniques for Doing Research Like a Professor" on p. 190 for more on this topic).

IOHO. Generally, it's better to incorporate brief quotes, or portions of quotes, into your own sentences than to set off long quotations in their own paragraphs. And be sure to always explain the quotes in your own words after you've reproduced them. The professor wants to know what you're seeing in the quote and what you take the quote to mean.

---

9. **Consolidate your argument.** As you read over the first drafts of your paper, consider taking out points that aren't central to the argument and developing more fully points that are. Often a more compact, more forcefully argued paper is a better paper; in any case, you should view your first draft as your first stab at properly capturing your idea, not the final, best-argued version.

10. **Deal the professor in.** There's nothing professors (and TAs) like more than helping good students construct excellent papers. Go to office hours with specific questions and problems, then follow up with e-mail as many times as is necessary or reasonable (for more on both of these topics, see "The 14 Secrets of Going to See the Professor" on p. 212 and "Etiquette for E-mailing Your Professor" on p. 217).

5-STAR TIP. **Review your product. Professors get really ticked off when papers contain spelling or grammar errors or have sentences with words left out or that don't make sense. Especially infuriating is when students misspell the name of a key author in the course (Jeremy just finished grading a set of papers in which the name of the eighteenth-century philosopher George Berkeley was spelled "Berkley" in more than a few papers; Lynn regularly gets papers in which Rembrandt is spelled "Rembrant."). Become the professor for a few minutes. Read your paper as if you had never seen it before, and make whatever changes are needed to make it more coherent and readable. You'll be amazed at how much difference a few minutes of polishing up will make in the overall impression your paper gives. And, in many cases, the overall grade.**

BONUS TIP. Know when to stop. At a certain point, endless revising serves no purpose (other than to make you upset). Sometimes it can even weaken your paper by disrupting the natural flow of the points that you first wrote. If you tend to be a perfectionist, learn when to put your pen down. Or to click "Save," then "Send."

10 Things Your Professor Won't Tell You About Grading

For most professors, mum's the word about grading. The less said, the less possibility of argument later when the student doesn't get the grade he or she wants. But do you ever wonder about what's going though the professor's mind as he or she doles out the grades? Here is a look behind the curtain at what the professor is really thinking —but won't tell you.

1. **"It's 15 minutes—then on to the next."** You might think that your grader will spend upward of an hour grading each of your assignments. Guess again. Given that an instructor may have 30, 40, or even 70 papers or tests to grade in a week, he or she is likely to try to get three or four students' papers done in an hour. This is why it's important for you to get right to the point, make your claims clearly and succinctly, avoid extraneous or irrelevant material, and take the trouble to really explain your points. (See "10 Tips for Writing the Perfect Paper," on p. 179, for more.)

2. **"I often outsource the grading."** In large courses at large colleges, the professor giving the lectures isn't always the person actually doing the grading. Instead, there's a cadre of low-paid grad students (or, at some universities, even undergraduates) who do the grading: could be your TA or some other person hired solely to grade the tests or papers. Some professors actively manage the graders, going over sample papers and setting the grading scales; others are happy to delegate the whole job to the underling and never set their eyes on any student work.

3. **"It's not nearly as subjective as you think."** Many students understand that on "objective" tests (like multiple-choice or

short-answer tests), there's no question about whether you got the answer right or wrong. But they think that the grading on essay tests or papers is "just a matter of opinion"—the grader's subjective feeling about how good the piece of work is. Not so. If you were given a stack of 50 essays on the same topic (and if you had a good grasp of the material) you could know right away which are the A's, B's, C's, and D's. Sure, there's some judgment around the edges: a grader sometimes has to think a minute, and look over the essay a second time, to decide whether it's a B, B+, or B/B+. But the major grade "breaks" are almost never matters of opinion; that's why there can be different TAs, all of whom will assess your paper the same way.

4. **"A's are often in short supply in my courses."** While some students think grade inflation is rampant in college, in truth most professors give about 10 to 25 percent A's in introductory classes and perhaps 25 to 40 percent A's in more advanced courses. And, contrary to what you may have heard, some courses have a "heavy bottom." If you're at the kind of university that most students in this country attend, there may well be a significant number of people getting C's and D's. And, believe it or not, in a large intro class of 300 students, there may be up to 10 percent F's.

REALITY CHECK. You may have thought it's pretty easy to get good grades at college given grade inflation. But to see what the real story is, check out Professor Stuart Rojstaczer's WWW.GRADEINFLATION.COM. An interesting and comprehensive site, very much recommended.

5. **"Grading is usually not a zero-sum game."** In classes that are graded on a curve, your grade is in fact determined by your position or ranking relative to other students. But except for the sciences, most college courses are not curved. So relax.

The reason you didn't get an A on the midterm isn't because you best friend stole the last available A. It's just that the level of your work didn't quite rise up to the level of excellent work.

6. **"First impressions count . . ."** Because your grader is working at breakneck speed to make a decision about what grade to give, nailing the main point in the very first paragraph sets your essay on the path to an A. Keeping the grader in suspense about when, if ever, you're going to answer the question, or, worse, larding your essay with all sorts of long-winded introductions or irrelevant filler, both pave the royal route to a C. (Check out "10 Tips for Writing the Perfect Paper" on p. 179 for more details.)

7. **". . . and last impressions, too."** Often by the time the grader gets to the end of your essay, especially if it's a long one, the grader may not remember each of the points you made or their significance. That's why it's a good idea to offer a brief summary at the end of your exam or paper, showcasing for the grader the points you most want him or her to take into account in determining your grade (not a bad idea to number them, if there are more than one or two).

8. **"Excuses cement C's."** Sometimes you haven't prepared the relevant material for the test, or you've run out of time before completing your answer, or you realize you didn't follow instructions quite right. And then you write a profuse apology giving all the reasons for your missteps. Bad idea. When the grader encounters all your excuses, it throws into high relief the deficiencies of your answers—which the grader might not even have noticed or have been tempted to overlook. Let your work stand on its own.

9. **"I'm on the lookout for cheating."** Though professors don't always announce it in lecture, they have many mechanisms in place to ensure that you don't string together passages from the Web, hand in substantially the same paper as your friend, or copy from a book or journal. Some use professional software like WWW.TURNITIN.COM, others search the Web for

unusual words or sentence constructions, others compare student papers one against another, while still others know the relevant literature like the back of their hand. Hey, when you read as many papers as we do, you get pretty good at sniffing out work that isn't the student's own.

10. **"Grade disputes almost never work."** Sometimes students who don't get the grade they think they deserved want to argue about the grade. Sure, most colleges have official procedures for disputing a grade—sometimes involving the TA, the professor, the department chair, or even the dean. But you should be aware that grades very, very rarely get changed—and only in case of procedural irregularity (such as incorrectly adding up the points, failing to read a page of the answer, or not following course policies on the syllabus or the rules of the college). Arguments we hear all the time but that almost never work include: "My friend wrote the same paper but got a better grade than I did," "Another TA grades easier than mine," "The assignment wasn't fair," or "The TA had it in for me." If you haven't gotten the grade you want, in most cases it's best to just suck it up and ask how you can do better next time. Which you can usually find out.

How to Turn a B into an A

One of the most common questions we get asked is "What can I do to turn my B paper into an A?" This is one of the hardest things for a professor to put into words, because every case is different, and in any case there's often no one thing you need to do to get over the threshold from good to excellent work. Nevertheless, here are 10 things you can do to increase your chances of bagging that much-sought-after A:

10. Offer a more subtle and nuanced thesis (rather than the most obvious one).

9. Probe the relations between the parts of, or the issues treated in, the question.

8. Give more examples or illustrations.

7. Draw distinctions, if they are relevant to the question(s) asked.

6. Bring in material from the assigned readings or from extra articles selected in conjunction with the professor.

5. Use the methods, techniques, and analytic tools of the field (like the ones the professor used in the class).

4. Reach a firm conclusion (rather than wimping out).

3. Pick a better topic next time—one that has more depth or about which you have more to say.

2. Get feedback from the professor (or TA) as you're writing the paper (not after the fact, once you've gotten your B).

And the number-one tip for moving from a B to an A:

1. Think harder. We know you can do better than this B paper.

14 Techniques for Doing Research Like a Professor

Once in a while you get hit with it. The dreaded 15- to 25-page research paper, aka the term paper or semester project. This is your chance to join the community of the 20 percent or so of college professors who are actually doing research. How do they do it? And how can you? Have a look at our 14 best tips for doing research—like a professor:

1. **Start from where you are.** The professor has his or her research program. You have your paper assignment. Carefully consider all the assigned paper topics, trying to pick one that seems interesting to you and about which you think you'll have something to say. If the professor is requiring you to propose a topic of your own, scour all the course materials (lecture notes, readings, syllabus, handouts, discussion sections, course bibliography) for possible topics. Then meet with the prof to see whether your proposed topic is one you could actually do, given what you know and what there is to know. A bad topic will not only net weeks of frustration, but will also lead to a bad paper in the end.

 IOHO. In many cases, good research can be seen as answering a question, rather than just surveying an area. If you're having trouble getting started on your paper, try phrasing your topic in the form of a question.

2. **Look for "gateway" sources.** Many students are inclined to start their research with Google or Wikipedia. Nothing wrong with that if you're prepared to accept the good, the bad, and the ugly: some links point to good material, and some articles

are written by real experts, but others could be written by a 14-year-old in his basement in Brooklyn. You might do better by starting with broadly conceived scholarly sources that survey the problem, area, or subject that you're researching and also point the way to further, more specific studies. They might have names like *Cambridge Companion to X, Stanford Encyclopedia of Y, Grove Dictionary of Z, Oxford Illustrated History of A*, and so on. (Ask your prof or TA for names in your field.) And whenever reading any source, look to the footnotes and bibliography for direction to further sources you might read.

5-STAR TIP. In picking sources, it's always best to start with any books or articles the professor has listed on the assignment or put on reserve (either print- or e-). You'd be amazed at how many students don't think of this.

3. **Drive your sources (don't let them drive you).** Always keep your investigation focused on the issue or problem you're studying. Just because some other guy makes some point—no matter how good it is—doesn't mean you have to include it in your paper, especially if the issue isn't really within the scope of your project. Keep in mind that *you're* the researcher here, so take control of the source material.

EXTRA POINTER. Keep it current. Although every investigation is different, you should be attentive to the dates of whatever sources you are using. At least arguably, science and learning move forward, so in many cases you'll do better with an article dated December 2012 than with one from the late 1890s. Besides, one of the things the professor might be looking for is your acquaintance with up-to-date journal research. (Of course, if you're studying primary sources—a fifteenth-century manuscript, nineteenth-century settlement records, or, if you're really lucky, a fourth-century B.C. Greek vase—older is better.)

4. **Use e-resources.** At most universities much of library research is done electronically, through journals or databases of journals that your library has paid big bucks to subscribe to. Start with the library web page: there you'll find "top ten lists" (love those) of the most frequently used e-reference tools; aggregated lists of journals by subject, where you can search for scholarly articles across many journals; links to the interlibrary loan (ILL) department, where you can order electronic materials from other libraries; and, usually, a link to WorldCat, the master list of all content products worldwide (and which libraries own them). (For an excellent discussion of all sorts of electronic resources, see Harvard librarian Cheryl LaGuardia's piece, "Top 10 Tips for Doing E-Research" on p. 196.)

5. **Embrace the Zen of research.** All research—especially good research—is a process that involves considerable uncertainty, doubt, recasting, and often a lack of quick or black-and-white answers. That's how, in most cases, discoveries are made. Get used to it. All of these are signs that the research is going well.

6. **Don't fixate too quickly.** Often in doing research—especially creative or original research—you'll find that your ideas change as you read new sources or think out an issue for yourself. This too is a good sign, and the process can be artificially aborted if you decide too soon on your final answer. Let ideas evolve naturally, and don't close the door on refining your ideas too quickly.

7. **Torture the data.** One of the main differences between superficial and really good research is that really good research picks something narrow to investigate, studies the topic in depth, and draws more nuanced or more meaningful conclusions about it. Of course, you should always consult with your professor or TA about how to conduct your research, but don't think of first-rate research simply as the mindless collecting and surveying of loads of data.

8. **Test your ideas.** It is important that you consider vulnerabilities in or possible objections to your hypothesis. (This is something your professor goes through every time he or she submits a paper for publication.) Try out your idea on a friend (if you have a friend who is reasonably smart and reasonably knowledgeable about the field) or go see the professor or TA and see what he or she has to say. It's especially good if you can meet at an early stage in your work, so that you can forestall going off in the wrong direction or even tweak your idea somewhat in response to some comment. (See our "10 Biggest Hesitations About Going to See the Professor—and How to Get Over Them" and "The 14 Secrets of Going to See the Professor" on pp. 208 and 212, respectively, for lots of tips on just how to do this.)

9. **Record and conquer.** Be sure to take complete and easily readable notes as you do your research. You'll never be able to keep straight what each of the authors has said if you don't have detailed records of what you've read. And be sure to keep *complete* bibliographical citations (name of article, journal, author page number, URL, and so on). You'll need that information later, when you write your footnotes and compose your bibliography, and it's an incredible pain—and major time-waster—to have to go back and find the sources again.

---

5 **5-STAR TIP.** Writing research papers will be 100-percent easier (or at least your paper will be 100-percent better organized) with reference-management software. If your college library doesn't provide it free, try EndNote, RefWorks, Zotero, or WizFolio.

---

10. **Take a stand.** Your research should always culminate in some definite result or conclusion about what you've investigated. No real researcher—or, at least, no *good* real researcher—would

conclude his or her study by saying "In the end, we can't be sure about . . ." or "Though I haven't shown this in this paper, my personal opinion is . . .". (These are real conclusions we've seen. Hey, you can't make this stuff up.)

11. **Fear not the footnote.** Some profs have a pole up their you-know-what about footnote styles. Why give them grief? Learn which of the many competing styles (APA, MLA, CBE, APSA, AIP, and others) your professor thinks is most important for the field.

ON THE WEB. Techies and nerds will enjoy HTTP:// RESEARCHGUIDES.LIBRARY.WISC.EDU/CITING, HTTP://LIBRARY.DUKE.EDU/ RESEARCH/CITING/, and OWL.ENGLISH.PURDUE.EDU. All the styles you'll ever want. And then some.

RULE OF THUMB. Words or ideas not your own = must footnote. Most universities have significant penalties for "borrowing" work that's not your own—that is, plagiarizing— and you wouldn't want to find out what they are.

12. **Don't pad your bibliography.** Unless instructed otherwise, don't include in your bibliography sources you didn't use. Most likely, your professor knows the literature and is interested only in how you used the materials.

13. **Leave time for writing.** It's one thing to do A-plus research; it's quite another to write a good research paper. Be sure to leave enough to time to write—and revise and edit—your paper.

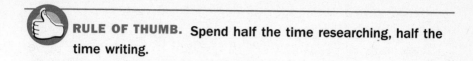

RULE OF THUMB. Spend half the time researching, half the time writing.

14. **Make the deadline.** No professor wants to get the work late, especially if it's accompanied by some cockamamie excuse for why it was late. As you move on in the academic world, you'll find that journals have drop-dead deadlines, so why not get in the habit of submitting your research on time, now?

Top 10 Tips for Doing E-Research

The situation: you've just been given your first 15-page college research paper assignment. Your professor wants you to use books and scholarly journals in writing your paper and not rely solely on Google and Wikipedia to do the research. What do you do? You could call your parents or ask advice from a friend. But a far better idea would be to follow these top 10 tips, offered by Cheryl LaGuardia, research librarian at Harvard University's Widener Library:

1. **Start with Google and Wikipedia.** Sure, your professor doesn't want you to rely *solely* on these e-sources for your research. But they're both good for giving you an overview of your topic. Once you get a general view and some descriptive words from Google and Wikipedia defining your topic, you can move on to the meaty stuff.

2. **Proceed to your library's website.** Once you've Googled and Wiki-ed to your satisfaction, you'll be ready to use more serious, scholarly sources that will provide you with dependable information. Go to your college library's website and consult the online catalog. The main library home page ought to give you detailed instructions about how to search.

ON THE WEB. Here's an example of a library catalog that requires you to search a certain way for keywords, authors, titles, and subjects: HTTP://HOLLISCLASSIC.HARVARD.EDU/. Some library catalogs have you search the way you do in Google; one example is HTTP://HOLLIS.HARVARD.EDU/.

3. **Use your library's online databases.** Although the online catalog helps you find books, it doesn't usually let you find

individual articles within scholarly journals. For that you have to
go into online library databases (to see how scholarly journals
differ from non-scholarly materials, and for more information on
sources generally, take a look at HTTP://USINGSOURCES.FAS.HARVARD
.EDU/). Usually there's a way to locate databases by subject.
Databases you'll find on your library's website may include
*Academic Search Premier, InfoTrac, JSTOR, ProQuest Central,
Readers' Guide*, and *Science Citation Index*. Be sure to read the
instructions on the opening screens of databases to learn how
to search them; it's worth taking the few minutes, because this
is where you're going to find the current information your
professor wants you to use. A bonus in using these databases
is that you may get the full text of articles on your
computer—a real time saver.

4. **Try Google Scholar.** Another good resource for finding scholarly
   articles is Google Scholar, which combines ease of use and
   rich content. If you go into Google Scholar from the public link
   HTTP://SCHOLAR.GOOGLE.COM, you can search the system and get
   full-text access if you'd like to pay. However, your college library
   may have a link into Google Scholar in its list of library
   databases, in which case—big money tip—the full text of the
   articles will be f-r-e-e.

5. **Use online research guides.** At many colleges and universities,
   librarians create online library research guides for use by
   students and others.

---

www **ON THE WEB.** **To give you an idea of the kinds of research
guides you may find at your college, here's a link to the online
research section of my library's website:** HTTP://HCL.HARVARD
.EDU/RESEARCH/GUIDES/.

---

6. **Evaluate websites.** In the course of doing research, you may
   need to use some websites on the open Web. You should

evaluate these sites for authority, bias, currency, documentation, and delivery.

7. **Use real print books.** You may find many research materials online, as new books and journals are increasingly appearing in electronic format. But you may also find a wealth of research material in books and journals that are not yet online—and the "secret bonus" is that many of your peers will not go after that material, so you'll do the better, more complete research—and probably get the better grade.

8. **Use ILL.** One resource that beginning students aren't always aware of is the interlibrary loan (ILL) department. Here students can borrow books from other university libraries—usually at no charge and quite quickly. To find out which library has the books you need, check out *WorldCat* (used to be called *FirstSearch*) at your library or in its public version: WWW.WORLDCAT.ORG/.

EXTRA POINTER. If it's an article you're looking for, many ILL departments can get a scan from another library the very same day.

9. **Use citation tools.** It's smart to create your paper's footnotes and bibliography as you go along (it saves time and backtracking later). There are lots of different software programs for doing this; your college will probably give you access to one of these, or you can go online and locate free software.

ON THE WEB. Here's a guide that outlines the citation tools in use at my library: HTTP://ISITES.HARVARD.EDU/ICB/ICB.DO?KEYWORD=CITATIONTOOLS&PAGEID=ICB.PAGE148723. And here's an example of a free online citation tool: WWW.EASYBIB.COM/.

10. **Ask a librarian.** As soon as you get that 15-page research paper assignment, go to the library and find a librarian who can help you. Librarians can save you enormous amounts of time, help you find research materials you otherwise wouldn't, and help you get the "A" as painlessly as possible. Locate a librarian as a first-year student and (with any luck) you'll be set for your entire college career.

6 INTERFACING WITH THE PROFESSOR

You might think that taking a college course is just about going to class and hitting the books. And you wouldn't be wholly wrong. But you'll be most successful in your classes if you add some social networking into the mix. With your professor, that is. Developing a relationship with the prof can pay off in all sorts of ways. Maybe the professor can clear up a misconception that's causing you to leave each lecture in a fog of confusion. Maybe he or she can help you get the thesis of your paper right or tip you off to what's going to be on the exam—thus averting disaster. Or maybe it's some special consideration you need—an extension, a makeup exam, or the review of a grade—or perhaps just a little encouragement to get you through the course.

Whatever the case, you're going to have to approach your professor and interact with him or her. But students generally don't have much of an idea of how to manage their relations with the professor. Some students are simply not interested in engaging the professor; others see the teacher as an enemy to be avoided at all costs. And lots of students are terrified of going to an office hour lest they somehow seem stupid or lost, or encounter a professor who has no interest in seeing them.

But it's well worth the time and effort to overcome these obstacles. It's really not that hard to interface well with your professor once you know how to do it—and once you understand the professor's perspective. And in the end, it'll make your educational experience exponentially better and—a few incompetent professors and SOBs notwithstanding—more fun, too.

In this chapter you'll learn:

▶ 15 Ways to Make Your Professor Love You

▶ 10 Biggest Hesitations About Going to See the Professor—
   and How to Get Over Them

▶ The 14 Secrets of Going to See the Professor

▶ Etiquette for E-mailing Your Professor

▶ 10 Surefire Ways to Piss Off Your Professor

▶ Top 10 Things Professors Never Want to Hear and What They
   Think When They Do Hear Them

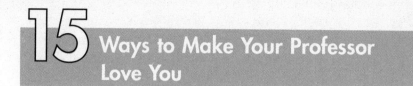

15 Ways to Make Your Professor Love You

Hey, professors are human beings too. With real human feelings. How your professor feels about you can influence how much time he or she is willing to put in to help you with the course, and even how good a recommendation he or she is willing to write for grad school or for a job. Surprisingly enough, only 1 in a 100 students thinks about this. Assuming you're one of the other 99, we offer you our 15 best tips on how to ingratiate yourself to your professor:

1. **Look interested.** Professors like nothing better than to see alert and engaged students seated front and center in their classes. Even if they're usually too polite to mention it, professors do notice students who sit there yawning or looking bummed out—or, worse yet, openly texting, reading e-mail, or selling on eBay (don't laugh, Lynn has seen it). If you look as if you're following, actively taking notes, and showing an interest in the material, you'll stand out from the huddled masses.

2. **Say hi to the professor when he or she enters the room.** Seems obvious, but take a look around sometime to see how few students do this.

3. **Ask a question.** Most professors regularly interrupt their presentations to give students a chance to ask questions. And when professors do, they're hoping for some kind of response—not the apathetic silence that often greets them. Your question will light up your professor's day. Make sure it's a question about the material, not one of those much-hated questions like: "Will this be on the test?" "Could you repeat what you just said for the past fifteen minutes?" or "When is the paper due?"

EXTRA POINTER. Bonus points will be given if your question demonstrates an understanding of material presented in an earlier class. Your professor will think, *Wow—a student who came to class and actually remembers something from last week!* It's also good when your question shows you have a more-than-passing acquaintance with the reading. Your professor will think, *Wow—someone is actually poring over that dull-as-dishwater textbook I assigned!*

4. **Put in your two cents' worth.** Another way professors break the monotony of the 50-minute lecture is by asking questions of the students. At times, running a class discussion can be like pulling teeth. So you're sure to win the professor's favor if you pipe up with an answer (or at least a stab at an answer) to the professor's query. And don't be afraid to be the first one in, either. Professors understand that it's sometimes hard to think on your feet.

5-STAR TIP. Do not take this as a green light to offer up whatever thought you have, no matter how dumb or unrelated to the question asked. If you just shoot your mouth off, without giving any thought at all to what you're saying, you're likely to become a major thorn in your professor's side *and* incur the wrath of your fellow students.

5. **Volunteer first.** You have a golden opportunity to earn your prof's affections if you are the first to volunteer when your professor is dividing up tasks for later in the semester—for example, seminar presentations, debates, or discussion leaders. Some professors even give special breaks on the grading for those brave enough to step up to bat first.

6. **Continue the conversation outside of class.** You will surely get on your professor's good side if you approach him or her outside of class to talk about issues raised in class. Usually the best venue is during office hours, but some professors have time to chat before or after class. Keep in mind that the more you can display your interest in the course material for its own sake (rather than for a good grade on the paper or test), the better. If you are shy, an e-mail to the professor following up on some issue raised in class can also do the trick (for tips on this approach, see "Etiquette for E-mailing Your Professor" on p. 217).

7. **Read the comments.** You can't imagine how many students come to office hours to go over a paper or test and haven't even read the professor's comments. Professors especially appreciate those students who *have*, because it shows that you actually want to learn from what the professor has to say. And it's a time-saver for the prof, too: who wants to say again what they just finished writing down the night before? (Also see "The 14 Secrets of Going to See the Professor" on p. 212.)

8. **Join the team.** Some professors offer students the opportunity to work with them on a joint research project or an internship. This can be one of the best ways to forge a great relationship with your professor and gain valuable training in your field. If no research or internship opportunities are available, see if you can at least take a small class or seminar with some professor you would like to work with.

9. **Ask the prof what he or she is working on.** Many professors spend lots of years working on a research project. And there's almost nothing professors like to talk about more than their own research. But it's a rare student who thinks to ask the professor about it. This is something that'll surely set you off from the crowd, and, hey, you might even learn something about the Siberian poetry of the late 1820s or the synthesis of amino acids.

10. **Participate in departmental activities.** Professors will take note of you when they see you at departmental events such as outside lectures, colloquia, or meetings of the departmental student club. Your participation shows you really care about the field. (Professors are suckers for that sort of thing.)

11. **Alert your professor to current events related to the class.** Bringing in a newspaper item or web article that has relevance to the course is a surefire way to win approval from your professor. Not only does he or she see that you are engaged enough with the class to recognize its relevance to real-world activities, but it gives the professor some valuable ammunition to prove to the rest of the class that—despite what they've been thinking—someone actually finds the course useful or interesting.

12. **Congratulate the professor on an achievement.** If you read on the college website or student newspaper that your professor just published a book, won an award, or has gotten tenure and/or a promotion, it's a very nice thing to offer congratulations. Everyone likes his or her accomplishments recognized, even professors.

13. **Tell your prof you like the class.** Students rarely realize that professors worry about how a class is going and would desperately like to hear that students are enjoying it. Look for an occasion when you can slip in, in a casual but sincere way, that you like the class. It would be a special touch if you could come up with some specific thing about the class that you are enjoying, but even a general expression of appreciation would surely be welcome.

EXTRA POINTER. It's one thing to compliment a professor and another to lay it on too thick. Once you slip into sucking-up mode, the professor realizes it's more about your trying to get a good grade than about him or her being a good professor. Never a good idea.

14. **Thank the professor when he or she does you a favor.** You might not realize it, but professors aren't obligated to do a lot of the things they do for students. Like making special appointments, answering e-mails on evenings and weekends, giving extensions and makeups, and providing help with picking other courses in the department. Professors remember the students who thank them—in person or at least by e-mail—for any special considerations that the professor might have offered. Which will come in very handy when you need another favor or two.

15. **Always be positive.** Whenever you have any interaction with the professor—whether in the class, in the office, or even in the hall—always be upbeat and enthusiastic. No one likes a sourpuss.

10 Biggest Hesitations About Going to See the Professor—and How to Get Over Them

Life doesn't offer you that many golden opportunities. But college offers you at least one: the chance to meet individually with your professor. Take advantage of this opportunity, and you can get feedback on your in-progress paper—or help in preparing for the exam, or an explanation of some point in the reading or the lecture that you didn't quite understand. Of course, nothing is guaranteed, but often a well-timed tête-à-tête with the professor (or TA) can net a major grade improvement—not to mention a real insight into some problem or issue. And yet, many students would rather go for a root canal than go see a professor. You can call off your trip to the endodontist if you follow our 10 best tips for overcoming your hesitations about going to see the professor:

1. **"The professor will think I'm a dumb ass."** If you're not doing all that well in a class, you may think that the professor will think you're an idiot if you disclose all the things you don't understand from the lecture or reading. But relax. If the professor has been teaching for more than a semester, you're not the first student to be asking about whatever you're asking about. And besides, whatever you don't know is probably going to come out in your exam or paper, so why not get it corrected while there's still plenty of time.

2. **"The professor will be mean to me."** Among the almost two million professors in the United States, some are bound to be total jerks. But, for the most part, those who chose teaching as their profession would actually like to teach—and help students learn. And, if that weren't enough, at many schools the promotion and tenure of the prof depends on student

evaluations, so there's extra incentive for professors to be helpful and welcoming to students. So take the plunge, put aside your apprehensions, and get to the office hour. You're likely to be surprised at how well you're treated.

3. **"I don't want to bother the professor."** Such consideration of the professor's feelings is surely appreciated, but consulting with students is a required—and for many professors, fun— part of the job. That's not only because the professor gets a chance to think about the material in a one-on-one setting (as opposed to the sea of blank faces he or she usually confronts in lecture), but also because the professor feels that he or she is really making a difference in the intellectual growth of individual students. And when things really go well, the professor learns something about the material from hearing the students' observations. Perhaps even yours.

4. **"I'm too shy to go."** Sure, many people are shy by nature, and facing up to some big expert in the field can be a daunting activity. But shyness can be overcome; it shouldn't be something you give in to when it stands in the way of success at college (and beyond). It may be easier for you to first ask a brief question before or after class. And some students find it more comfortable to correspond by e-mail, where the situation is much more controlled and you're not on the spot (for some tips about e-mailing your professor, see "Etiquette for E-mailing Your Professor" on p. 217). After you've succeeded in making initial contact with your professor (and hopefully gotten a friendly response) you might be able to step up and have a face-to-face meeting in an office hour.

5. **"What would I say?"** You don't need to have a prepared speech, together with a PowerPoint presentation, to go see the prof. It's just fine to come in with a few simple questions, such as "I was wondering if you could tell me if I'm on the right track with this paper" or "I'm not sure I fully understood what point you were making in the lecture about ____." Professors are very good at running with the ball, and you'll have a very

fine discussion if you come in with even one or two focused questions.

6. **"I don't have the time for extra activities for this class."** An office hour meeting usually lasts 15 or 20 minutes (30, tops). Wouldn't it be worth a few minutes out of your jam-packed schedule to ward off the 72 on your midterm or the red C+ on your paper?

7. **"I'm just taking this course to fulfill a requirement, so why invest more time in it than absolutely necessary?"** Yes, going to see the professor represents a greater investment of time or energy than just showing up for class, but the little extra effort may be worth your while. Failing a distribution course will force you to sit through the same old course again (you'd be amazed how many students have to retake, and in some cases retake again, the same required course). And even if you scrape by with a pass, your GPA doesn't distinguish between elective and forced courses. Who knows? The discussion with the professor might even increase your interest in and enjoyment of the course.

8. **"It won't help, anyway."** Sometimes, when the course is a living nightmare, it's easy to feel defeated and think that failure—is actually *inevitable*, rather than being only one possible outcome. If you're feeling this way, that's exactly why you need to make an appointment to see the professor. He or she will be able to help you objectively assess your situation and give you directed, customized help about how to make the best of your situation.

9. **"I can't bear to face the grade."** Sometimes the purpose of going to see the professor is to go over the test or paper and better understand better why you got the grade you did. And sometimes that's too much for you to handle. But of course, you've gotten the grade you did, and so it would be good to understand the mistakes you made—and, more important, to get some tips from the prof about how you can improve on the next one. Ostriches don't generally do that well at college.

10. **"I might actually have to *do* what the professor recommends."** This is the most irrational worry: that the meeting might actually go well and, as a result, you'll have to invest more time in improving your work. Sometimes students come to an office hour asking for some minor help on a paper they think is done and are stunned when the professor suggests the unthinkable: a reconsideration of the main idea of the paper, a tracking down of five more sources, or a rewrite to make the main idea more clear and forceful. In short, more work. Now, nobody is happy to get this news. But that's a short-term way of looking at things. The long-term outlook, for those who follow the professor's suggestions, includes a much better grade and, even more important, the experience of really advancing your own take on the material. And isn't that what you came to college for? Now, aren't you happy that you overcame your hesitations and sought out the professor?

The 14 Secrets of Going to See the Professor

Now that you've recognized the value in reaching out to your professor, you may wonder how best to conduct your office visit. When should you go? What should you say? How should you respond to what the professor says? These and a hundred other questions may occur to you once you've decided to seek out your professor. You'll have an easy time figuring out what to do once you've considered our 14 insider tips about how to make that office hour really count.

1. **Go while there's still time.** It's best to go as early as a week or two before the test is to be held or the paper is due. That way you'll have plenty of time to apply the suggestions the professor might make. And you'll avoid the interminable line of students outside the office the day before the assignment comes due.

2. **Go it alone.** Even though you may feel more comfortable going with a friend or partner, the office hour will go better if it's just you and the professor. You'll get in more questions, the discussion will be tailored to what you need the most help with, and two-party communication is almost always more productive than committee work. Your friend can wait outside for the postmortem.

3. **Don't make 'em wait.** If you can't make the official office hours, most professors are willing to make individual appointments to help you out. If you're lucky enough to land such an accommodation, though, be sure you're right on time. There's nothing that ticks a professor off more than making him- or herself available for a custom office hour only to find that you don't care enough to come on time. Moreover, the professor may give up and leave after 10 minutes, making your

trip a total loss. (See "10 Surefire Ways to Piss Off Your Professor" on p. 220 for 9 more ways to get on your prof's bad side.)

4. **Come ready to work.** If you're meeting with the professor to go over a paper or test, or to ask questions about a particular lecture or reading, make sure you bring that paper or test, or your lecture notes or a copy of the article. The professor isn't going to remember what he or she thought about your individual piece of work (especially if 49 other papers on the same topic were in the stack to be graded). On the other hand, a quick read-over of your paper or test should do the trick, especially when the professor has his or her comments to refer to (be sure to give him or her ample time to read them over). If your paper is about a specific reading or portion of the lecture, be sure to bring that article or book, or your own lecture notes, so the professor will be able to refer to these, too.

5. **Come in with something to say.** Office hours almost always go better if you bring a few specific questions to the meeting. It's almost never a good idea to start a meeting with general comments such as: "I didn't understand what you said about [main topic of the course]" or "I couldn't understand any of your lectures last week." It is much better to come in with two or three conversation-starters about a specific concept, point, or problem you didn't understand. Keep in mind that in a 15-minute office hour (which is how long these things usually last), two or three questions are usually the most you'll have time to discuss.

---

⑤ 5-STAR TIP. Go for the meat. It's usually best to ask questions about the main ideas, rather than about little facts or tiny details. Focusing on the central and most far-reaching issues will also help you on the test or paper, because professors usually ask about the most important points, not picayune details.

---

6. Start the conversation yourself . . . You've come to have your concerns addressed. You should start the conversation by asking a question or raising an issue.

. . . But let the man (or woman) talk. Be sure you also let the professor get a word in edgewise. Sometimes students come in prepared with so many things to say that the professor never gets a chance to get his or her two cents in. Net result? You don't get the benefit of the professor's suggestions and guidance, which is—when you think about it—what you came for.

RULE OF THUMB. When the professor starts talking, no matter how briefly and how tentatively, you stop talking. Always works.

---

7. Follow up with follow-ups. Once you've gotten a good discussion going, it's good to probe issues more fully by asking directed questions about what the professor just said. The most productive office hours occur when new—and unexpected—ideas are generated during the conversation. Your follow-ups, even when you're not sure where the discussion is going, will help generate such ideas.

8. Don't be coy. No point being shy or pretending. If the professor says something you don't understand (or directs your attention to something in the lecture or reading that you can't identify), it's always good to say, simply and forthrightly, that you haven't understood. Professors, who have often gone over the same material with different students, simply don't realize that you're not taking in what they just said—unless you tell them. And they'll appreciate your honesty and real desire to learn.

9. Don't dispute balls and strikes. It's perfectly all right to go to the professor and ask why you got the grade you did. It's not all right to mount a pitched battle with the professor about each point the grader took off. A better idea would be to focus on the concepts you didn't understand—and on the (less-than-successful) strategies you used in writing the paper or taking the test—so that you can do better next time.

BEST-KEPT SECRET. Most professors, when they smell a grade dispute coming, do the best they can to shut down the discussion. Keep this in mind when you shift the discussion from the course material to why you got the grade you did (often not worth it).

10. **Get it down.** It's always a good idea to take notes. Points often go by very fast in conversation, and you'll be pleased to have a record of what the professor suggested when it comes time for writing the paper or studying for the test. And don't be embarrassed: professors themselves are very used to taking notes at meetings.

EXTRA POINTER. If the professor suggests additional readings or reference materials, make sure you get down as full and exact a citation as you can. You'd be amazed how often students can't find the article afterward because they've written down only a few key words (or misspelled the author's name).

11. **Don't make it personal.** It's almost never a good use of office time to confess your personal troubles, problems with your life, your roommate, your family, and so on. The professor is not a confidant, and even if he or she were, airing your problems in this venue won't help you in the course.

12. **Ask—and ye shall receive (maybe).** It's generally not such a great idea to ask for an extension or a makeup exam (either of which just puts off the pain). But sometimes such accommodations would really, really, really help you out (for example, when you've got two other exams on that day). Always ask. Politely, of course. Sometimes professors have hidden course policies that allow them latitude for such special cases. And what's the worst that can happen? They'll turn you down.

13. **Be a mensch.** It's always nice—and prudent, too—to politely greet the professor with an upbeat "Hello, Professor So and So" at the beginning of the meeting and to thank him or her at the close for taking the time to meet with you. Professors respond to such niceties, especially when you mean them.

14. **Beg for more.** It's often good to try to set up an additional meeting if you still have questions and would like to continue the discussion. And don't forget about e-mail. Professors are often very happy to answer (specific and focused) questions by e-mail or even to read drafts or at least paragraphs of papers before you hand them in.

BEST-KEPT SECRET. Many professors are starting to use Skype as a way of communicating with students outside of office hours. Ask whether your professor is one of them.

Etiquette for E-mailing Your Professor

Like everyone else, professors have gone electronic, which means that in addition to the one-on-one office hour, they're almost all willing to communicate by e-mail (indeed, at some schools e-mail is slowly but surely replacing the office hour). Here are some things to consider before clicking "Send":

▶ **E-mail is forever.** Once you send it off, you can't get it back. Once your professor has it, he or she owns it and can save it or, in the worst case, forward it on to colleagues for a good laugh. At your expense.

▶ **E-mail goes where it's told to.** Check—and double check—to see that the right address appears in the "To" line. Just because your mom and your professor are both named Lynn is no reason to send all your love to Professor Lynn.

▶ **Professors may not be using the cruddy university e-mail system.** So send it to the address they actually use, not the one on the university directory. (Check the syllabus or assignment sheet for clues.)

▶ **Professors may not open mail sent from luckydogpig@thepound.com.** They prefer to open mail sent from more reputable addresses, like your.name@theCruddyUniversityE-mailSystem.edu.

▶ **Subject lines are for subjects.** Put a brief explanation of the nature of the e-mail (like "question about paper") in the subject line. Never include demands such as "Urgent request: immediate response needed." That's the surest way to get your request trashed.

► **Salutations matter.** The safest way to start is with "Dear Professor So and So" (using their last name). That way you won't be getting into the issue of whether the prof has a PhD or not, and you won't seem sexist when you address your female professor as Ms. (rather than Professor) or, worse yet, Mrs. So and So.

► **Clear and concise is best.** Your prof may get 25 to 30 e-mails a day. So it's best if you ask your questions in as focused and succinct a way as possible (hint: it's often good to number your questions). And if your question is very elaborate or multifaceted, it's best to go to an in-person office hour. You'll get better service that way.

EXTRA POINTER. Before sending a draft of a paper to a professor as an attachment, confirm that he or she is willing to accept such long documents. If not, find out whether he or she will look over a page or even a central paragraph of your work incorporated into the body of the e-mail. And, if you don't have your e-mail set to automatically keep a copy in your Sent folder, be sure to cc yourself any time you send a piece of work—who knows the fate of the document you're sending?

► **Always acknowledge.** If your professor deigns to answer—or to send you the handout or reference that you asked for—be sure to tell him or her that you got it. That way he or she will think kindly of you next time you need something.

► **THIS IS NOT A SHOUTING MATCH.** Don't write in all uppercase letters (which is an e-mail convention for anger or other strong emotion). No one likes being yelled at.

► **No one really likes emoticons and smileys.** Trust us on this one.☺

► **This is not Facebook.** So don't write to the professor in the same way you'd write on your friend's wall.

► **This is not IMing.** So pls dun wrte yor profeSR llk ur txtN. uz abbrz @ yor own rsk. coRec me f lm wrng. (Translation courtesy of WWW.TRANSL8IT.COM, which features a neat little Facebook widget.)

► **This is not CollegeHumor.com.** So resist the temptation to talk about the "badass" paper you need help with, your "loser" TA who didn't teach you what you needed to know, or the "crappy" grade you just got on the midterm.

► **This is not RateMyProfessors.com.** The professor doesn't want your comments about his or her performance in the class. Save those for the end-of-semester evaluations, where you'll be able to spout off. Anonymously.

► **Spelling mistakes make you look like a doofus.** So always use the spel check and proofread yyour e-mail, two.

► **Sign-offs and signatures count.** Always end by thanking the professor for his or her time and closing with "Best wishes" or "Regards" (or some other relatively formal, but friendly closing). And always sign with your (entire) real name, not some wacky nickname like Ry-Ry or Biff.

► **Your prof doesn't want to hear your philosophy of life.** Skip the cute quotes or statements of your religious or political views at the bottom of your e-mail. You never know what may offend.

► **Don't lay it on too thick.** It's one thing to be polite and friendly in your e-mail; it's another thing to wind up with a brown nose.

10 Surefire Ways to Piss Off Your Professor

Like any other relationship between two people, the student-professor interaction depends on goodwill from both sides. Things go wrong when one party—for example, the student—does something that offends the other party—for example, the professor. In some cases, the student isn't even aware that he or she has done something to irritate the prof. Lest you unwittingly make a misstep, here are ten of the most common ways students get on the wrong side of their professors—and how you can avoid these *faux pas*:

1. **Making excuses for missing class.** Many students feel guilty when, for whatever reason, they don't show up for class. But the professor does *not* want to know that your family reunion was more important than his or her class, or that your cramming for your P-Chem exam took precedence over yet another boring lecture. Suggestion: carefully think out what excuses you're going to make for missing class; better yet, don't make any excuses at all.

    EXTRA POINTER. If you must make an excuse, either because the professor takes attendance or because he or she asks you why you weren't there, it's best to be as brief as possible. Simply saying that you weren't feeling well, that your kid was sick, or that there was an accident on the freeway will work well.

2. **Misbehaving in class.** It's very easy for students to think that the prof pays no attention to what they are doing in a lecture. The class is huge, so why should the teacher even care what

the audience is doing? Surprisingly enough, though, the professor often notices—and sometimes remembers—the student who's busy IMing in class or whose cell phone goes off or, worst of all, who nods off during class. And although few professors will dock your grade for such questionable behavior, it can come back to bite you when you need some help with a paper or an extension of a deadline, or when your score is on the borderline between two grades.

3. **Challenging your professor publicly.** It's one thing to ask a pointed question or propose a different interpretation; it's another thing to suggest (however implicitly) that the professor has no idea what he or she is talking about or that no one has understood anything he or she has said so far. Before asking a question in lecture, make sure you're not going to show the professor up or otherwise embarrass him or her. It's not worth it.

4. **Disputing a grade like a "mad dog."** Even though it's the least pleasant part of the job, all professors realize they're obligated to entertain student questions and disputes about their grades. But professors really hate it when some student comes in frothing at the mouth and complaining that the grade on their paper is unacceptable, unfair, wrong—or all of the above. One likely result of such behavior: the professor will reread your paper like a gymnastics judge at the Olympics, replaying everything in slo-mo, looking for any possible deduction. And in many cases will come to the conclusion that the initial grade was way too high for such a lousy piece of work. Tip: consider the dispute from the side of the interaction that counts. *The professor's.*

5. **Seeming really stupid.** From time to time professors encounter stupidity the likes of which they've never seen. Students who can't remember who painted the Mona Lisa. Students who say they can't come to a 12:30 p.m. office hour because it's in the middle of the night. And students who don't know their "its" from their "it's,"—or their "their" from their "there" from their

"they're." Seeing this kind of stupidity from college students can really tick off a professor. (On the positive side, it does make for some great cocktail party snickering with the professor's faculty friends.)

6. **Giving lame excuses for handing in a late paper or missing an exam.** Some excuses wear really thin with professors. Computer ate your paper (have you ever heard of backups?). Alarm clock didn't go off (as if I've never heard that one before). Grandmother died (amazing how many grandmothers go to meet their maker the day of the midterm). But some excuses really go off the deep end. Like the student who vehemently argued to Lynn that he was never told about a course rule because his syllabus was missing a page—all the while holding that very page in his hands. On the flip side, the *best* excuses we've heard include: "I couldn't get to the test because I was in jail" (how can you argue with that one?) and "I couldn't do the paper because Ozarks Electric hasn't restored the power to my house fifteen days after the ice storm" (it's true).

7. **Treating the professor like your servant.** You're guaranteed to offend the professor if you leave phone messages or send e-mails that say: "ABSOLUTELY MUST SEE YOU TOMORROW TO DISCUSS MY EXAM. I HAVE CLASSES FROM 10:30 TO 12:30, LUNCH 'TIL 2 AND HAVE TO WORK FROM 3 TO 5. SO I AM AVAILABLE BETWEEN 2 AND 3. PLEASE RESPOND IMMEDIATELY." Yeah, right.

8. **Plagiarizing in super-obvious ways.** No professor likes students who cheat. But even worse than plagiarism is copying in a way that's so transparent and obvious that anyone with half a brain could detect it. Like what happens when the professor enters the first few words of your paper into a Google search and finds, word for word, parts of your paper in the first entry. Look—professors think plagiarism is intellectual stealing and, as the antilittering signs in New York City say, "disgusting and filthy, so don't do it." But you add insult to

injury when you copy in so obvious a way that your professor would have to be a moron to not be able to find your source.

9. **Comparing your prof to other profs.** No professor wants to hear how he or she stacks up against other professors you've had or against professors teaching other sections of the course. Even a casual comparison can offend, so think before you compare.

10. **Going over your prof's head.** No prof will be happy if you go to the department chair (or worse yet, the dean) with complaints about the course or about how the professor is treating you. But it's possible to wind up offending through no intention of your own. Say you encounter the department chair, either in the hall or at a departmental function, and he or she asks you, "So, how's that course X with Professor Y going?" You answer, "Not so great, given A, B, C, and D." After which, the next time the chair sees that prof, he or she says, "So I hear your course X is having some problems," and when asked, casually mentions your name as the source of the "observations." You wind up in the doghouse with the prof, when all you intended was to be friendly with the departmental chair. Moral? Be careful where you bad-mouth your professor—what you say can come back to bite you.

Top 10 Things Professors Never Want to Hear—and What They Think When They Do Hear Them

10. **"I missed class yesterday. So, did you do anything important?"**

Of course not. I just stood up in front and ran my mouth about nothing, like I always do.

9. **"I lost the syllabus. Oh, and the paper assignment, too. Would you mind e-mailing them to me?"**

Sure, last time I checked my job description, it included research, teaching, and being at your beck and call.

8. **"Can we go over my test?"**

Don't you think reading the whole thing through once was more than enough for me?

7. **"I'm terribly sorry my paper wasn't in on time; my dog ate my printer."**

Time for obedience training. For you.

6. **"My friend and I worked together on this paper. How come I got a B and he got an A?"**

Hmm . . . in addition to being better looking than you, your friend is also smarter.

5. **"I really need an A in this class."**

Well, if I were parceling out A's on the basis on need, I'd be giving them to all those D students. They need 'em more than you.

4. **"This C is totally unacceptable to me. I'm an A student."**

Not in my class.

3. **"I'm leaving early for my ski vacation. So can I take the final early?"**

Now there's a deal I can't refuse: I do double work making two finals, and you spend more quality time on the slopes.

2. **"I'd do anything for an A."**

Anything?

And the number one thing professors never want to hear:

1. **"B-? You've got to be kidding. I paid good money for that paper."**

7

IN CASE OF EMERGENCY . . .

College is not always a luxury cruise. Sometimes it's more like a boat that's sprung a few leaks. Or worse, one that's taking on water and about to take a Titanic-like plunge to the bottom. When you see signs of major trouble, it's easy to start the blame game: *It's the college's fault*, or *It's the professors' fault*, or (if you're in a really confessional mood) *It's my fault*. Then panic sets in: *OMG, what should I do next? Everyone is doing better than me. How will I survive this semester?* And finally, sometimes you want to simply give up on the whole thing: *I'm never going to be able to do college. I shouldn't even be here. Where's the exit?*

We advise a different course. Instead of going off the deep end, make a careful, rational assessment of what's gone wrong, and then make a plan to fix things up. This chapter can help. The tips here cover a wide range of problems—some that might come up early in the semester, others that tend to hit around the midterm, still others that arise only when the semester is in its dying throes. Even when the situation looks hopeless, a few practical, and sometimes surprisingly simple, techniques can turn the thing around.

In this chapter you'll learn:

▶ 10 Things to Do When You Can't Keep Up with the Lecture

▶ Top 10 Signs You've Been Cutting Too Many Classes

▶ What to Do When You've Bombed the Midterm

▶ 7 Best Last-Minute Strategies for Saving Your Grade

▶ 10 Signs You're in Real Trouble at College

▶ What, Then, to Do? The 7-Step Approach

10 Things to Do When You Can't Keep Up with the Lecture

One of the biggest—and most common—problems students have at college is not being able to keep up with the lecture. No matter how much you try, you're always a few steps behind and never quite able to get it all down. What to do? Consider our 10 tips for getting your note taking up to speed:

1. **Hear clearly.** It's very difficult to take good notes when you can't clearly hear all that the professor is saying (even the words he or she mutters under his or her breath). So pick a seat that's in direct earshot of the lecturer. And keep in mind that because bodies absorb sound, it'll be harder to hear when the room is full and when your compatriots are also muttering under their breath.

2. **Come prepared.** Doing the reading or polishing off the problem set before the lecture will give you important advance information on what the lecture is going to be about. It's easier to follow and take notes on a lecture when you know what it's going to cover.

EXTRA POINTER. If weird names and foreign terms are giving you trouble, prepare a cheat sheet with important names and terms, and bring it with you to the class. This will save you having to figure out on the spot how to spell these things—thereby saving you valuable note-taking time. Some students even devise three-letter abbreviations for exotic names of people and places.

5-STAR TIP. Be sure to check the syllabus (including any schedule of readings and lectures) and the course web page for lists of topics, and sometimes even outlines, of what's going to be covered in the lecture. The more information you have in advance—especially about the central points and the structure of the lecture—the easier it'll be to get it all down.

3. **Don't take mental breaks.** As long as the professor is up there dishing out material, keep focused on what's being said and get it down into your notes. Now's not the time to be zoning in and out (save that for your study time, when you're in control of the speed at which the content is being presented).

4. **Write fast—really fast.** Most college students can text with blazing speed with just two thumbs, but when it comes to note taking the old-fashioned way, they shift into a paralyzingly slow pace. Write in script as messy as you can read and use whatever shorthand will make sense to you. (Keep in mind that it'll have to make sense to you at 11 p.m. the night before the test, so don't go overboard.) Or use an electronic device: especially good for note taking are mini tablets, which typically weigh less than a pound, have an eight-hour battery, are about two-thirds the size of a normal tablet, and will set you back only $250–$350. (For more information about different devices, see our "10 Things to Consider Before Buying a Tablet, E-Reader, or Laptop for College" on p. 62.)

5. **Capture the professor's thoughts, not his or her exact words.** Note taking is not about creating a word-for-word transcript of the lecture, but about getting down the main ideas (and the most important details) of what the professor has said. So don't waste time trying to decide whether the prof noted "close parallels" or "lots of similarities" between this and that. Trust us—the professor isn't going to remember the exact language, so you don't need to either.

EXTRA POINTER. Of course, if it's a key technical term, a crucial distinction, or a theorem or equation in a problem, it *is* important to get down word-for-word what the professor is saying. Try to focus 100 percent on what the professor is saying at these points, and be sure to copy down (as fast as you can) anything he or she writes on the board or displays in a PowerPoint.

6. **Look for importance—and structure.** In any given lecture, not every point is of equal significance: some are the key ideas, some are expansion and embellishment, some are examples or illustrations, and some are just things that occur to the professor as he or she is talking. Moreover, in any lecture the points are put together in a certain order and with a certain direction and logic: there usually is a reason that points come at the place they do and stand in the relationship they do. Always be on the lookout for the most important points and their structure. If you can locate the key points of the lecture and figure out their arrangement, it'll be ten times easier to take notes.

7. **Don't panic too soon.** Professors almost always sum up and repeat the main points at various times in the lectures, so if you missed something the first time around, it's likely to come up again. The summary at the end of that section or at the end of the lecture can be particularly useful if you missed a point the first time around.

8. **Keep practicing.** With note taking, as with most things in life, practice makes perfect. As you keep at it, and as you get more accustomed to your professor's lecturing style, your notes will get better.

REALITY CHECK. A good time to check whether you're getting down enough of the lecture material—and the right points—is after the first test. If you see many things on the exam that were talked about in lecture but did not make it into your notes, you should try to diagnose the problems you're having with taking good notes. And for many students it's a good idea to go see the professor or TA—armed with your notes, of course—to see what suggestions they might have about improving your note-taking techniques. Teachers are often surprisingly interested in seeing how well their students are getting down the main points and often are very willing to offer suggestions about how to take better notes.

9. **Use "aids."** If you're really having trouble taking notes, it may be useful seeing whether official lecture notes are sold at the bookstore (many universities have these for beginning classes). And you might ask the professor whether you could record the class so you can listen to it, with breaks, at your leisure. Just don't get too addicted to these aids. Because the real skill is learning to take notes yourself, these short-term fixes aren't to your advantage in the long term.

IOHO. Recently a number of online note-taking services and communities have arisen. We think that, although in theory these could be good, in practice they're not so great to get started with. It's easier to cut class if you think someone else in the community will be doing your dirty work for you. And besides, the note takers could be significantly less good students than you. Most important, taking notes yourself is one of the key ways you're actively processing, and learning, the material. So suck it up and do it yourself. Leave the social networking for *social* networking.

10. **In the worst case, bail.** If, after trying all these tips, you still can't keep up with the note taking, maybe the problem isn't your note-taking skills, but that the class is too hard for you. If so, forget about improving your note taking, and drop the class. No shame in that.

Top 10 Signs You've Been Cutting Too Many Classes

10. You show up Wednesday at 9 a.m. only to find the class meets Tuesdays and Thursdays from 3 to 4 p.m.

9. You're so confused by the lecture that you can't get in your usual zzz's.

8. Your classmates roll their eyes when you do show up and "contribute" to the discussion.

7. You ask when the midterm is going to be, only to find out it was held three weeks ago.

6. It's the tenth week of the semester and the prof mistakes you for a prospective student.

5. You ask the professor what you can do to catch up, and he or she starts laughing like a hyena.

4. You discover that while you were gone your Russian class has mysteriously moved from singing the alphabet to reading *War and Peace*—in its entirety.

3. The hottie you had your eye on is now married to your classmate at the end of the row.

2. You find a really interesting class for next semester, then realize you're currently in it.

And the number-one sign you've been cutting too many classes:

1. You arrive at the final only to find out that the professor gave an in-class final and the course is already over.

What to Do When You've Bombed the Midterm

It's the eighth week of the semester, and you thought you were doing great. But you just got back your midterm and—can you believe it?—it's a C (or worse). Panic sets in. *Drop out of college? Crawl back home to your parents?* Here are some better ideas:

▶ **Figure out the real score.** Sure, you know you got a 75 on the midterm. But have you considered the impact of that mess-up on your total grade in the course? Though you may not have thought about it in the depths of your despair, in many courses the midterm counts one quarter or less of the whole course grade. That's because most professors want to give students a chance to screw up and still have some motivation to keep working throughout the course. So all may not be lost—yet.

▶ **Ignore the neighbors.** Despite what you have been able to glean by glancing surreptitiously at other folks' A papers, you are not the only one in the class with a lousy grade. So don't assume that everybody is doing better than you. They're not.

▶ **Don't miss the going-over-the-test.** No matter how bad you think the test went, don't cut on the day the tests are returned (or the section meeting that week). That's the time when most professors (or TAs) can't help but whine, berate, or tell the class how badly they did—all the while revealing the components of the perfect answer. This is a golden opportunity for you to see what they were really looking for. So listen up—and take notes.

5-STAR TIP. Pay special attention when the professor lists points that could have gone into the good answer. Get most of these points, you'd have had an A; half or more, a B; and not too many at all, some sort of C. Live and learn.

▶ **Look in the rearview mirror.** Now is the time to figure out what went wrong in your preparation, so that you can correct it before the next test (which probably will be quite similar to this one). Pinpoint your problems. Did you miss key lectures or not fully understand the lectures? Did you skip the reading or focus too heavily on it? Did you blow off studying, study in the wrong way, or study with the wrong comrades? Did you fail to answer exactly what was being asked, or did you make mistakes in your answers? Figure it all out, and you'll do better next time.

▶ **Feed on the feedback.** Your test will no doubt come back with plenty of red ink marking places where you lost points and, if you're lucky, loads of comments explaining how you could have done better. This is your individualized interface with the prof, so read your teacher's words of wisdom with great care. Yeah, these comments were written pretty quickly while your prof was struggling to get through the stack and get on with his or her life. But the professor was still focusing on your work—one of the few times this happens in the typical semester.

EXTRA POINTER. Give the grader the benefit of the doubt. Things will go better if you read the comments with the aim of learning how to improve, instead of demonstrating how incompetent the grader is.

▶ **Get some face time.** A trip to your professor's office hours—or in some cases your TAs—can provide a fount of knowledge about how to avert future disasters. Professors regularly see students seeking help after getting bad grades, so why let your friends with the C's get a leg up on you?

BEST-KEPT SECRET. Professors will usually really open up and offer all sorts of aid if you go to them and say, "I didn't do so well on the midterm, and I see from the comments that x, y, and z. Could you explain a little more fully how I might correct this problem on the next test?" (This works because it shows that you've read the comments, are not angry, and would like to improve). Less good: "I'd like to go over my test and see why I got the grade I did." (Professors think that's what the comments were supposed to accomplish.) Least good: "Here's my exam—could you find some extra points for me?" (Professors think grade grubbing is *your* job.)

▶ **Turn over a new leaf.** Now's the time to make strategic changes—the ones that will address the specific ways things went wrong. Not changes your parents, friends, and even advisers suggest without having a clue about what you did right and what you did wrong. Above all, don't keep using the old strategies that got you into deep doo-doo in the first place.

▶ **Lighten the load.** In some cases, dropping the course may be the right thing to do—like when you're so far behind that you can never catch up, even if you studied day and night for the rest of the semester, or if the skill level will kick up a notch or two after the midterm (for example, in a language course or math class). And don't worry—there's nothing wrong with a W (for withdrawal) on your record. There's much more wrong with a grade that sucks.

7 Best Last-Minute Strategies for Saving Your Grade

Sometimes even the best-laid plans go wrong. And sometimes you never had a plan in the first place. But whatever the reason, toward the end of the semester some students find themselves in a ginormous hole. But there's no reason to fold just yet, at least not before checking out our seven things to do to salvage the semester:

1. **The extension.** Even if the due date for the paper is accompanied by copious threats, many professors will give students extra time to complete a paper. To get an extension, you have to ask. Make your request face-to-face (no e-mail, Twitter, Facebook, or snail-mail notes) and during an official office hour, not before or after class. Explain your reasons simply and concisely: a sob story is OK if it's believable and lasts no more than 20 seconds. Be honest and super nice: these qualities can outweigh even a flimsy excuse. And propose a firm date for completion of the work—say, an extra week or two. Tests are more dicey: many professors aren't even allowed to give makeup exams. But ask anyway. You never know. . . .

5-STAR TIP. You can turn your request for an extension on a paper to your advantage by highlighting the *academic* reasons for the needed additional time. For example, you might point out that in doing your research, an additional issue emerged that requires further investigation; or that in framing the argument, an additional objection came to mind. Professors are usually overjoyed to hear that you want to devote additional study to your topic and are often willing to give you the extra time to push your ideas forward.

BEST-KEPT SECRET. At many schools you're entitled to an automatic extension if you have more than two finals on the same day. If you find yourself in this situation, be sure to request that extension.

---

2. **The incomplete.** If you're way, way, behind—or missing more than one piece of work—an extension won't do the trick. What you need is an incomplete—that is, an I in the course plus several months to complete the work (often the university sets the completion date as some particular week of the next semester). Incompletes may temporarily appear on your record, but they'll go away when you submit the outstanding work. The real drawback, though, is that they are a bear to complete outside the structure of the class. Many a student happily goes off with an incomplete, only to see it lapse to an F when he or she never gets the energy or motivation to finish the work in the allotted time.

3. **The withdrawal.** If you have a sudden or serious situation—an accident, serious illness, or family emergency—you may be eligible to withdraw from a class. This is often the best solution when you have not been able to do any or most of the work in a class. Keep in mind that withdrawals are often controlled by the dean or registrar's office (rather than the professor) and are subject to strict rules. In some schools, past a certain date you may be required to withdraw from the entire semester (which is good if you have done no work in any course, but not so good if you are behind in only one course). And keep in mind that in most cases there are no refunds. Makes it hard to just walk away from the semester.

4. **The suck-it-up.** You might find that the best solution is to just take an F on one piece of work in the class and see whether you can still eke out a passing grade with the remaining work. This is often a good strategy when you stand half a chance in

your other courses, and investing more time and effort in this course would be throwing good money after bad.

BEST-KEPT SECRET. Some professors have hidden rules that won't allow you to pass the course without doing all the tests and/or papers; others average in a zero on a hundred-point scale (rather than an 0.0 on a 4.0 point scale) for work not submitted. So before you blow off a piece of work, check with your professor to find out the cost.

5. **The do-over.** A hidden gem in your college's rule book may be the grade-forgiveness policy. This is a policy that allows you to retake a course you failed (or got a very bad grade in) and replace the grade with the one you earn the second time around. Before you decide to go this route, make sure you understand all the fine print in this rule. Usually you have to take the exact same course; this can be a bummer if the course is offered only every two years. Also, most colleges allow you only one or two chances at this. So don't expect to keep pulling the same trick.

EXTRA POINTER. At some schools the grade-forgiveness program may have a cap on how much forgiveness you get: you might get a maximum of a C replacement grade or the average of the grades. Look before you leap.

6. **The dispute.** If you're up-to-date in the class work but not happy with your grade, you might consider "inquiring about"— or, in street language, disputing—your grade. Normally, this has to be conducted with the professor of the class: going to a higher-up (such as the department chair or the dean) rarely works and really angers your professor like nothing else. (See "10 Surefire Ways to Piss Off Your Professor" on p. 220 for

more on this.) You can, however, go over the head of your TA to the professor, because TAs are low enough on the food chain for you to get away with this, and who cares if they get pissed off, anyway?

Grade disputes work best in cases of computational errors, or when a grader has accidentally not read parts of an exam or a paper, or—sometimes—when the comments show that the reader hasn't understood what you meant. Your chances of success are nil, however, when you argue for a better grade simply because you "tried hard" or "just aren't a B student." Whatever your tack, go in person and be polite and respectful, but make your case firmly and straightforwardly. It's a good idea also to offer to leave your work with the professor for his or her review.

5-STAR TIP. In an effort to discourage exactly the activity you're engaged in, some professors reserve the right to lower (as well as raise) grades upon review. You may want to ask—discreetly and delicately—whether your prof does this.

7. **The request.** If your professor is a real softie, he or she may give you a chance to improve your situation through extra-credit work, exempting you from a piece of work, letting you redo a paper or test, allowing you to count some piece of work twice, or giving you some other sort of bonus. Here it really helps to be unbelievably nice and throw yourself on the mercy of your instructor.

One thing you never want to try is

The cheat. Cheating is disgusting, filthy, and immoral. Besides, you're only cheating yourself. And what's more, you could get caught. If you think you're in a hole now, you might find yourself in the Grand Canyon if you get caught cheating. Spare yourself the grief.

10 Signs You're in Real Trouble at College

Some college students are in serious trouble but don't even recognize it. They think that nothing is really wrong, that everyone else is in the same boat, or that college is just supposed to be hard. Other students are just not sure: *Am I doing bad or* really *bad*? they wonder. *Should I take some bold action or just wait it out, hoping it'll get better?* To help you decide whether you're in serious difficulty or just caught up in the ordinary ebb and flow of college, here are 10 signs that you're in real trouble at college. If you exhibit any of these signs, it's time to do some major reassessment—and make some big changes:

1. **Your grade point is below C or you're getting D's in some of your courses.** Don't kid yourself: C is a bad grade, and D is even worse. A lot of students in college are getting A's and B's (at many schools the average GPA is between B and B+). So if your quizzes and tests are coming back C's and D's, be aware that you are learning very little (and in some cases, virtually nothing) in the courses you're taking. As you move into more upper-level courses, you're likely to find yourself unable to muster even C's and D's and instead will be ending up with F's.

2. **You're constantly asking for (and even getting) extensions and incompletes.** Extensions and incompletes are supposed to be the exception, for very special circumstances, not the rule. If you find yourself depending on them as a regular educational crutch—one day the reading took longer than you were expecting, another time you couldn't get enough pages written, a third time you were too busy with your four other courses to bother with this one—you're demonstrating that you aren't able to keep up with the pace of college.

3. **You can't follow what the professor says in lecture—ever.** Most students have moments when they can't understand a point the professor makes in lecture (see "10 Things to Do When You Can't Keep Up with the Lecture" on p. 228 for things to do in this case). But if all of your lectures are incomprehensible to you, every time, then consider yourself to be in way over your head.

4. **You're spending every waking moment of the day doing the reading or the homework problems.** Professors are well aware of the time constraints placed on students taking five courses a semester and often working part- or even full-time, as well as participating in extracurricular activities. So the assignments are geared to be done in a manageable period of time: somewhere between one and three hours per class. But if you're missing by a mile—always—you probably are lacking the basic skills expected for the course or are using wholly wrong study strategies (see "The How *Not* to Study Guide" on p. 104 for some of these strategies).

5. **You're living off your credit cards.** If you can't afford your dinners or textbooks without relying on credit, then you are stretched too thin financially. Going to college is a big commitment of both time and money, and trying to get an education at the edge of bankruptcy is likely to put more pressure on you than the average person can manage.

6. **You can't get through the basic requirements.** Some students find themselves unable to pass even the lower-division requirements in math, English composition, and history—and in some cases the developmental courses in math and English required before getting to these requirements. Being unable to pass these or needing multiple attempts to pass them is a sign that you aren't academically ready for college.

7. **You're on the cell phone with your parents five times a day.** Hand-holding and support are one thing, total dependence (or codependence) another. If you're unable to make any break

from your parents, you might not be ready for the independent living—and thinking—that go with college.

8. **You can't get through the day without self-medication.** We're not talking about prescription medications you might need for a medical problem or chronic condition, but meds, drugs, or alcohol that you use for recreation or for altering (or balancing) your moods. Many students indulge in some partying at college, but once you get into heavy substance abuse, it's impossible to maintain the discipline and mental focus needed for success at college.

9. **You spend every waking moment on some medium.** It's perfectly fine to interact on Facebook for a bit each day. But when you're texting, tweeting, and tagging without stop—you can't live for fifteen minutes without a device—you leave yourself no time to study (or to do much of anything else). If you find yourself unable to get through a day without your computer or cell, consider yourself to have a media addiction that needs to be broken.

10. **You feel overwhelmed—all of the time.** It's normal to feel pretty stressed out at the beginning of each semester, and of course at midterm and finals times. But if you find yourself struggling every week of the semester—waking up each day hating where you are—something is wrong. Really wrong.

What, Then, to Do?
The 7-Step Approach

So maybe you've recognized these symptoms in yourself or in someone you know and love. But what should you do? Here's our 7-step plan:

1. **Pinpoint the problem.** It's easy to feel overwhelmed when you're hit with the perfect storm. Everything's screwed up: your schoolwork, your health, your relationships, your grades. But usually there's one problem that's more serious than the others, and that's spilling over into the others and making them worse. Find the single most acute problem—the one that, if you could change just one, you'd change *it*—and begin to work on it. If the problem you select is at the root of the others, you may be able to solve a number of issues in one fell swoop.

2. **Figure out whether it's solvable.** Not every problem can be solved. And not every problem can be solved in the short term. If you're in serious grade difficulty, you're not going to be able to dig yourself out in one semester. If you're chronically depressed, a few visits to a counselor are not going to make you happy. If you're in major debt, a part-time job will not take care of your whole problem. Still, it's worth making a plan and getting started—because you'll start to feel better as you take a positive step, and even a little progress toward solving a problem is progress.

3. **Make use of campus resources.** Colleges invest a tremendous amount of money in providing academic, financial, psychological, and clinical services to their students. And because colleges often attract the best minds, the professors, advisers, counselors, and clinicians who provide these services

are often very gifted individuals. Check out the college website, your adviser, or a professional whom you feel you can trust for direction. And if you're at your wit's end and can't bear negotiating the university bureaucracy, call the dean of students and ask for advice: he or she will know what to do. For peer-to-peer counseling, try your dorm counselor or resident adviser.

FLASH! If you're using your health insurance to pay for psychological (or in some cases, behavioral) counseling, you'll be happy to know that, due to the Mental Health Parity and Addiction Equity Act, many insurance companies now provide the same coverage for mental illness and substance abuse as they do for physical illness. Inquire, if this is relevant to your situation.

---

4. **Talk to a confidant(e).** If you're ashamed of your problem—or don't want the university to know about it—find a trusted friend, parent, minister, doctor, or lawyer outside the university and talk to him or her. Most professionals are bound by confidentiality laws (if in doubt, ask) and can either offer help themselves or point you to community resources that will work with you to help solve your problem. And simply having someone to talk to about what's bothering you may provide some immediate relief.

5. **Enlist a professional.** Certain problems are more serious. Significant legal difficulty, serious health problems, various addictions, or overwhelming debt—these are problems that require extended and professional treatment. In some cases, you will not be able to solve the problem while remaining a full-time student (or sometimes a student at all). Colleges know about these sorts of problems and are sympathetic (after all, they've made an investment in you). So once you've figured out a plan of treatment, go to your college—often the dean of

students is the right contact point—and request a *leave of absence*. You may be surprised to hear they'll hold your place and in many cases keep your financial aid, too. Much better than to stay enrolled and mess up.

6. **Accept the realities (change is difficult).** If things aren't going well for you, accept the fact. Sometimes you've made mistakes that put you in the position you are in, and sometimes things go badly through no fault of your own. But in many cases change is possible, though difficult. Some problems are habitual—they've been reinforced many times by ill-advised behaviors—while some problems arise swiftly and suddenly. In either case, you should make peace with your situation and realize that the problem won't be solved in a day.

7. **Decide what to do.** Your best shot is to take decisive action. Identify the problem, get help, devise a few alternative remedies, pick one—then do it. You may not be picking the perfect solution—who can, when the situation seems dire? But you will have done something that will, to one degree or another, help you with your problem. Sure beats sitting on your hands and doing nothing.

8

THE SECOND HALF

As you make your move into the junior and senior years of college, you'll face an increasingly broad array of choices. Many of these center around what to do in your major and what you plan to do after college. Some more far-sighted, goal-oriented students may have already been thinking about their postcollege life from the very first day they walked onto campus. Others have the "drink no wine before its time" mentality: they face finalizing their choice of majors, and ultimately the choice of career, only when they absolutely, positively, without a doubt, must.

But whichever type you are, the second half of college can be a wonderfully exciting time: a time to decide who you really are and what you want to devote (at least the next part of) your life to. Part of the reason it's so exciting is that the stakes are high. When you invest a lot of time and money in pursuing a college degree, you want to be sure what happens at the other end—the real-world end—is a fitting culmination to all you've put in.

In this chapter you'll learn:

▶ 10 Must-Do's at the Halfway Point of College

▶ 13 Skills You'll Need for a Career—and How to Get Them at College

▶ 10 Strategies for Women Considering a Career in STEM Fields

► Transfer Tips—from Community College to Four-Year College

► Summer School Pros and Cons

► Top 10 Myths about Study Abroad

► Top 9 Tips for Taking Out Student Loans

► 10 Tips for the Senior Thesis

10 Must-Do's at the Halfway Point of College

So you've aced the first two years of college—or at least gotten through them. Now you have only two (or three or four) years to go. But you're about to make a leap: from the lower-class years, in which you've been occupied largely with the lower-division (or introductory) program—to the upperclass years, in which you'll be working in a much more focused way on your major and on upper-division (or more advanced) courses. Ready to cross the threshold? You'll *burst* over it if you follow our 10 best tips to get yourself ready for the second half of college:

1. **Assess where you are.** At critical junctures, it's always good to take a look backward before planning for what comes next. So consider for a moment how your first couple of years of college turned out. Which classes went well and which were real losers? Which professors did you like and which were, well, less distinguished? What things did you do that advanced your intellectual and personal goals, and which activities were complete wastes of time? What could you have done differently—or better—and how might you change your ways? Having a detailed—and honest—view of your successes and, perhaps, failures in the past can usher in real change for the years to come.

2. **Reevaluate your major.** If you're like most students, you declared your major when you entered college (rather than enduring the shame of being the only one you knew to remain "undeclared"). But by now you've had a chance to take at least a few higher-than-introductory courses, so you know what the work in the major is really like. Now would be a good time to ask yourself: "Am I really happy with this major, or am I just

slogging my way through the work?" "Am I doing at least reasonably well, or am I struggling to get a low B in every course?" "Am I looking forward to taking the six or seven remaining courses in this major, or is each just another hurdle to be gotten over?" If your answers show that you're not really all that gung-ho about your major, you should consider switching to another. Better sooner than later: why add two more years onto your time to degree?

3. **Develop a focus.** People who get the most out of college and develop the best trajectory out of college are those whose college programs are more than just a motley assortment of required courses and courses in their majors. Instead, they make their degree more than the sum of the parts by developing a specific focus to their studies. For example, they don't just study business, they focus on the use of radio-frequency identification (RFID) in inventory management; they study not just industrial engineering, but carbon nanotubed-based computers; not just history, but American diplomatic history of the second half of the twentieth century; not just astronomy, but exoplanets and their importance. Narrowing your research interests within a specific field will not only establish your distinct intellectual personality, it will also help you get internships and guide your study abroad; it will ease your finding a topic for a senior thesis (if your school has those); and it will lay the foundation for a convincing graduate school application or a powerful job search.

4. **Get your mind around the requirements.** Many students have only a vague idea of what courses and other activities are required to complete the major and the degree—and when they are offered. Scour your college or department's website—as well as any departmental brochure, booklets, or handouts—to find out all there is to know about the structure of the major and the advanced level requirements. And check with your adviser or the college website to see what courses are left in your degree plan. The sooner you know exactly what's left to do, the better you can plan to actually do it.

5. **Get a departmental adviser.** Whether you have been getting advised in the general college advising center or doing it yourself online, now is the time to start working closely with the specific departmental adviser. The departmental adviser is much more likely than the general advisers to be able to direct you toward courses that are best suited for your interests and goals, and he or she has the knowledge to keep you away from classes and professors that you'd best avoid (and that everyone else should probably avoid, if the truth be known).

6. **Establish a relationship with a professor.** Once you've established a specific focus within the major, it'd be good to find a professor who is a specialist in your area of interest and would be willing to consult with you on your work. Sometimes, more learning goes on out of class, on a one-to-one basis, than in class, on a one-to-five-hundred basis. Moreover, no matter what your plans are for beyond college, you're going to need established professors—not lowly TAs or just-out-of-grad-school starting professors—to write letters of recommendation to employers, graduate schools, or professional schools. Start scouting out the choices right away, and take steps to get these people enthusiastic about your work. (For some tips on seeking out the professor and getting him or her to write, see "The 14 Secrets of Going to See the Professor" on p. 212 and "Top 10 Tips for Getting Bang-Up Recommendations" on p. 289.)

7. **Participate in departmental events.** Most departments offer many activities designed to supplement their courses and provide further enrichment for their majors. The bulletin boards—electronic and physical—are likely to be filled with announcements of lectures, colloquia, field trips, and clubs. And some departments even have weekly e-blasts of the week's activities, which you should be sure to sign up to get. Getting involved in these extras not only will add to your store of knowledge, but also will get you better connected with the department and its faculty. You'll enjoy your courses a lot more if you take them not as a bummed-out student but as part of a vibrant intellectual community.

8. **Leverage your summers.** At this point you should really try to make your summers more than just earning bucks working retail. Find activities that will build skills and experience for your post-college life. Consider things such as internships, study abroad, volunteer work (in areas related to your major), or taking courses at another institution that aren't offered at yours. (See "Top 10 Myths about Study Abroad" on p. 268 and "Summer School Pros and Cons" on p. 264 for more details.)

9. **Improve your skills.** Success in a particular field often requires developing a cluster of skills or a competence in a contiguous or neighboring area. Make sure that you don't neglect abilities in areas that might not be strictly required by your college. For example, you might have a better shot at that bang-up job at Procter & Gamble if you know Mandarin as well as marketing, or at Caltrans if you know transportation engineering in addition to civil engineering, or at Acxiom if you know computer programming in addition to data analysis. Have a look at your coveted job- or grad-school website and imagine what you could do to get a leg up on your future competition.

5-STAR TIP. If you don't know what you need, find someone at the company that you have your eyes on or the graduate school you'd give your left arm to get into, and ask what things you can do to bolster your skills or improve your knowledge. Amazingly, these contacts will usually tell you.

10. **Turn it on.** However much you might have slacked off or partied in your first years at college, now is the time to get serious. The final years of college are what really set you up for your life after college. Putting the effort in now is sure to pay off.

13 Skills You'll Need for a Career—and How to Get Them at College

In the twenty-first-century economy, students are more worried than ever about what kind of career awaits them. The best way to increase the odds that the job you'll get won't involve waiting tables or flipping burgers is to get the career skills you need while you're still in college. But what are those? Here is a baker's dozen of the most critical job skills that every college student should try to get:

1. **Writing clearly and forcefully.** Students often don't recognize how important writing skills are in many professions. Many students, without a trace of shame, proclaim "I can't write" and consistently avoid courses that require papers. But the "I can't write" excuse won't cut it later on, when you have to write a strategic plan for your business, draft briefs for your legal case, or pitch your advertising plan in a report to the client. Actively seek out college courses that give you lots of opportunities to write. And use the feedback you get on each writing assignment to impel you to improve on the next.

2. **Systematizing and organizing data.** Many jobs require employees to do quite a bit of number crunching and to create numerous spreadsheets and tables. Be sure you take courses that teach you the skills to do this kind of work—math, statistics, and the like. Even students in liberal arts majors should come out of college able to handle a reasonable range of quantitative tasks once they hit the real world.

3. **Doing research.** In this internet age no one seems to be actually reading books in a library much. But there's more information out there, so being able to conduct research is even more important than before. Courses that include research assignments—usually upper-level classes in the

humanities and social sciences—will give you experience with a number of research tools, many of them electronic, that you can use when you come up against research assignments at work. (See our "14 Techniques for Doing Research Like a Professor" on p. 190 for more on e-research.)

4. **Presenting material orally.** In many jobs you'll spend more time than you can possibly imagine attending meetings or giving presentations. Needless to say, when your boss asks you to comment at a meeting or give a presentation, it's not so great to plead shyness or fear of public speaking (as many college students routinely do when asked to present material in class). College offers you many possibilities for training in public speaking. Yes, there's the speech or communications class or going out for the debate team, but smaller classes and seminars often require presentations too (see our "15 Strategies for Painless Presentations" on p. 118 for some tips).

EXTRA POINTER. Make sure you become proficient in some kind of presentation software, such as PowerPoint, and learn to use all its features, including video and multimedia.

---

5. **Taking notes.** Maybe you like to sit back in lecture and enjoy the passing show without bothering to take down a single note. Or maybe you write only from time to time as you focus in on what the prof is saying. Not a good idea for college. And even less of a good idea someday when your boss asks you to remind him or her in detail of what plans for the big campaign were brainstormed in last week's three-day retreat. Every college class gives you an opportunity to become an ace note taker, so don't blow the chance. (See "10 Secrets of Taking Excellent Lecture Notes" on p. 109 for some pointers.)

6. **Reading carefully.** When you get that high-paying job as a financial analyst, you'll have to interpret every word of the minutes of the Federal Reserve Board for clues about what changes they're planning to make to the discount rate. Almost

every college course has assigned readings, which you can use to polish your skills at careful reading and interpretation of difficult texts. (See "15 Ways to Read Like a Pro" on p. 113 for our best tips.)

7. **Basic computing.** Most jobs today require even entry-level employees to know their way around many software programs. And college courses allow many opportunities to become proficient not only in Microsoft Word, but also (depending on the course) in Excel, InDesign, Photoshop, Final Cut Pro, and many other field-specific programs. Take advantage of the free training.

5-STAR TIP. It's a good idea to fully master a software program when given the chance, rather than just learn enough to do the assigned project.

---

8. **Making deadlines.** At college, some professors are softies who will offer extensions, makeups, and incompletes for a wide variety of justified (and often unjustified) reasons. But one of the most common shocks experienced by students once they hit the real world is that most clients and bosses expect them to actually meet their deadlines—no matter what unavoidable (and avoidable) events came up in the meantime. Get in the habit of taking your college deadlines seriously and meeting them without exception.

9. **Working on a team.** Teamwork is often a key factor in job success. What worker is a one-man (or -woman) band? Group projects at college and work with study groups can give you valuable experience in working in a common effort with other human beings, even ones you may not like. Doing an internship or participating in a research project with your professors can also give you ways to practice working well with others.

10. **Getting along with a boss.** In college, the professor (or TA) is your boss. Learn to get along with your prof, whether what he

or she is saying is what you'd like to hear or not. Think of each office-hour meeting, each Skype session, or each informal encounter after class as an occasion for practicing your interpersonal skills with a higher-up. Collegiality—that is, getting along with others—is one of the key business skills.

11. **Multitasking and time management.** A college load of four or five courses, each with different sorts of assignments and schedules, is the perfect training ground for developing your skills at doing lots of things at once and balancing the time needed for each. If you hone your abilities for handling the end of the semester—you know, that time when you need to turn in three papers and take five finals—you'll be in a great position to handle the crunch season at work.

12. **Seeing a big project through to its end.** You'll be in a better position to easily handle jobs that involve large, complex, long-term projects if you've worked on and completed a major term paper, a junior or senior thesis, or a protracted science experiment while you're at college. Sustaining interest and motivation over the long haul is a special skill that lots of students have trouble with. Now's a good time to know thy enemy—at least as regards big projects—and learn how to conquer it.

13. **Creative thinking.** You may not know it, but what really characterizes A-level work at college—and distinguishes it from B-level work—is some creative spark that allows select students to see the issue under consideration in a deeper and more insightful way (for more on this topic, see our "How to Turn a B into an A" on p. 189). You can develop your creative skills in almost any course—not just courses in the arts or creative writing (which are also fine ways to stimulate your creativity). Try to always go beyond the most obvious points, striving for deeper levels of meaning and more imaginative ways of expressing them. Creativity shines through at any job interview, and beyond, once you get your once-in-a-lifetime job.

10 Strategies for Women Considering a Career in STEM Fields

There is growing concern at American colleges about why women get a disproportionately low percentage of STEM (science, technology, engineering, or math) degrees and come to hold less than a quarter of STEM jobs after college. Though more than half of undergraduates are women, according to a 2009 study, 138,000 STEM bachelor's degrees went to men whereas only 88,000 were earned by women; and, according to the 2009 census, although 48 percent of the workforce is made up of women, only 24 percent of the STEM jobs go to women.

A recent—and quite interesting—meta-study, sponsored by the National Science Foundation and the American Association of University Women, identified eight factors that contribute to the disparity between the numbers of female and male college students electing the sciences:

- ▶ Accepted beliefs about intelligence

- ▶ Stereotypes

- ▶ Students' self-assessments

- ▶ Spatial skills

- ▶ The college student experience

- ▶ University and college faculty

- ▶ Implicit bias

- ▶ Workplace bias

We were interested in finding out what advice could be offered to women in male-dominated STEM fields. So we invited Sara Seager, professor of planetary science and of physics at MIT, to share her very best tips. Here's what she recommends:

1. **Join a support group of peers.** It will be reassuring to have a specific group of peers to meet with. Such "women in physics" or "women in engineering" groups not only provide a group of people in a very similar situation to yours, but have also organized practical connections such as resources and advice. And consider attending one of the growing number of conferences for undergraduate women in different STEM disciplines.

2. **Find a mentor.** A mentor is someone who can provide you with guidance and advice. Many colleges have formal mentoring programs to connect mentors and mentees; if yours doesn't, seek out a mentor on your own. The mentor need not be a faculty member; a graduate student, a senior undergraduate, or even a peer with good insight are all suitable possibilities.

3. **Get involved in a research project.** Listening in classes and completing homework is very different from any kind of work done in an actual scientific or engineering career. To learn whether or not a science, technology, or engineering career is really for you, it is important to try the research environment. Seek opportunities during term or in the summer, at colleges with professors, or with summer internships in industry.

4. **Organize your time.** College can be overwhelming in the rate of new material you are expected to learn as well as all of the possibilities for extracurricular activities. Especially in science, math, and engineering fields, with their heavy course loads and challenging problem sets, time management is a must. Get a calendar and use it. Plan ahead for big due dates such as term papers or exams. Clear blocks of time each day for homework and studying. With so many new opportunities in college, it's tempting to overcommit, but it's better to do a few things very well than to struggle with an unrealistic schedule. (See "Top 10 Time-Management Tips" on p. 96 for some ideas.)

5. **Don't be afraid to be assertive.** Ask questions in class. If you're not understanding material from class or homework assignments, visit your professor or teaching assistant during office hours. It's their job to help you, so take advantage of it. Many departments also have tutoring programs, peer or otherwise, that no one should feel embarrassed to take advantage of. Beyond classes, ask specific professors or other individuals about internships, mentorships, or other career-related opportunities, even if formal ones do not already exist.

6. **Have confidence.** A common stumbling block for women college students is lack of confidence. Remember that you were accepted to your college because of your qualifications and accomplishments, and you belong there. It may sometimes appear that some other students are excelling effortlessly. Whether or not this is the case, it should not interfere with your reaching your goals at college: to become educated and train for a career.

7. **Look out for yourself.** Another pitfall for women is the tendency to help others before helping themselves. In a science career, where individual accomplishments are used as the main basis for judgment, this is detrimental. Regardless of whether the research environment is collaborative or competitive, make sure your own interests are being met.

8. **Avoid taking comments personally.** Inevitably, rude or sexist remarks from others will occasionally happen, even though they are not supposed to. The worst ones attack women's abilities in science, engineering, or math. These remarks are unfounded, so don't take them personally. Women students can often fall into the trap of taking even healthy criticism and scientific debate personally. Don't do this; it will hinder your progress.

9. **Strategize for the future.** When approaching the senior years of college, always look a step ahead. Try to identify internships, graduate school, or other interesting options well in advance. Find out what it takes to be admitted to these programs, and

then put in the effort needed. For example, your college's alumni database could be useful for finding contacts who are willing to help you identify what it takes to be admitted or hired.

10. **Enjoy yourself.** The secret to a successful career in science, technology, engineering, or math is to find something you both *like* doing and are *good* at. Take your time in college to explore and find what suits you.

FLASH! For an interesting recent article from *Inside Higher Ed*, "Attracting Women to STEM," go to WWW.INSIDEHIGHERED.COM /NEWS/2010/03/22/STEM. For the NSF/AAUW meta-study, go to WWW.AAUW.ORG/RESEARCH/WHY-SO-FEW/.

And for the very interesting U.S. Government Chamber of Commerce report on women in STEM fields, go to WWW .ESA.DOC.GOV/SITES/DEFAULT/FILES/REPORTS/DOCUMENTS /WOMENINSTEMAGAPTOINNOVATION8311.PDF.

Transfer Tips—from Community College to Four-Year College

Community colleges are hot—even among those students who go on to get a bachelor's degree at a four-year college. The Regents of the University of California report that 30 percent of UC graduates attended a community college before transferring to the UC. And among all those earning a bachelor's degree in Virginia, a third began at, or supplemented their education with, classes from a Virginia community college. Here are 10 tips for making the leap from community college to the big U from Glenn DuBois, chancellor of Virginia Community Colleges:

1. **Complete your associate's degree.** National research shows that community college students who finish their degree program go on to complete their baccalaureate at a much higher rate than those who transfer with just a grab bag of credits.

2. **Shop around.** Examine all of the options available to you as a transfer student. Consider both public and private four-year institutions to decide which will be the best fit for you. The four-year institution that you had your heart set on in high school may not ultimately be the best choice for the subject you want to pursue.

3. **Plan ahead.** The earlier you begin to prepare for transfer, the better. Visit your top choices, collect transfer materials, and find out whether there are any transfer agreements between where you are and where you want to go. The more information you have, the easier it will be to make a decision.

4. **Know which courses actually transfer.** Make sure you are picking courses that are transferable to colleges and

universities. There are websites, tools, and advisers at both community colleges and universities to help you choose wisely.

---

5 **5-STAR TIP.** Many states have "articulation agreements"—negotiated documents that make clear what's needed to transfer from one higher education institution to another. The benefit to you as a student is that the agreement takes the guesswork out of the process by telling you in black and white what classes you need to take and what grades you need to make to avoid losing hard-earned credits when you transfer. Many states have websites with detailed information about articulation agreements and the process of transferring. Some of the best are:

Virginia: WWW.VAWIZARD.ORG

Arizona: WWW.AZTRANSFER.COM/CCSTUDENT

Texas: WWW.TCCNS.ORG

Illinois: WWW.ITRANSFER.ORG

California: WWW.CPEC.CA.GOV/ONLINEDATA/TRANSFERPATHWAY.ASP

---

5. **Don't be shy.** Meet regularly with advisers at the community college. Keep your adviser informed of your transfer plans, and as transfer approaches, set a time to meet with an adviser at your *target* institution. If you try to navigate this process without the help of advisers, you may not be able to maximize your community college courses.

6. **Choose a major.** Pick your major early, and seek advice about the best courses to take to meet requirements. By choosing your major early, you can take the prerequisites that you need for that program at the university. Well-planned course taking will help you finish your transfer program more efficiently, saving you time and money in the long run.

7. **Get admitted.** Make sure you apply to both the institution and the program you want to attend at that institution. If you get

admitted to the university, often that does not mean you are admitted to the specific program you want to study, such as engineering or nursing. The deadlines for the university admissions materials and the program admissions materials may be different. Do your research!

8. **Make them show you the money.** Be sure to fill out the Free Application for Student Aid (FAFSA) at WWW.FAFSA.ED.GOV. Call the university admissions office to see whether they have scholarships set aside for transfer students—many institutions do. Make sure you meet all of the deadlines for financial aid. Otherwise you may miss out on assistance that is available to you.

9. **Attend orientation.** You may think you do not need this because you already are a college student. But navigating the university is different. Take advantage of the opportunities the university has created for transfer students. These orientations will help ease the transfer process.

10. **Stay focused.** This one is easy to forget. Whether it's your associate's or bachelor's degree, finishing on time is not easy. But it can be done if you are focused and work hard. Keep your goal in mind, even when you're working in your hardest class, which you don't much like. It will all pay off.

Summer School Pros and Cons

Many upper-division students think about taking courses in summer school to fill out their major or required cognates. But is this such a hot idea? To help you size it all up, here are some advantages and disadvantages of extending your college experience into the dog days of summer. First, the pros:

Pro #1. You can get out of college sooner. With the average time to degree running at five to six years for a BA (and over three years for an associate's degree), you can trim some years off if you take courses over the summer. And if you have just a course or two left for graduation, it could be cheaper to "buy" it in summer session than to register—and pay—for a whole other semester.

Pro #2. The courses are actually "open." Because enrollment in summer school is significantly lower than during the regular school year, there are likely to be spaces in classes that normally have ginormous waiting lists. And you can often get times you like—in the morning, for instance, rather than at 5 in the evening.

Pro #3. You might be able to get courses not offered during the year. Sometimes professors take the opportunity to teach courses during summer session that they aren't able to offer during the year because of other teaching obligations. Or sometimes there's fresh blood in the instructor pool—for example, visiting professors from other schools who provide offerings not available during the year. These classes can be real finds, especially if you're at a small school with relatively limited course offerings.

Pro #4. The classes may be smaller. It's not at all uncommon to see classes that usually have 500 students being offered over the summer with only 25 students. Avoiding the monster classes at your mega-U is a real plus. You could actually be able to see and maybe even get to know your prof. Now that'd be a first.

Pro #5. You might actually get a time you want. As opposed to the regular semester, when you're stuck with a course at 8:10 a.m. or 4:45 p.m., you might be able to get a 10 a.m. or 1 p.m. Wouldn't that be something?

Pro #6. The classes have a more relaxed atmosphere. Everyone tends to loosen up a little during the summer, even professors. Some might even shed their tweed jackets or pencil skirts and show up in shorts. Whether these are fashion *faux pas* or not, what's not to like about a more laid-back instructor?

Pro #7. You'll get a more intensive study of a subject. Summer school often runs for fewer than half the number of weeks of the regular semester, with classes meeting several hours every day. As a result, you get a rare chance to truly concentrate on the subject you're studying. Which is great if you're really interested in the topic of the course.

Pro #8. You can complete a prerequisite for a course you want to take in the fall. Summer can be a great time to knock off those pesky prereqs so you can finally take a course you need for your major or are just really excited about. Preplanning pays off.

Pro #9. You can hook up with a friend taking summer school. Sometimes you hear that a buddy—romantic or otherwise—is planning to sign up for courses in just the fields you want to study. What better opportunity to strut your stuff than sitting next to your pal five days a week?

Sound great? Ready to trade in your summer in Bimini for the classrooms of University Hall? Now have a look at the cons:

Con #1. It's *too* intensive. Summer school classes are very compressed: they almost always meet an hour or two a day, five days a week. For some people, having both class and homework every day, as well as tests and papers due at much more frequent intervals than usual, is more than they can bear.

Con #2. You might not get the regular faculty. Many faculty members, especially the well-paid ones, don't want to be bothered with summer school teaching. So it's quite possible that there are folks teaching summer school who aren't on the regular staff—and who may not be as qualified as the regular staff (think: TAs, faculty from other schools in the city, unemployed academics).

Con #3. The class may not really cover all the material. Yes, technically a summer school class is supposed to do the same stuff that the regular-semester courses does, but many faculty find it difficult to actually accomplish this. Cramming 15 weeks' worth of material into just 6 weeks requires very careful planning, and, hey, it's hard to cram effectively when it's 100 degrees outside.

Con #4. Summer school costs extra. You've already paid thousands and thousands of dollars for fall and spring (and, at many schools, you can take as many courses as you like then). So why pay twice?

FLASH! The Student Aid and Fiscal Responsibility ACT (SAFRA) of 2010 made important changes to whether Pell grants can be gotten for summer school (in short, it depends on whether you've maxed out your entitlement during the regular year). Read about the current state of affairs at HTTP://PELLGRANTELIGIBILITY.NET/, an excellent site to consult periodically.

Con #5. There's a smaller selection of courses. Summer school classes tend to be weighted toward required courses that can net enough tuition-paying students to make it worthwhile to offer. So they may not offer exactly what you want. (Gotta love that capitalistic spirit.)

Con #6. It's too darned hot to learn. Who wants to be inside some un-air-conditioned classroom when it's so hot and humid that the only sane place to be is at the beach?

EXTRA POINTER. If you are going to take a summer school class, get the room number off the schedule of classes, and then go to the room and see whether it really is air-conditioned. You can't be too careful.

Con #7. You deserve a break today. After two long semesters—or (gasp!) three quarters, for some lucky folks—you may be much in need of some R&R. In this case, you may want to give summer school a pass. Don't worry; no one will hold it against you. And you'll still finish in the four—or five or six or seven—years you had planned.

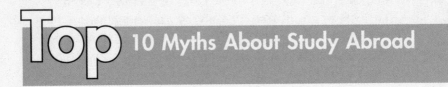

Top 10 Myths About Study Abroad

Thinking you might want to study abroad? For some, it'll prove to be one of the most rewarding, life-enhancing experiences of their college careers. For others—well, enjoy the fish and chips. Here are the 10 most common misconceptions about study abroad from Sara Dumont, director of Study Abroad, American University. Get over these and you're guaranteed a bon voyage:

1. **"With the state of the world today, it's just too dangerous."** It's always wise to keep abreast of world events and to avoid study in a region that is currently at war or has a high level of civil unrest. But not surprisingly, study abroad programs usually aren't offered in those regions. Your school's study abroad adviser will be able to help you assess the relative risks of various regions.

 5-STAR TIP. Check online resources especially designed for students studying abroad, such as WWW.GLOBALED.US/SAFETI.

2. **"I can't afford to go."** For most students, affording a semester, a term, or even a year studying abroad is perfectly doable. If you will earn credit toward your degree for your experience abroad and you receive federal financial aid, then that aid can be applied to your study abroad costs. In addition, many colleges allow their own institutional aid and scholarships to travel with the student.

EXTRA POINTER. Be wary of those who try to talk you into studying on a summer or January break, claiming that short programs cost less than semester-length programs. Although the program price may be lower, financial aid is rarely available for study outside the regular semesters.

3. **"All programs are alike, so I just need to pick my favorite country."** There are many different types of study abroad programs designed to meet the wants and needs of all kinds of students. Ask yourself, *Will I study with foreign students or other Americans? Will I have foreign professors or American ones? Will I live in a dorm, in an apartment, or with a family?* Let your study abroad office help narrow your choices, or talk to a student from your college who has already gone on the program.

 5-STAR TIP. Some universities abroad have special institutes or divisions for students coming from other countries (like the United States). This isn't necessarily bad, but you should find out whether you'll be taking the regular courses with the regular faculty or special (sometimes less qualified) teachers the school has instead hired to teach the "imports" (namely, you).

4. **"I don't speak a foreign language, so I can't study abroad."** Don't forget that English is the native language—or at least one of the commonly spoken languages—of England, Scotland, Wales, Ireland, Australia, New Zealand, parts of India, and a host of countries in Africa. And many European and Middle Eastern countries—especially the Netherlands, Scandinavia, Israel, and Jordan—are now offering a range of courses in English, too. But even if you pick a non-English-speaking country, you'll find many universities offering hybrid programs: some of your courses will be in the native language (here you'll attend lectures, take notes, and take the tests in the language of the country), and others will be in good old English.

5. **"I'm not in humanities or social sciences, so I can't get the courses to count for my major."** Although students majoring in subjects like history, political science, and languages tend to have the widest range of courses and programs available,

students in any major can study abroad and stay on track for graduation (provided they choose programs and plan carefully). Consult the university website, catalogue, or study abroad office to see what's offered in the sciences, mathematics, or whatever your major might be.

6. **"It's too late for me to study abroad."** Don't worry if it's late in the fall semester and you haven't done any planning to study abroad for the spring or summer. Normally, you apply for study abroad midway through the semester in advance of the one you want to be away in. And even if you miss the application deadline, check with your study abroad adviser, because many programs will still have space and can accept late applicants.

EXTRA POINTER. Sophomores and juniors aren't the only ones who study abroad—seniors do it, too. Just keep in mind the need to plan, if you need specific courses. And be aware that some countries require students to get visas, so if that process takes a significant amount of time, you won't be able to go to some countries if you are a late applicant.

7. **"I'd like to study abroad so I can become completely fluent in the language."** Get real. Learning a language to the point of fluency is a challenging and lengthy process for most people, and even a year of immersion usually isn't enough to get there. Be realistic about your goals—if you aren't, you will become frustrated and not make the most of your experience.

8. **"I'm going to make lots of local friends and travel as much as I can."** These two expectations are incompatible. If you spend all your free time traveling and away from the place where you're studying, you won't have the needed time in your new temporary home to make new friends. If traveling is what you think is most important, then realize you may end up traveling mostly or exclusively with other Americans.

9. **"I'm paying the same fees as I do at my home university, so I should get the same level of services, extracurricular opportunities, and technology."** NOT! You're in a different country; things will be different. Savor the culture you're visiting—and its distinctive character.

10. **"I'm not going abroad to sit in a classroom or a library."** Um—yes, you are. This is *study* abroad, after all. You'll be getting academic credit toward your degree, so guess what? You'll be expected to do the work—reading, writing papers, showing up for tutorials, and participating in classes. Having experiences (the "fun" part) is great, but collecting experiences without the intellectual underpinnings (that is, without the "study" part) can be very superficial, and study abroad is meant to be profound. At least in the best case.

Top 9 Tips for Taking Out Student Loans

Many students think, wrongly, that once they're in college the financial aid game is over: you've gotten whatever money you're going to get, and that's the end of the story. But it turns out that money can be had every year: either your grant needs to be renewed or you can probe for new sources of money. So we asked our friends Isaac Bowers and Radhika Singh Miller, program managers of Educational Debt Relief and Outreach, at Equal Justice Works, to offer their best tips for getting you the loot. Here's what they had to say:

1. **Fill out your FAFSA—every year.** The Free Application for Federal Student Aid (FAFSA), available online at WWW.FAFSA.ED.GOV, is required to apply for federal student aid in the form of grants and loans. In addition, many states and institutions also use information from the FAFSA to determine eligibility for their different grant and loan programs. Don't make the mistake of thinking filling out the FAFSA is not worth your time—the vast majority of students qualify for some form of aid.

2. **Look for free money.** Scholarships and grants provide you with money to pay for college that you don't have to pay back. That's a great deal. Before you take out loans (which you *do* have to pay back—with interest), see whether you are eligible for federal programs such as Pell grants (WWW2.ED.GOV/PROGRAMS/FPG/INDEX .HTML) and federal work study (WWW2.ED.GOV/PROGRAMS/FWS/INDEX .HTML). Then seek out private scholarships and grants: in addition to your college financial aid office, WWW.FASTWEB.COM and WWW.SIMPLETUITION.COM are sites worth checking out. Don't assume you won't qualify—you never know unless you try!

BEST-KEPT SECRET. As you move into your upper-class years, be sure to check out your major department for sources of gift aid. In many cases, there are special endowments that are used to give fellowships—or awards and prizes—to students excelling in a particular major. And if you are a member of a special group—for example, a minority student, first-generation student, veteran, or returning student—be sure to check out the university financial aid office or website; there's often special dedicated money for these, too.

3. **If you borrow, borrow federal first.** Federal student loans are far better deals than private bank loans for almost all student borrowers: they have important borrower protections such as fixed interest rates, access to a variety of repayment plans, and options such as deferment and forbearance (see "Top 10 Tips for Paying Off Your Student Loans" on p. 303 for more on these). By contrast, paying for college with private loans is like paying by credit card: they usually have a higher interest rate, and you take on the debt with no real protection, except the ability to discharge the debt through bankruptcy.

EXTRA POINTER. Federal loans are limited to $5,500 for the first year, $6,500 for the second year, and $7,500 for the third and fourth years. So you may have to take out private bank loans in any case.

4. **Know before you owe.** A recent survey from Young Invincibles (WWW.NERA.COM/NERA-FILES/PUB_STUDENT_LOANS_0312.PDF) found that a disturbing number of borrowers misunderstood or were surprised by various aspects of their student loans: for example, repayment terms, monthly payment amounts, and interest rates. Read the fine print before taking out loans, make sure you ask questions about anything you don't understand, and take the exit counseling process seriously when you graduate. Chances are you will be paying back your loans for 10 years or more, so set yourself up for success by knowing what you are taking on.

5. **Manage your loans while you're in college.** Unsubsidized federal loans and private loans accrue interest while a borrower is in school. This interest adds up quickly, and when you enter the repayment period you find yourself owing a considerable amount more than you originally borrowed. If you can swing it, pay off the *interest* on your student loans *while* you're in school. And keep an eye on what you need and what you're using. If you're not using all your loan money for college costs, don't blow it all on spring break; save it and borrow less next year. You'll thank yourself later.

6. **Lower your tax bite.** To some degree, the pain of out-of-control tuition increases has been lessened by a slew of tax deductions and credits. Students in college, borrowers in repayment, and parents with children in college should be sure to educate themselves about these benefits. Take care to calculate your deduction or credit for each to see which one gives you the maximum benefit.

ON THE WEB. Very good information about federal tax deductions and credits (including family-income caps and other requirements) is available at the IRS' *Tax Breaks for Education: Information Center* at WWW.IRS.GOV/NEWSROOM /ARTICLE/0,,ID=213044,00.HTML. Gluttons for punishment can read the entire 87-page IRS publication at WWW.IRS.GOV/PUB /IRS-PDF/P970.PDF.

---

7. **Be wary of campus debit cards.** At the beginning of a term, many students receive financial aid refunds that can help cover

costs like rent, transportation, food, and textbooks. An increasing number of students have the option to receive their refund on a debit or disbursement card. Unfortunately, these cards often come with a full panoply of fees (such as fees for overdrafts, insufficient funds, reloading, PIN transactions, replacement cards, balance inquiries, disputes, and using another bank's ATM). Before wasting money on these fees, read the fine print on the card agreement so you understand and can avoid them. Or pass up the shiny new plastic in favor of an old-fashioned paper check or cash—schools are required to offer these options—or have the funds direct deposited into your bank account.

8. **Minimize your spending.** Treat yourself occasionally, but resist the urge to spend money you've borrowed too freely. First, because you might run out—but also because by the time you've paid off your purchase plus interest, you will have paid two or three times the current cost of the item (that double grande vanilla mocha from Starbucks might not seem so tempting every day if you remind yourself that each one will ultimately cost you $10).

9. **Get your mind around your repayment options.** As you approach graduation, make sure you know what comes next. Use the National Student Loan Data System at WWW.NSLDS.ED.GOV to keep track of your *federal* loans, and obtain a free credit report from each of the three credit-reporting agencies at WWW.ANNUALCREDITREPORT.COM to keep track of any private loans. Figure out when each payment is due and how much it will be (our "Top 10 Tips for Repaying Your Student Loans" on p. 303 examines many of the alternatives). And check out our new eBook, *Take Control of Your Future: A Guide for Managing Your Student Debt* (WWW.EQUALJUSTICEWORKS.ORG/ED-DEBT/EBOOK), available as an e-book at the Kindle Store, which will not only tell you everything you need to know about your student debt but also help other students by supporting Equal Justice Works' Educational Debt Relief Program.

ON THE WEB. Follow Equal Justice Works on Twitter @EJW_org (use #studentdebthelp) and on Facebook at /EQUALJUSTICEWORKS. Also, check out our Student Loan Ranger blog on *U.S. News & World Report* (WWW.USNEWS.COM/EDUCATION /BLOGS/STUDENT-LOAN-RANGER) to stay informed about what's coming down the pike, such as President Obama's new Pay As You Earn repayment plan, funding for Pell grants, the upcoming doubling of the interest rates for subsidized Stafford student loans, and proposed legislation like the Student Loan Forgiveness Act. Then get involved by expressing your support (or opposition) to your representative and senators.

10 Tips for the Senior Thesis

Many schools offer students the possibility (or even the necessity) of writing an extended paper in their final year of college. For some students this paper, aka the senior thesis, represents a golden opportunity to leave college with a fancy honors degree—and to get their first taste of working on a more professional level in their chosen field. But for others, this is a dreaded, seemingly insurmountable obstacle standing between them and that fancy piece of paper with the university seal. To give you your best shot, we offer you our 10 best tips for surviving and thriving while doing the senior thesis.

1. **Think before you leap.** If your school requires a senior thesis, then you're stuck. (Sorry.) But many schools do not require a thesis at all, or require it only for those seeking honors degrees. In this case, you should do some serious reflection to determine whether you're really up for this. If you hate writing and sweating out 5-page papers, maybe signing onto an 80-page project might not be the right choice for you.

2. **Pick a prof.** The success of your project depends more on your faculty adviser than you might think: for it is he or she who helps you pick the topic, guides your research, and shepherds you through the final defense before a faculty committee (if your school has that). It's best if you can pick someone who is an expert in the specific field you're working on: acridology (grasshoppers and locusts), ornithology (birds), or phycology (algae). Also, there's less risk if you pick a prof you've already taken a course or two from, and it wouldn't hurt if you got along well with your sponsor.

EXTRA POINTER. If you're not sure whom to pick as a thesis adviser, ask the departmental undergraduate adviser or, for more inside tips, a current senior who's working with the professor in question.

---

3. **Pick a topic.** A bad topic guarantees a bad thesis. So devote a lot of time up front—in careful consultation with your adviser—to finding a good topic. Make sure it's not too broad (say, requiring 500-plus pages to cover) or too narrow (after 3 pages you have nothing more to say). And often it's best to focus on a question to be answered rather than an area to be surveyed. Simply talking in general about a topic usually nets a descriptive report, not an analytical paper—and reports come in on the lowest rung of the intellectual food chain.

 IOHO. It's often a good idea to develop a topic by expanding a paper you wrote in a previous upper-division course. This allows you to hit the ground running rather than spending the first month (or two or three) feeling your way around in the dark.

---

4. **Get psyched.** You're going to be living with this project for a year, or at least a semester, so it's important that you muster a fair amount of excitement at the start. You should feel some real desire to be able to do in-depth work on your topic—and feel you have a good idea to pursue. Needless to say, most of that desire will have long since faded by the time you finish the project, but it'll be much worse if you begin it bummed out. Feeling bummed out already? Consider another topic (or consult tip #1).

5. **Set a schedule.** A senior thesis is a marathon, not a sprint. Unlike other courses, which have built-in deadlines for papers,

quizzes, and tests, the only deadline for the thesis is the submission or defense date, which is usually a long way off—that is, until it gets way too close for comfort. Solution: at the very beginning of the project, create your own firm deadlines for the various tasks (research, experiments, writing, editing, and so on). Adjustments may at times be necessary, but be as assiduous about meeting your self-imposed deadlines as you would be about externally imposed ones. View this as practice for a real life in which you're the manager, not the managed.

6. **Have regular consults.** Throughout the project it's important to meet regularly with your adviser. These meetings not only make you accountable to your professor (and yourself), but also give your adviser the opportunity to correct you if you seem to be going off course. Most students—because this usually is their first time doing a sustained project—make missteps. Correcting missteps is just part of the process, so get used to it.

EXTRA POINTER. Depending on your project, there may be a number of scholars at your university who could give valuable input into your work—by helping direct your research or your thinking on an issue. Check with your professor about whether it would be worthwhile to consult with additional faculty members, either within the department or in neighboring departments.

7. **Spread out the writing.** Many students underestimate the time needed to do the actual writing of the thesis: they end up spending about 90 percent of their time researching—which means that they don't actually start pulling together their ideas until it's already too late. And because good senior theses require multiple drafts, be sure to allow enough time for revising—and rethinking—your points as you go along.

8. **Don't overwrite.** Many, many students think (wrongly) that the whole game is to come up with as many pages as possible. But most professors judge by quality, not quantity: even the nicest professors can have smoke coming out their ears after reading scores of pages of pure, unadulterated filler or, worse, BS. Ask your adviser what the appropriate length of the project is. Some professors are looking for a 70- to 80-page *magnum opus*, but others would rather see a strong journal-article-size length of 25–40 pages.

9. **Be kind to the outside readers.** Most schools require a couple of additional readers to help judge the quality of the paper and to give input into the work. Don't screw them over. Give them the draft of the essay with plenty of time to read it before the deadline. And be informed about whether it's expected that outside readers will give you comments on the paper and— more important—whether you're expected to make revisions based on these comments prior to submitting the final version. Make sure you act in accordance with any such expectations.

10. **Prep for the oral defense.** At many schools, the senior thesis is capped by an oral exam: a committee of two or three faculty members hold court and ask you questions for an hour or two about what you've shown. This can be the time during which the grade—or level of honors—is determined. Make sure you know what's going to be expected of you at the oral exam— and take the time to prepare for it (no matter how tired you are at this point). If in doubt, ask your adviser about how the meeting is likely to go.

5-STAR TIP. Be sure to come to your oral defense equipped with a statement of what you think your work has shown (the most likely first question). And have it prepared in short, medium, and long versions. Sometimes the committee members want a few-sentence rendition of the highest points of your thesis, but sometimes they want to hear a 10-minute presentation of the highlights of your work.

BONUS TIP. As your project draws to a close, it's especially important to assess where your work stands in the field and what original contribution it makes. This is something you will need to communicate in both the paper and your thesis defense (if you have one). The whole idea of the senior thesis—or capstone project—is for you to start being a player in the field. You can't really play unless you know your position and who else is playing.

9

MOVING ON

No matter how much you love being a college student, it ultimately has to come to an end. And so, especially in your last year or two of college, you'll find yourself spending significant amounts of time preparing the materials that hopefully will propel you to your life after college. For some students, it'll be that dream job that the excellent work you've done in your major will put you in first place for. For others, it'll be more school—perhaps law school, or med school, or business school.

Whatever the next stage in your life will be, it pays to do the preparation that'll put you in the best position to grab the brass ring from the merry-go-round of life. And, just like all the other activities you've done in college, there are better—and worse—ways to do what is needed.

The tips in this chapter will help you make the right choices in the last year and a half of your college career. And the good choices you make in the waning time can propel you into continued success—long after your days at the big U have become a distant and beautiful memory.

In this chapter you'll learn:

► The 10-Step Program for Thinking about Grad School

► Top 10 Tips for Getting Bang-up Recommendations

► 8 Tips for Finding a Job

► Top 13 Tips for Acing the Job Interview

► Top 10 Tips for Paying Off Your Student Loans

The 10-Step Program for Thinking About Grad School

No one should lunge at graduate school. Getting an advanced degree can take four years in the best case (ten years in the worst) and can costs tens of thousands of dollars if you're not lucky enough to land a fellowship. And no one should begin planning for graduate school in October of their senior year. Putting together a good application—one that can really sell—is the product of a number of years of careful planning and doing the right stuff to get yourself ready for graduate work in your desired field.

What to do? Follow our step-by-step guide to getting ready for the graduate school of your choice:

1. **Don't fixate too early.** There's no point in making a decision about whether to go to graduate school until you've finished about half of the courses in your major—especially the upper-division or advanced courses. Only then can you see whether you like the field enough to devote yourself full-time to working in it. And whether you're good enough in it to make it your profession.

 REALITY CHECK. You ought to be getting mostly A's (or at least more A's than B's) in your major area if you're seriously thinking about graduate school. At many of the better schools, only one in ten applicants gets in, and it's likely that the one won't have had too many B's and C's. (Even at less competitive schools, you're typically expected to have all B's or better to stand a fighting chance of getting in.)

2. **Get the tools.** Many graduate programs expect you to have certain skills by the end of your undergraduate career—perhaps the ability to read in one or more foreign languages, proficiency in statistics, or competence in some particular sciences. Make sure you know what's needed for your field and that you've taken the courses—even if not required for the undergraduate major—that furnish the relevant skills. Otherwise you might have trouble getting into grad school in the first place, or have to play catch-up once you get there.

EXTRA POINTER. If you're not quite sure what's expected, check out the departmental web page for the graduate program you're considering. Often they're surprisingly forthright about what you need to get in—and what won't help you any.

---

3. **Don't overload with one professor.** It's tempting to take four or five courses with one prof, especially if you like him or her and are getting good grades in his or her courses. But there's a pitfall: exposure to too few points of view might stifle your development in the field, might give you too narrow a "take" on what the field is like, and, in any case, will hamper your ability to get three (or more) expert letters of recommendation to apply for graduate school. (See "Top 10 Tips for Getting Bang-Up Recommendations" on p. 289 for more on this.) Cast your net too narrowly and you'll come up short, come application time.

4. **Take the professional-level courses in the department.** Focus on the harder courses and be sure not to skip the junior seminar, senior colloquium, undergraduate thesis, or capstone course. This is where you can distinguish yourself as a serious player in the field, at least among the undergrads. Just what you need to do to position yourself for grad school.

EXTRA POINTER. Skip the throwaway courses—those courses taught by less rigorous professors or intended for the general university population (and hence too easy to prepare you for grad school). Your undergraduate adviser can steer you away from these, if you only bother to ask.

5. **Try before you buy.** If you are able to do so as a senior, take a graduate course (especially if there's one in the subfield in which you are interested). Or do an internship or join a research project with a faculty member in your area of interest. That way you'll get a taste of graduate school or graduate-level projects—all the while building up those relationships that are going to net you those stellar letters of recommendation.

6. **Get at least 150s on your Graduate Record Examinations (GREs).** Most top graduate programs expect good scores on your GREs. Common *average* scores for ranked graduate programs include 155 for the verbal reasoning section, 165 for the quantitative reasoning section, and 4.0 (though there's some variability here) for the analytical writing section. (All of these are according to the newer, post-August 2011 scoring system). If your scores fall significantly short of these, take the GRE again (this time better prepared)—keep in mind, though, that many schools take into account all the times you take the test.

5-STAR TIP. It wouldn't hurt to invest twenty bucks in one of those telephone-book-sized GRE test-prep books. You'll have an easier time on the test if you know the kinds of questions that'll be asked.

ON THE WEB. One very nice site that gives you average scores from representative universities is WWW.MSINUS.COM /CONTENT/AVERAGE-GRE-SCORES-US-UNIVERSITIES-219/. Check it out and see where you stand.

7. **Line up letters of recommendation.** Grad schools pay lots of attention to both what the letters of recommendation say and whom they are from. As you begin your search for grad schools, start to think about who will be able to write nice things about you.

8. **Give a great sample.** Many graduate schools ask you to provide a writing sample, and the sample can be critical after the first cut in the admissions process. Be sure to submit a strong sample—one that has a topic, methodology, and quality of argumentation and of writing that demonstrates your readiness for graduate-level work. And pay special attention to the suggested length. A school that expects a 20-page journal-sized article will not be happy to receive your 100-page senior thesis. (Conversely, a school that's looking for a substantial piece of work won't be bowled over by your four- or six-page short paper.) If in doubt, ask your adviser what's expected.

9. **Write a killer personal statement.** The personal statement you submit should focus on the one or two *projects* you'd like to pursue once you get into graduate school—not just general fields or areas of study. Be sure to include evidence that you can actually do the project(s)—that is, that you have the intellectual tools and the background necessary for carrying out what you're proposing (there's no point in bluffing or blowing smoke). Also, your personal statement is meant to be an *intellectual* plan—not a general autobiography, your musings about the state of the field, or a testimonial about how much you love the field. At least not if you hope to get into graduate school.

5-STAR TIP. Cognoscenti may want to tailor their applications to particular grad schools (rather than sending the same statement to all). That way, if you've done some work or have some interest that would particularly appeal to some graduate school, you can highlight that in your application.

IOHO. Be careful about mentioning a particular professor you want to study with. You run the risk of offending someone if you mention one professor to the exclusion of others, and you can easily go wrong if the faculty member you mention has announced his or her intention to leave the school. Better idea? Highlight the areas and topics you want to study, not the folks you want to work with (the schools know who they have in which fields, in any case).

10. **Don't romanticize grad school.** There's lots of drudge work and many courses to be taken in all aspects of the field you're going to be studying. If you're going to grad school in psychology, for instance, don't assume that every course will be about probing the minds of death row inmates or improving your parenting skills. And keep in mind that grad school is a long haul. Four to ten of years of your life could be a big bite if you go in merely thinking *Economics might be kinda fun—gee, I can figure out whether the Dow will hit 20,000 in my lifetime.* Make sure grad school is really for you—and you know what it really involves—before you send in that application.

BONUS TIP. Once you've narrowed your choices down to one or two, be sure to visit the graduate schools you're thinking about. While you're there, sit in on a class or two, talk to some of the professors you're thinking of studying with, and, most important, ask lots of questions of the grad students who are already there. They have been where you're going.

Top 10 Tips for Getting Bang-Up Recommendations

One of the least-fun parts of applying for graduate or professional schools—or for scholarships or jobs—is rounding up the necessary letters of recommendation or reference. Who likes going to someone in a position of authority to beg (that is, ask) for an assessment of one's intellect, character, or body of work? Especially when the evaluation could make the difference between a good grad, law, or med school and a less good one—or between a great entry-level job and one on the path to nowhere. That's why it's important to approach this delicate task with great care. Follow these suggestions and your applications will be happily accompanied by five-star reviews:

1. **Know your target.** Before you approach any potential recommenders, be sure you know what kinds of letters, and how many letters, you need. Study all the information available for the place you're applying to—whether it's a scholarship selection committee, a potential employer, or an admissions committee—to get a better sense of what they're looking for. There's no point sending in a letter from someone attesting to your character when the place is looking for evidence of your *academic* achievements.

5-STAR TIP. Always begin your quest with the school website (for graduate or professional schools) or the job posting (for employment opportunities). When institutions are forced to describe themselves, they usually highlight what is most important in their conception of themselves—and what they're most looking for in potential graduate students or hires.

2. **Give them what they ask for.** Some people think more is better, but if you are asked for three recommendations, you should probably give them three—rather than five or six, which might make you look desperate or unable to follow directions. Also pay attention to any instructions about what issues the recommenders need to address; what forms (if any) the recommenders have to submit; whether the recommendations are to be submitted electronically, by snail mail, or by phone; and the due date for the recommendation or reference. (You'll want to convey this information to the recommender when you see him or her, so be sure you get it right.)

3. **Pick the right person.** Grad schools are sensitive to whom the letters are from. The best letters come from tenured faculty who have a national reputation, have given you an A, and can talk knowledgeably about your work. Less helpful letters are those from people whom no one in the field has even heard of; from faculty in fields other than your major field (except in cases where you're applying to a joint graduate program or the second field directly bears on your course of study); from TAs (rather than professors); or, worst of all, from family members, Facebook friends, or (gasp) your parents.

REALITY CHECK. It sometimes happens that you've taken a course, even in your major, with a TA. In many such cases, there is a professor overseeing or responsible for the course. Bring your work to that person, and ask him or her for a letter of recommendation. Usually, he or she will consult with the TA and, if not write the letter, at least sign the recommendation written by the TA.

EXTRA POINTER. For jobs, you might consider getting letters from people outside the university. A practitioner in the industry, someone you have worked for (either during the semester or over the summer), or even a minister, priest, rabbi, or imam could be of use if the job is looking for an evaluation of your character, work history, or personal interests.

4. **Pre-screen your recommender.** Grad schools and employers also pay great attention to what the letters say. Some deciders even take out their yellow highlighter (real or virtual) and mark specific words and phrases that describe the candidate. So it's most important to figure out what exactly your proposed recommender is likely to say. How to find out? One way is to ask him or her, in person, whether he or she can recommend you "enthusiastically and without reservation" (these are good words to use). Then wait, and carefully attend to the answer. If you see any signs of hesitation—a long awkward pause or some hemming and hawing—you might say something like, "I would really value a letter of support from you, but I do have other possible references, so if you don't feel that you could write a strong letter for me, I'd appreciate you letting me know." (Of course, it's best, if you say this, to actually have those other letters of recommendation on tap.)

5. **Show up with samples.** Be sure to save all your graded work and give it to the professor when asking for a letter of recommendation. That way the prof will be able to incorporate specific information about the nature and quality of your work, rather than just writing how nice you are to be around.

6. **Bring the full application materials.** These would include information about what you're applying for; your resume, list of achievements, or *curriculum vitae;* your personal statement; and, of course, information about how and when to submit the letter. Provide the professor with this "personal packet," and he or she is likely to write a more detailed—and better—letter.

7. **Waive your rights.** Legally, you are entitled to see your letters of recommendation unless you waive this privilege. But in practice it is not a good idea to ask to see your letter. That's because professors (like all other human beings) are more guarded in making judgments about someone when they know that that someone is going to see the evaluation. So resist the temptation for transparency; in a way, you already know what your professor thinks of you from the grade you got in his or her course.

> **BEST-KEPT SECRET.** In an *open* letter (that is, a letter that the student is free to read), the professor is unlikely to make any comparative judgments in the form of "Mr. X was one of the two best students in my Biometrics 457 class" or "Ms. Y was one of the two or three best students I have had in my 30 years of teaching at the five best universities on the planet." But these are exactly the judgments that get you into the best schools in the country or the best jobs in creation.

8. **Allow plenty of time—and follow up.** Many professors are overworked and/or have lots of recommendations to write. So be sure to approach your professor as soon as you can— September or early October is best—and check back with him or her a couple of weeks before the due date if you haven't received confirmation from the school or employer by then.

9. **Be super-nice throughout the process.** One thing you may not have considered is that professors have considerable discretion in how they write these letters: there's no one telling the prof how to shade your various achievements. So it's always good to be polite and respectful to the professor for taking the time to write for you. The warm feeling the professor

has for you can carry over to the tone of the letter, especially in borderline cases or judgment calls.

10. **Share the good news.** Once you've been accepted into the program you applied for or gotten the job you wanted, be sure to tell your recommenders that their letters did the trick. It's always nice to express appreciation for something nice that someone did for you. And even if you didn't get the prize, it's still a good idea to thank the recommenders for their efforts (if you don't want to face your profs in person, a brief e-mail would be sufficient). Who knows? You might need another recommendation from these people some day.

Tips for Finding a Job

Many students are worried about how they'll finish college. We hope this book has helped them. But some students are even more worried about how they'll find a job after college—especially given the lingering, iffy employment outlook for recent college graduates. What is the best way to approach the job market?

When you are actually looking for a job, it is always a "bad" market. The market in the last few years just happens to be a little more so, especially if you happen to be an auto worker or a Big Law associate. But although many people lost their positions during the Great Recession of 2008–2009, others have found interesting and rewarding jobs since then. There is no one magic formula for finding a job, but there are ways to take control of the process and enhance your odds. Here are eight tips for finding a job from Susan Schell, director of career services at the University of Arkansas Law School:

1. **Know what it takes.** Different fields have different application requirements, and you need to know what those are for the field you are interested in. Do you need a resume, a cover letter, a writing sample, a portfolio, and so on? You also need to know what these materials look like in your field, and which skills and experiences you need to emphasize. A legal resume is different, in both form and content, from a management resume, which in turn is different from a marketing resume. Don't have a clue? Try to arrange an informational interview with a professional in the field to which you aspire and learn what it takes.

2. **Perfect your application materials.** Always have your application materials reviewed by someone who is a better editor than you. After polishing and massaging your resume a hundred times, you are probably too close to it to see the nits that need to be picked. Have your materials reviewed again

whenever you make revisions or add updates. Don't know any good editors? If you are in school, try your career services office.

3. **Activate your network.** Tell everyone you know what type of job you are looking for. There is no sin in looking for employment, so you need to get everyone in your network working for you. Although your hair stylist is not a lawyer or a management consultant, he or she may know one. Follow up every lead you are given; you never know who knows the person who can get you the job you want.

5-STAR TIP. **If you have a professor who's worked in industry or in extra-university work in the field you're considering, make sure to invite him or her to use his or her contacts. Often even an informal recommendation from a professor can open doors.**

EXTRA POINTER. **If a parent, family friend, older brother or sister, or employer of yours works in the field you want to go into, enlist that person's help, too. You never know who has the contacts that count.**

---

4. **Join a professional organization.** Most occupations, from restaurant managers to engineers, have professional associations. Join one. (Many have student rates.) Attend meetings, go to seminars, and read the materials. Just as an anthropologist would, you should learn the language and customs of your field, be aware of the issues of the day, and identify the key players. That way, when you land an interview you will "speak the language" like a native.

5. **Be patient and persistent.** Set aside time every week to check for postings, to do research on employers in your field, and to send out a manageable number of applications. It is probably not realistic to try to send out 20 letter-perfect, individually tailored applications in a weekend, so pace yourself. It is better to send 5 high-quality applications than 20 generic applications. Treat the job search as a marathon rather than a sprint. When you work on the job search regularly rather than in fits and starts, it is easier to stay focused and control the stress that inevitably accompanies it.

ON THE WEB. Three of the many websites that will help you in your job search are WWW.JOB-HUNT.ORG, WWW.WETFEET.COM, and WWW.CAREERJOURNAL.COM. They provide job search tips, career research information, company profiles, and many other features. Check 'em out.

6. **Prepare carefully for your interview.** If you are fortunate enough to land an interview, treat it as an opportunity to establish a professional relationship with the interviewer. Know the employer and be prepared to ask intelligent questions. Engage with the interviewer, and do not be shy in letting the interviewer know how much you know about the employer and how much you want to work there. Be enthusiastic, not desperate. (For more tips on putting your best foot forward at the interview, see "Top 13 Tips for Acing the Job Interview" on p. 298.)

BEST-KEPT SECRET. It's always a good idea to do a little web research on the company before the interview—and, when possible, on the individuals who will be interviewing you. You'll make a much better impression when you know what the company is doing—and how you might fit in. And while you're at it, Google yourself and check out your own Facebook page to see what your interviewer might be learning about you (this will indicate what you'll need to try to explain away).

REALITY CHECK. Although there are bills pending before various state legislatures to prevent employers from accessing your social media profiles as part of their job search, many are still taking a peek—and, no doubt, will continue to do so no matter what the law is (wouldn't you?). So consider setting your privacy settings to restrict public access—especially if you have stuff up that you wouldn't want any employer (no matter how liberal-minded) to see.

7. **Practice out loud.** Try to anticipate the types of questions you will be asked at your interview, and practice your responses. If you lack experience or feel uncomfortable in interviews, find someone to do a mock interview with. As with other skills, communication skills get better with practice. And although you may think you have a perfect answer in your head, you won't know it until you actually articulate it. In an interview there is the answer you plan to give, the one you do give, and the one you wished you had given. With practice, those three answers come together.

5-STAR TIP. It's always a good idea to do a "mock interview"—that is, a trial run in which someone knowledgeable about the business sits down with you for an hour and asks you the sorts of questions that are likely to come up. Good "interviewers" are faculty in your major, people actually employed in the relevant profession, and professional career counselors. Your department or campus career counseling office can point you in the right direction.

8. **Be positive.** Stay upbeat throughout the job search. Remember that there is no "perfect" candidate; just be the best you can be.

Top 13 Tips for Acing the Job Interview

One of the main—and most feared—steps in getting a good job is the interview: the tête-à-tête with the potential employer in which you try to show your stuff. It'll go great if you follow our baker's dozen of time-tested tips:

1. **Dress right.** Be sure to show up at your interview clad in appropriate clothing (though it's usually a good idea to dress at least one step higher than the dress code for the job you're applying for). You can get some idea of what's customary by looking at how folks are dressed on the company website (try to make sure they're holding the same level of job as you're applying for), or by consulting with someone who has a similar job in a similar kind of company. You wouldn't want to show up in a dress suit if everyone is wearing a blue polo and khakis; conversely, you wouldn't want to be wearing a T-shirt and shorts if all the interviewers are dressed in three-piece suits and sheath dresses.

2. **Show up on time—and relaxed.** You can't do a good interview if you're huffing and puffing, and sweating buckets. So allow yourself extra time to get to your destination (factoring in the possibility of getting lost or having trouble finding parking). You'll also want to give yourself enough time to collect your thoughts prior to the interview and maybe even to get a cup of coffee or tea (be sure not to spill the coffee on yourself—hard to interview in wet clothes).

3. **Play the part from the start.** At some companies you're under observation from the moment you set foot in their place. Be respectful to everyone you meet (you never know who that person walking through the waiting room really is). And don't

make stray comments about the job. You never know who might overhear your offhanded remark that "one would have to be crazy to want to work for this firm."

4. **Great everyone enthusiastically.** Interviewers start forming opinions from the very first moment they meet you. Be friendly. Shake everyone's hand firmly (but don't draw blood). Smile as you say how pleased you are to meet them (you ought to be, given that they have a job to offer). Be forthcoming if they ask you a question or two informally: don't offer one-word, nonresponsive answers (no one likes that).

5. **Answer the questions head-on.** Rather than just dishing up canned answers that don't really address what's being asked (and, in any case, seem artificial), respond to the specific questions you get. And don't be afraid to take the discussion in a direction you hadn't planned. Sometimes the best interviews display the ability to think on your feet and to explore previously unprepared territory. Sometimes, spontaneity and authenticity can outrank completeness and exactness.

5-STAR TIP. It's especially nice to address the interviewer(s) by their name and proper title when you answer their questions. Pay special attention to how they introduce themselves; that's how you'll know what to call them.

---

6. **Strive to fit in.** Each company or organization has its own corporate culture, and interviewers like candidates who seem like they would fit in. Indeed, many interview questions are actually not designed to test your knowledge or background, but rather to determine what it would be like to have you sitting at the next computer. Be alert for questions such as "How interested you are in doing _____ [fill in the blank]?" or "Would you be able to handle a work environment that is _____ [fill in the blank]?" If you detect this sort of question, your answer should not just be, "Sure, whatever," but should

communicate real excitement and enthusiasm about
_____ [fill in the blank].

BEST-KEPT SECRET. In many job interviews, the interviewers are performing a thought experiment: *What would it be like if the candidate were working with us starting Monday?* Try to make it seem that it would be a good experience for them if you were.

---

7. **Showcase your qualifications and achievements.** You'd be amazed by how many candidates shoot themselves in the foot by answering questions in ways that put down their own abilities ("Well, I'm not really that great at math, but I bet if I worked at it I'd be able to do it more or less OK . . ."). Don't put yourself down in your answers. On the other hand, don't be a show-off, or come off as if you think your you-know-what doesn't you-know-what.

8. **Don't get frazzled.** Often interviewers ask questions that are *meant* to be hard. Do your best to answer all the questions, but don't fall apart if one or two strike you as incredibly difficult. Even if you screw up a question or two, hiring is a composite judgment involving many factors—and sometimes many deciders—so one slipup does not necessarily kill your chances. (Throwing up your hands and giving up, though, can torpedo your chances.)

9. **Be yourself.** Obviously, you want to make a good impression, but you want to do it while still being who you are—or at least who you are on a good day. Interviewers don't like people who come off as fake. Even if you can fool them at the interview, your posing could come back to haunt you when you actually land the job and the employer quickly discovers the real you.

REALITY CHECK. If the "real you" includes strong opinions about controversial religious, political, or social topics, it's best not to show *that* you. Employers are very concerned to maintain a cordial and nonconfrontational workspace these days, and they won't want someone guaranteed to stir up trouble by bloviating at work.

10. **Ask *them* a question or two.** Most interviews include a time when you're asked whether you have any questions. This is a golden opportunity to cement the good impression you've already made. Always have a few questions on tap; not having any questions conveys to interviewers that you're not all that interested in the job.

11. **Don't show too many of your cards.** Telling your interviewers about other places where you are under consideration (even if they ask) can be dangerous. If you seem like you have interviews at much better companies or organizations, your interviewers might figure you'd never accept their offer and therefore there's no point in making one. But if you divulge a lack of other opportunities, or interviews at much worse places, the interviewers might conclude you're a loser—and not make an offer, either.

12. **Don't jump the gun.** Job searches unfold according to a certain timetable. You look bad if you inquire about details of the benefits package or of the salary at too early a stage in the process. Also, try not to make comments or ask questions that appear as if you are rushing the process (such as "When will you be making your decision?" or "When can I expect to hear back from you?" or "How are you going to be deciding, anyway?"). Keep in mind you're playing one side of the net, and you shouldn't be stepping onto the opposing side.

IOHO. A post-interview thank-you note is nice; a telephone call or email to find out where you stand, less so.

13. **Don't take it personally.** There can be many reasons why your interview didn't net you the job—many of which don't depend on you. It could be a lack of fit, budget shortfall, or disagreements within the company about who to hire. Or there could be a better candidate than you (or a candidate who better fits the needs or perceptions of the company). And sometimes it's simple bad luck: the cards flipped, but not your way. Whatever the case, stay positive and keep on interviewing. In many cases, it takes a long time to get a job and the worst thing you can do is panic too soon.

Top 10 Tips for Paying Off Your Student Loans

For most students, the end of college means the beginning of debt. And lots of it. According to the most recent statistics, over two-thirds of last year's college graduates have taken out student loans, with the *average* amount being $26,600. And, for the first time in U.S. history, the total amount of student debt exceeds the total amount of credit card debt. The sheer size of the debt forces many students to delay important life events. Buying a car, getting married and having a family, buying a first home, and, yes, even having an apartment of your own can be put on the back burner while you return to your parents' house and your childhood room. It can be pretty grim. And so we invited financial guru Mark Kantrowitz, publisher of FASTWEB.COM and FINAID.ORG, to offer some tips on paying off your student loans after college. Here are his 10 best ideas:

1. **Start from where you're at.** At the exit from college to the world beyond, it's very important that you assess where you stand with your loans. Key is a student loan checklist. Virtually every college provides one on their website (search for "loan checklist" or "student loan repayment checklist"); commercial ones are also available, such as WWW.FINAID.ORG /STUDENTLOANCHECKLIST, recommended by many colleges. In addition, you'll want to attend—fully prepared—the exit counseling available at many colleges and mandated by federal law (if you have a federally guaranteed student loan). Most students who are late with a loan payment are late with the very first payment, so get educated about what's in store for you.

ON THE WEB. Keep track of all your *federal* loans at the National Student Loan Data System website: WWW.NSLDS.ED.GOV.

---

2. **Set up automatic monthly payments.** Not only will you reduce the likelihood of missing a payment, but also many lenders offer discounts to borrowers who sign up for auto-debit. The federal government's Direct Loan program, for example, will reduce the interest rate by 0.25 percent if you repay your loans by auto-debit with electronic billing. So too, many private lenders offer a 0.25-percent or 0.50-percent interest rate reduction for auto-debit. Keep in mind that even a fraction of a percent discount can really add up over a ten-year (or in some cases twenty-year) repayment period.

3. **Claim the student loan interest deduction.** The student loan interest deduction lets you deduct up to $2,500 in interest on federal and private student loans as an above-the-line exclusion (that is, a deduction you can take from your gross income) on your federal income tax return. Note that you can take the deduction even if you don't itemize, which is a real money-saver for the other 99 percent.

WWW **ON THE WEB.** Full details about the student loan interest deduction can be found at www.IRS.GOV/TAXTOPICS/TC456.HTML. The most detailed information about education tax benefits generally is available at www.IRS.GOV/PUB/IRS-PDF/P970.PDF. Happy reading.

4. **Accelerate repayment of the highest-interest-rate loans first.** If you happen to have some extra bucks lying around, ask your lender to apply the payment to the loans with the highest interest rate first. They are required to do this, but they may or may not do this on their own. Be sure to keep a copy of any correspondence you send them, and check your online statement to make sure they have properly credited your account. There are no prepayment penalties (that is, additional fees) for doing this, so any minimally rational college graduate will request this from their lender.

5-STAR TIP. If you're making an extra, nonrequired payment, be sure to request that it be applied to the principal, not credited as prepayment of a future payment. This will lower your interest over the entire remaining term on the loan.

5. **Look into alternate repayment programs.** Many students struggle to repay their student loans—which, unlike other consumer debt, cannot be eliminated in a bankruptcy—so if you find yourself unable to keep up, consider some of your options. *Deferments* and *forbearances* (ways of delaying payments) temporarily suspend the monthly obligations, but at a price: interest continues to accrue while you are sitting on your hands. Other options that you might consider (if appropriate) include the Public Service Loan Forgiveness (PSLF) program, for those working in a wide variety of public-service jobs; the Income-Based Repayment (IBR) program, for those with a very high education-debt-to-income ratio; and Loan Repayment Assistance Programs (LRAPs), available from a variety of colleges, employers, and federal and state governments.

ON THE WEB. An excellent website that describes all the alternate repayment programs, in sympathetic detail, is www .EQUALJUSTICEWORKS.ORG (click the "Ed Debt" tab, then the "Post Grad" tab).

6. **Be careful about consolidating.** Consolidation can streamline repayment by replacing multiple loans with a single loan. But if your loans have interest rates that differ significantly, it will prevent you from saving money by accelerating repayment of the highest interest rate loan first. If you have *private* student loans, though, listen up: here you can sometimes save money.

Private consolidation loans have changing interest rates based on the borrower's current credit score. Often your credit score will decrease with each successive year in school due to the added debt. But when you have a few years of full-time employment after graduation, and repay all your obligations (not just student loans) on time, your credit score will improve enough to qualify for a better interest rate.

 ON THE WEB. If you're thinking of consolidating your federal student loans, check out the article at WWW.FORBES.COM /2009/04/15/STUDENT-LOANS-MONEYBUILDER-PERSONAL-FINANCE -CONSOLIDATE.HTML and this useful calculator: WWW .LOANCONSOLIDATION.ED.GOV/.

---

7. **Talk to your lender before you default.** If, for whatever reason, you just can't pay (and you don't qualify for any of the programs just described), talk to your lender. Ignoring the debt—most people's immediate impulse—will not make it go away, and it will make a bad situation worse. You will lose options if you default first. And if you owe money to Uncle Sam, the federal government has very strong powers to compel repayment: it can garnish up to 15 percent of wages and Social Security benefits, and offset federal and state income tax refunds, all without a court order. Even lottery winnings can be seized by the government. There is no rational reason to default, because the monthly payment under income-based repayment is lower than the wage garnishment amount.

8. **Appeal to your folks.** Sometimes, when you're really in financial trouble, your parents or some other relative can step up to bat. If possible, it's good to get a "bridge loan"—or better yet, an outright gift—from someone who really cares about you. Don't be afraid to ask—especially if your creditor is breathing down your neck.

9. **Face the reality.** If you have significant amounts of student debt, you may have to cut back your lifestyle. First step is to create a descriptive budget: track every expense, no matter how small, for a month (no cheating; you're only cheating yourself). Record and categorize each expense with a spreadsheet or program like Quicken or Microsoft Money. Better yet, use the tools at MINT.COM or GNUCASH.ORG, both of which are free. Decide whether each expense is a *need* or a *want* (be honest): needs are those expenses that, if you didn't ante up, you would go to jail for—or (eventually) you would die; wants are things you'd really, really like to have but somehow could make do without. At the end of the month, compare the totals with your income. Hey, this is the real world; your college days are long gone.

10. **Get the whole picture.** Even after reading these tips, you may still have questions. Go to the two "bibles" of student loan information: WWW.PROJECTONSTUDENTDEBT.ORG and WWW .STUDENTLOANBORROWERASSISTANCE.ORG. There you'll find every fact known to humanity about student loans, including the ones you're looking for. And check out the Quick Reference Guide on Repaying Student Loans at WWW.FINAID.ORG/LOANS/ REPAYINGSTUDENTLOANS.PDF: four pages of info, including charts, web links, and phone numbers to call when things go wrong.

10 THE END— AND THE BEGINNING

A nd so we come to the end of *The Secrets of College Success*. Or do we?

Though you probably haven't been counting, if you've read the book straight through from the beginning, you've seen over 800 tips for college success (834, to be exact). But the three most important tips are still to come. The tips that *you* will write—and use.

Some students have found in this book many tips they can see themselves using. Starting right away. Others have thought up their own tips while reading ours. And still others—well, you're thinking that if you only thought about it for a minute or two, you'd be able to come up with *much* better tips than we have.

Whichever is the case for you, go get a pencil—or, if you prefer, your iPad, laptop, tablet, or other device of choice—and answer the following question (100 points, no time limit):

What are the three best tips for college success that you resolve to use—100 percent of the time, without fail, no matter what the situation?

5-STAR TIP #1.

_____
_____
_____
_____
_____
_____

5-STAR TIP #2.

_____

_____

_____

_____

_____

_____

5-STAR TIP #3.

_____

_____

_____

_____

_____

Congratulations! You've just taken the first—and most important—step on your path to college success.

 **10 People We'd Like to Thank**

#10. **Kate Bradford.** Our editor. Takes a lot of patience to be an editor. And a little vision, too.

#9. **Arthur Klebanoff.** Our agent and friend (good contract-writer, too).

#8. **Tom Hapgood.** Designed our website and keeps all our graphics modern and cool.

#7. **Michael Kohlmeyer-Hyman.** Our business manager and Jeremy's brother. If there's a better guy, we don't know him.

#6. **All the folks at Wiley in editorial, marketing, and production:** Lesley Iura, Dimi Berkner, Jen Wenzel, Nana Twumasi, and Justin Frahm. They've done yeoman's service in getting out this book in record time.

#5. **Our publicists at Wiley,** Mike Onorato and Samantha Rubenstein. They get the word out better than anyone.

#4. **Jeff Puda for the cover; Maureen Forys, Jon Schleuss, and Corrine Kohlmeyer-Hyman for the interior design and Sue Blanchard for the Professors' Guide™ logo.** How boring would the book be without them?

#3. **Professors David Christensen and Richard Lee for endless infusions of tips** (especially when we were running dry).

#2. **All our past and present students.** You were the beta lab that showed the tips work.

And the number-one person we'd like to thank:

#1. **You!** Without you there'd be no one to tell the secrets to. Bummer.

WEB RESOURCES

INDEX

Notes

Notes

Notes

Notes

Notes